REDUCE, REUSE, REIMAGINE

REDUCE, REUSE, REIMAGINE

Sorting Out the Recycling System

Beth Porter

ROWMAN & LITTLEFIELD
Lanham • Boulder • New York • London

Published by Rowman & Littlefield
An imprint of The Rowman & Littlefield Publishing Group, Inc.
4501 Forbes Boulevard, Suite 200, Lanham, Maryland 20706
www.rowman.com

Unit A, Whitacre Mews, 26-34 Stannary Street, London SE11 4AB

British Library Cataloguing in Publication Information Available

Library of Congress Cataloging-in-Publication Data

Names: Porter, Beth, 1988– author.
Title: Reduce, reuse, reimagine : sorting out the recycling system / Beth Porter.
Description: Lanham : Rowman & Littlefield, [2018] | Includes bibliographical references and
index.
Identifiers: LCCN 2018009452 (print) | LCCN 2018015543 (ebook) | ISBN 9781538105405
(ebook) | ISBN 9781538105399 (cloth : alk. paper)
Subjects: LCSH: Recycling (Waste, etc.)—United States. | Waste minimization—United States.
Classification: LCC TD794.5 (ebook) | LCC TD794.5 .P6745 2018 (print) | DDC 363.72/820973—
dc23
LC record available at https://lccn.loc.gov/2018009452

∞™ The paper used in this publication meets the minimum requirements of
American National Standard for Information Sciences Permanence of Paper
for Printed Library Materials, ANSI/NISO Z39.48-1992.

Printed in the United States of America

CONTENTS

ACKNOWLEDGMENTS

To Lynn and Andy, my mom and dad, you are my heroes. You both inspire me to see kindness in others, hold tight to integrity, and live to my values. Thank you for every single moment of support, wisdom, and joy you've shared. Thank you to Aunt Sandra and Shelley, for helping me talk through concepts as well as to laugh and not take things too seriously.

I am fortunate to live in a little ecosystem full of generous, brilliant, passionate friends and family. To everyone who took the time to ask, "How's the book going?" and offer one more gentle nudge to cross the finish line, this book was made possible thanks to each of you. To everyone who has taken the time to share your recycling queries with me and let me wander down roads of thoughts with you, I am deeply grateful. Every single question you asked has folded new aspects of a complex and important system into this book. I hope it answers any others you may have. (If not, please give me a ring! Let's figure out the answer!)

I'd also like to extend my sincere gratitude to those who aided in my research, writing process, and book design, including Suzanne Staszak-Silva and Andrew Yoder of Rowman & Littlefield, Emily Biondo, Iris Gottlieb, Susan Kinsella, Adam Ortiz, Neil Seldman, and my wonderful colleagues at Green America.

And to Michael Curcio and Corbin, I am eternally grateful for your encouragement and patience as I read sentences aloud while wandering through our home. Thank you for letting this book live with us for so long and helping to make it all possible. You mean the world to me.

I

THE ECOSYSTEM OF RECYCLING

In the forest, dozens of complex systems operate in quiet determination. Organisms compete for resources throughout their ecosystems. Tiny acorns work tirelessly for years to grow and burst into the top level of a tree canopy, while mosses envelope woodland floors and regulate soil moisture. Within every forest exists a myriad of systems striving for their individual success, while also contributing to the longevity of the larger ecosystem. This allows a community of organisms to thrive. But, ecosystems are not simply harmonious utopias. There is fierce, brutal competition and fatal tragedies. What allows these turbulent ecosystems to maintain their existence is not the absence of conflict, but the balanced use and replenishment of resources over time. When a resource is divisible, such as a tree used by many insects and animals for shelter and food, multiple species have access to its benefits—organisms vying with each other can coexist by using the resource at different times and in varying amounts. This is what prevents a catastrophic "race to the bottom," meaning the depletion of resources. Conversely, a nondivisible resource generally ends up under the control of a singular, dominant species. Species using the same limited resource in the same way at the same time cannot coexist for long. But, when different aspects of a resource are used in a variety of ways to serve multiple stakeholders, equilibrium can be achieved.

Ecosystems require balance to survive, and when that balance is compromised, as in the extinction of a resource or a species, disaster can strike the system as a whole. This vital management of resources can also be reflected in economic systems. A healthy ecosystem, like a healthy economic system, does not have a void of competition or effort. Instead, there are competing forces that sometimes work cooperatively to keep the larger system afloat. This single planet has finite resources. It is our responsibility as organisms of a shared global ecosystem to use them efficiently, equitably, and sustainably. In both nature and economics, we observe when a healthy distribution of resources is achieved, systems can not only function, but flourish.

The United States' recycling system has removed a ton of greenhouse gases from the atmosphere (actually, in the hundreds of millions of tons) and has the potential to remove much more. A functional recycling system can boost our economy by providing manufacturers with the means to generate new products, and benefits the environment by reducing the demand to extract raw materials. However, this potential has yet to be fully seen. Unlike the layers of systems operating in a thriving and healthy forest, our recycling system experiences bottlenecking and inefficiency. How can the United States—one of the leading nations on innovation and technology—lag behind in the most obvious of resource recovery systems? Where in our history of recycling did we go from a leader to a laggard, as we can't seem to exceed a 34 percent recycling rate,[1] while other nations have rates double that?

Our recycling process has many examples of dysfunction. However, it is still ripe with all the potential of an acorn when given water and healthy soil. What we need are policies to incentivize a large, systemic change—we need to make materials that can be effectively recycled, and we need standardized recycling rules so that individuals can easily understand the process. Nature knows how to recycle itself, decomposing waste back into the soil to continue the circle of growth. We should follow its lead.

Systems touch every part of our lives. Whether it's the traffic route a bus follows or the process of waiting in line for tickets to a show, systems help us navigate the world and can bring ease and comfort into our lives. The beauty of a working system is similar to a tall oak tree, with much of the mechanics going on underneath the surface, so much so that we may enjoy the results of all these grand designs without mulling over the minutiae of its operation. We might take for granted a working oven, as it systematically cooks our dinner. We also might take for granted the shade of the tree in our backyard. But when the oven is broken or a huge tree limb falls onto the roof, we notice right away. A system is most noticed when it's not working. In the case of the U.S. recycling system, the dysfunction is seen through the decreased value of recyclables from contamination or delays in processing residential materials. Or when neighborhood residents suspect their carefully placed recyclables are just dumped into the garbage truck. If one aspect of the system doesn't operate correctly or is trying to function without another key participant, the system staggers and can even break down.

When delving into the complex and multifaceted world of recycling, it is helpful to view this industrial web through a systems-thinking lens. Systems thinking is a term attributed to Barry Richmond, who defined it as the "art and science of making reliable inferences about behavior by developing an increasingly deep understanding of underlying structure." In short, Richmond says systems thinking allows us to view the forest and the trees, with one eye on each. Since Richmond developed this concept in 1987, there have been many adaptations of his original definition. But the common threads woven throughout all these interpretations are the interconnectedness of systems, the understanding of dynamic behavior, and the need to see a system as a whole rather than as its parts. Richmond affirmed that it is essential to take a systems view of a problem. We should seek to understand all parts of a web rather than solely elicit the perspective of one expert on one corner of it. He noted that only when this full-system scope has been achieved can we be expected to "act responsibly."[2]

A system is a regularly interacting group of items forming a unified whole.[3] This can be seen in the forest, as photosynthesis and decomposition chug along, accomplishing their respective tasks but also feeding into one another. In order to look at a process within a systems-thinking lens, one must consider these three parts: the system's elements, the interconnections, and the purpose. Let's make a simplified description of a forest ecosystem through these parts. The forest's purpose is to be a habitat for organisms and to process carbon while creating oxygen to maintain a healthy atmosphere. A few of the system elements would be the trees and animals, and the interconnections are seen in how they all rely on each other to survive. For example, many tree seedlings are dispersed by animals, and the trees will in turn grow to provide shelter and food for animals.

The purpose of recycling is both to lessen our society's negative impact on the environment, as well as to provide manufacturers with quality materials to generate new products that will bolster our economy. Residents, municipalities, waste management companies, transfer stations, sorting facilities, material brokers, manufacturers, and customers are among the many elements of a recycling system. Each of these elements, or stakeholders, has a vested interest and involvement in the production of recycled materials. Whether each stakeholder embraces that role and responsibility determines if the system will thrive or decline.

The interconnections, or interrelationships, are what exist between each of the elements. These connections can be found in everyday moments, like when a neighborhood resident looks up recycling rules from their city's website or when a company's new policy mandates buying more recycled materials from manufacturers. This is the time when different stakeholders (or "elements") overlap and interact with one another, like when the municipality educates its residents and the manufacturer sends prices to the company. Interconnections are also present when one element of the recycling system tries to shift its own agenda onto another area without fully taking into account the ramifications of that move. For example, when a city decides to have residents put all recyclables in the same bin (to reduce its budget and boost participation), it might not take into account how this will escalate contamination. This leads to materials like paper being damaged or even ruined from another container's residue, lessening the quality of that paper. The contaminated paper is no longer useful to manufacturers and has a higher likelihood of ending up in an incinerator or landfill than of being made into a new product.

Only looking at one part of a system in isolation leads to uninformed problem solving for the whole system. When only one aspect is explored, deeper systemic issues can go unnoticed, and all that receives attention are any visible symptoms of the core problem. Should we attend to parts of a system that need immediate attention? Yes. However, we should also take those opportunities to think of the other areas and how they may be contributing to the piece that is most obviously broken. This requires time and can seem overwhelming because the more aspects and stakeholders, the more arduous the task. But, it's worth the investment if the system keeps breaking. Over time, fixing symptoms one by one ends up being a longer commitment. As in most things with sustainability, an investment now means a lot more savings in the future.

Entities across the country, from schools to municipalities to amusement parks, each with their own resources and agendas, establish their own recycling programs. But there is no governing voice to help coordinate all these programs, leaving a significant gap in synchronizing efforts and often resulting in a waste of resources. Because the core objective of recycling is to save as many resources as possible, this lack of communication is ironic.[4] If every school in the United States had some form of a recycling program, there would be more than 130,000 sets of recycling rules and practices in our school systems alone. With this variation of programs, it seems obvious that recycling is not just driven by waste management's sustainability goals; it's also driven and expanded because people demanded it. People love to recycle and are proud to do so; however, every person has their own individual schedule and tasks to achieve every day, and most people are short on time. If a system requires too much effort and isn't an absolute necessity to meet immediate needs, then there's a good chance it will be a lower priority for most people. In order to increase participation in a system, it should be efficient, with steps that are easy to follow and not constantly changing. This way people can build it into their habits and not be concerned about when the system rules will change.

A method called single-stream recycling was introduced in the 1990s in California. The goal of single-stream was if consumers toss all recyclables into one bin, then the effort of residential sorting is removed, and participation will increase. Through the use of sophisticated technology, material recovery facilities (MRFs) would take on the task of appropriately sorting recyclables. Single-stream recycling does result in higher participation rates; unfortunately, it also raises the chances for material contamination. When different materials are tossed into the same bin, they can damage or even ruin each other simply by proximity throughout the journey from your curbside bin to your local sorting facility. Think of a plastic bottle that still has some soda in it and gets tossed in with old magazines, soaking them—this is a common scenario of contamination. The contaminated items are not as valuable for manufacturers and are either exported overseas or sent to the landfill. Cities might gain many benefits from implementing single-stream recycling, but the negative effects influence manufacturers and the other stake-holders in the system. Poor communication makes effective recycling more challenging and can undermine a system's goals. Within a system that demonstrates abundant interconnections, it is essential that communication between the elements is open and that the roles of each element are understood by one another. This allows the stakeholders to know what they are accountable for in making the system thrive and provides clear paths toward accountability when solving problems.

When systems fail, there can be catastrophic consequences for years after. On April 20, 2010, a system failure caused numerous injuries, the loss of human lives, and one of the worst environmental disasters in American history. The Deepwater Horizon rig explosions resulted in a deluge of oil pouring into the ocean for months.[5] Hundreds of millions of oil barrels plagued the waters, killing animals and plants, while also delivering a debilitating halt to the regional economy. The oil spill into the Gulf of Mexico warranted a government response of significant size and cost, so the disaster left not only a devastating environmental impact but also a strain on our national resources. Cited for reckless conduct, BP was saddled with 67 percent of the penalties in the lawsuits that followed. Also charged were Transocean, Limited, with 30 percent of damage costs, and 3 percent levied against Halliburton Energy Services.[6] Some experts argue that these penalties were a meager attempt to rectify the devastation these energy giants inflicted onto local communities.

There are many lessons to be learned from this system failure; most notably are the severe risks of offshore drilling and the costs of continuing to prop up unsustainable forms of energy. Commission reports have confirmed that the disaster could have been avoided, if not for human error in management and communication.[7] The involved companies failed to share important information. They cut corners and took risks that had serious repercussions. Mechanical failures occur and are sometimes unavoidable; however, the willful dismissal of necessary safeguards and the lack of communication led to the devastating magnitude of this particular system failure. By no means can the impact of the Deepwater Horizon oil spill be compared in exact parallel to the dysfunction of the U.S. recycling system. These are two very different examples of how system failures and lack of communication have consequences. The commonality is that taking a systems-thinking lens to a problem, with each stakeholder owning their responsibility, can curb system failures and allow it to function more seamlessly. And when problems do arise, they can be tackled quickly to curb damage.

An ecosystem is a complex community of organisms, or a group of living and nonliving things that all affect one another. An economic system is the production, resource allocation, and distribution of goods and services within an area.[8] While we observe competition in both system types, research has shown that such forest organisms as trees are not merely competitors but also communicators. Beneath our hiking shoes exists vast communication systems between trees that show not only their correspondence with one another but also their collaborative efforts to share resources. When one tree species experiences a restricted ability to absorb carbon, such as a deciduous tree having shed its leaves in the winter, a neighborhood evergreen species might share carbon through its root systems to aid the struggling tree. Forest ecologist and professor Suzanne Simard discovered these communication webs while researching the mycorrhizal network, an underground network of fungi connecting individual plants together.

Simard's findings have captivated audiences beyond forest ecologists, and this work will continue to shed light on the "conversations" beneath the forest floor. We can learn from her existing research and apply it to the recycling industry. It is beneficial for even competing organisms to regularly communicate and, at times, collaborate when their functions and resources overlap. Simard states that a "forest is a cooperative system," and that if a forest were all about competition, the dynamic and diverse qualities of the ecosystem would not be as plentiful.[9] What a forest produces would not be as rich, either. Forest "output" (from the human perspective), like oxygen and carbon sequestration, is needed to keep the air clean in the global ecosystem. What the forest creates is essential for its own functions and also contributes to the greater good of our entire planet.

A major objective of a system is the usefulness of its outputs. This requires appropriate inputs, like fitting data or effective materials. If the output of recycling is a valuable commodity to be sold to manufacturers, then the input must be of a certain quality (meaning not covered in wet food or other contaminants). A system's feedback is the process of measuring the output, like how good the results are or how much is achieved. This comparison can provide positive feedback (in which the system continues as is) or negative feedback (which provides us with information to improve the system). In this case, our recycling and contamination rates gauge how successful the United States is at producing great outputs in comparison to other nations.

Other key aspects of a system are its boundaries and limitations while producing its output. An open system engages with its environment by getting inputs and outputs to and from its boundaries. Its boundary lines are malleable, so it can connect with other systems outside itself to exchange resources and information. A closed system is less likely to take in new things from outside sources, and its boundaries are more defined and rigid. The problem for a closed system occurs when it declines in function because it can't adapt to new changes. It becomes less effective and risks becoming obsolete from this lack of adaption. An open system can adapt and move with its surroundings, but a closed one remains static, its functions unchanged by its larger environment.[10]

Now, back to the forest. Ecosystem boundaries refer to the line between different environments; one example is where the forest edge meets a field. The forest itself lives within a type of boundary. However, within the forest, there are many boundaries that are not as easy to draw as a line of trees meeting tall grass. If we apply systems thinking, examples of boundaries could be the maximum amount of carbon absorbed by an average tree in a year or the number of acorns available for small animals in a season. If processes and resources in an ecosystem were constantly running up against boundaries of scarcity or depletion, then it would put a strain on the environment to sustain itself. Ecosystems must cycle through materials with methods like decomposition to stay balanced (think of it as not living beyond your means). Decomposition is the end of a life and the beginning of another life. This cyclical process is what perpetuates growth and sustains life from the forest floor to the backyard compost pile. Decomposition is a collaborative effort of the detritivore community (like beetles), in which dead tissues are broken down into less-complex organic material to be used for food. These decomposers operate together or alongside each other, chowing down dead materials, with each detritivore responsible for an aspect of the process.[11] Some materials take more effort to get through than others, but in time, everything that has fallen is taken back into the soil to help facilitate new growth.

It's imperative that we deal with the waste our society generates, just as forests must decompose its own waste within a reasonable amount of time. However, what happens when the forest has too much to decompose and not enough time to do it or when factors slow down the decomposition process nearly to a halt? This problem has appeared in forests surrounding the Ukrainian Chernobyl nuclear power plant. More than thirty years have passed since an explosion at the plant led to massive evacuations as radioactive material seeped into the surrounding environment. Similar to the BP oil spill, this incident had consequences that still plague the area to this day, particularly on the nearby natural ecosystems. Studies conducted in 2007 show that organic decomposition rates of twenty forest sites surrounding Chernobyl were 40 percent lower than what is typical for the region.[12] This suggests that the radioactive pollution has increased accumulation of organic "litter" on the forest floor and negatively affected the growth of plants. Maintaining regular rates of decomposition is essential for soil health and, in turn, the forest ecosystem health as a whole. Imagine going on a stroll through your favorite forest only to find that the ground was still covered with dead trees, leaves, and other organic litter. There would be no forest floor to speak of, and your stroll would be shortened to the very edge of the woods. Essentially, imagine if nature were as inefficient with its waste as humans often can be.

In the United States, each person disposes of more than four pounds of trash every single day on average. From the packaging of the food you purchase to the receipt from the store to any remaining food itself that gets tossed, waste is generated in every meal, snack, and business transaction we make. Being a consumer is part of existing in modern-day society, but the choice comes in *what* and *how often* we choose to consume. While we must mitigate the trash we produce through processes like recycling, there are limits to our efforts. At some point, we need to get back to the root of the problem: We have too much stuff. As Annie Leonard states in *The Story of Stuff*,[13] we all should absolutely recycle, but that alone will never be enough. For every garbage can of waste your household puts on the curb, seventy garbage cans of waste were made to create all the trash that you are now throwing away.[14] There is a reason we are taught that reduce and reuse come before recycle. Even if we were able to recycle everything our households and workplaces dispose of, there is still the impact of *making* all that stuff in the first place. This book focuses on the recycling system, but it's crucial that we first reduce our overall consumption, repair and reuse existing items, and *then* recycle what remains. This point is expanded in later chapters.

Recycling needs many groups of people to function: waste haulers; sorting facility workers; manufacturers; and, of course, companies to buy and create a demand for recycled material. However, the single most influential group of people who has helped expand recycling and kept it within the national focus are community residents. These are people who push for more recycling programs in their neighborhoods, community centers, and schools. These are the people who care enough to think, "Can I recycle this?" before tossing something in the trash. People have seen recycling as more than an action they take for the environment. It is a habit that gives them a pride reminiscent of patriotism. If the general public does not use a form of waste management, it will not succeed. And the overwhelming (and sometimes surprising) fondness that many have for recycling shows that the action resonates with people.

It may often feel like we are living in a predesigned system and the decisions we make have essentially been made for us by lawmakers and capitalists. We move throughout this web and do the best we can to exercise control over our lives, perhaps trying to leave our corner of the web better than when we found it. And in many ways, these feelings are justified. The world operates as it does because people, for better and for worse, agreed for it to work that way. Not everyone had equal power in these decisions, and it's obvious this unequal decision making not only hurts many of us but also makes our society worse because of that unjust imbalance. However one thing hinging entirely on all people agreeing to do it, on all of us buying in and making it happen, is recycling. People have helped maintain recycling at different times in history by demanding it exist. People just like us woke up every day and wanted to have a better option to deal with waste to improve our world. These people made it possible by choosing to participate and grow a system that begins and ends with our individual actions.

This book raises awareness about this imperfect yet extremely powerful system we all manage. I discuss how it came to be this way, the communities through modern history who shaped it, and the challenges we currently face in allowing it to thrive. It is my hope you come away with a deeper understanding of the recycling system we take part in daily and the power individuals have in creating the society we want through small actions woven into the routines of our lives. You will learn about the stakeholders and industries overlapping in this system and who have responsibility for helping it, and yes, you will also learn if you can recycle pizza boxes.

My hope is to nurture the enthusiasm you may feel for recycling as problems within the system are solved, to harness that excitement for your irreplaceable role in making it work, and to empower you in that role to help the system flourish. In 2012, a three-year-old boy named Ryan visited his local recycling center near San Juan Capistrano, California. [15] This trip to an ordinary facility inspired Ryan to devote his time and energy to helping his neighborhood recycle better. By age seven, Ryan was a leader in his community for recycling advocacy. He now offers to collect recyclables from his neighbors for free, and has served 100 participants across a 20 mile radius. The local hauling company has celebrated Ryan's efforts to educate by awarding him and sharing his story on social media. With a contagious love of recycling, Ryan's message has reached people beyond his neighborhood and he now receives emails from fans worldwide asking recycling questions and sharing in his enthusiasm. He speaks to crowds about recycling in varying places from his local chess club to the headquarters of major corporations. Ryan is one young person who saw the wonder of engineering new treasures from our old trash, and used every platform he could to raise awareness for this system. Besides being a very endearing story about an inspiring child who has diverted hundreds of thousands of items from the landfill, this is a story about how people's excitement for recycling helps grow the process throughout our country. We need to remember this, as we untangle the complex knots in the system and find new ways to be better environmental stewards. Just as we look to nature to learn how it manages its waste, we can look to one another for inspiration.

2

WHEN RECYCLING WAS PATRIOTIC

Imagine seeing your neighbors frantically collect old, rusty wagon wheels; broken phonograph records; used-up wash pots and horse-shoes; and fallen-down fences. Now imagine your entire town cheering while all this refuse is piled high in front of your Town Hall, cherishing the collection of previously unwanted stuff. Instead of feeling annoyed or inconvenienced, a contagious sense of pride would spread as you worked together to find every discarded scrap of junk abandoned from fields to alleyways. In 1942, these scrap scavenger hunts were celebrated with parties and rallies. These items would be given a new life, and it wouldn't have been possible without neighborhoods like yours across the country digging for discarded and forgotten scrap. The resource drives during World War II proved how eager communities are to work together when there is a call to action with a sense of urgency. Recycling old trash suddenly became a staple habit of good Americans everywhere. Old pantyhose could become a parachute, cooking fat could help make black powder, and razor blades could have a new use in machine guns.[1]

There were modest monetary rewards (a typical payment was a penny per pound of scrap), but what seemed to be more compelling for participation was the community spirit the drives incited. There was the satisfaction of backyard junk going to help friends and family members fighting in the war. Turning old materials into newer items was not a concept born of the war effort, as there are records of recycling in classical civilizations. (The concept has deep roots, but the term recycling was not used until the 1920s.[2]) What was unique to this specific era was the energetic support and devotion this form of recycling received from the public.

Collecting scrap had been a business in the United States decades before it became a popular practice of the war effort, but it was not always so celebrated. Historically, owners of scrap firms were likely to experience blatant discrimination from the public, despite the efficient waste management and societal benefits their businesses contributed. Throughout the world, there are examples of disdain or disrespect for workers in waste management industries, and the United States is no exception. People have a tendency to look at waste management with a wrinkled nose, like one you might have if a garbage truck drives by, wafting the scent of all the trash we produce in your direction. We like to have trash hastily removed, and people may not care where it goes or who escorts it there, as long as it's away from their homes.

Beyond discrimination against sanitation workers, there is overt prejudice in placement of where our trash is taken, as indicated by the proximity of waste disposal sites to underserved communities of color. In Gerald Gutenschwager's 1957 dissertation about Chicago's scrap industry, he discovered that the concentration of scrap businesses in African American neighborhoods was significant, and he drew a series of maps showing the relation. These maps, dating from 1919 to 1956, show junk shops were placed in residential areas made up of at least 25 percent African American population. If anything, we would learn this was a modest estimate. Much of the public wanted nothing to do with trash, so the industry was an undesirable field to work in. This meant there was space for individuals who were less easily deterred (or had fewer options) by the negative perception of the industry. The scrap trade of the 1880s–1920s offered a unique opportunity to immigrants to open a business requiring little startup capital and could offer prosperous returns in just a few years.[3] These business owners, who later labeled themselves the "original recyclers," continued their work despite being called "filthy" and "un-American" by those who looked down on them and their industry. The perseverance paid off, as scrap businesses had a fast escalation in profit. This proved that the need to dispose of trash and the need for raw material for manufacturers outweighed the social scorn much of the public felt for the industry.

Scrap dealers were also not supported by the government, and in many cases, legislators tried to reduce the businesses' ability to legally collect raw materials. The government cited safety concerns as reasons to block the industry. Collecting and sorting scrap was dangerous work with safety hazards, such as jagged-edged pieces and rusty items that could cause tetanus. The concerns were valid, but at the end of the day, the discarded stuff had to go somewhere. Scrap dealers used marketing campaigns to influence the public perception of their work. They proudly claimed an identity as a crucial component of fighting waste and inefficiency to bolster domestic manufacturers. The industry aligned scrap collection with commendable conservation for the sake of the country because it would be harder to argue with such a patriotic justification.

The tables turned as the United States became entrenched in World War II. There was a dire need for scrap metal supplies, as steel factories experienced deficits across the country. Henry Doorly, publisher of the *Omaha World-Herald*, read an article lamenting the supply shortage and set out to organize a scrap drive competition in Nebraska, having counties compete for prizes and war bonds (a loan to the government that people bought to invest in the war with the promise of repayment).[4] The target goal was to collect one hundred pounds of scrap per Nebraskan over the three-week period. Despite the grumblings of some who scoffed that 3 pounds per person was the best the state could hope for, in July and August 1942, Nebraska collected 67,000 tons of scrap, the equivalent of 103 pounds per state resident.[5]

Nebraskans recall how the daily routines of their towns stood still. The focus was to gather scrap, and citizens did so with efficiency and pride. Organizers made the drive successful by relying on methods that would unify residents and ensure wide participation. First, they acknowledged every contribution as important, regardless of its size. Second, conversion factors were used to help the public conceptualize what their scrap could become and envision its utility to the soldiers (we use a similar method today on recycling posters, for example, emphasizing that ten plastic bottles can be made into a T-shirt or plastic lids can become a new picnic table). And finally, the spirit of competition with prize incentives motivated the counties. Through this fruitful drive, we can see that creative planning, incentives, and a strong sense of unity can mobilize a community to achieve meaningful goals.

Nebraska's initiative inspired the federal government to announce a nationwide scrap drive, and states began competing, with no need of any enticing cash prize for the winner. Franklin Roosevelt's call for scrap was heard loud and clear, as citizens throughout the country, hungry for ways to contribute to the war effort, eagerly began collecting old materials. Government agencies used every method of media to promote the drive. Requests were made through posters, radio shows, public rallies, and newspaper articles to mobilize residents. Thousands of drives began in cities and towns, led by local businesses, schools, and other community groups to gather household waste.

Each state had a monthly quota, and communities were exceedingly creative in ways to collect materials. For example, the Biltmore Hotel in Dayton, Ohio, hosted a "fur ball," charging partygoers to donate fur garments as the admission fee. The donated items were used to make nearly 50,000 fur-lined vests to keep Allied merchant seamen warm while they transported supplies across the ocean.[6] Paper was another essential resource, used for packaging vital goods for the soldiers, and people in all industries were finding opportunities to use less of it in order to divert more to the war effort. Newspapers and magazines used fewer pages, while tissue and other light paper products were made even thinner. Typesetters narrowed page margins to maximize words per page. All of these measures were so impactful at salvaging that paper mills requested a temporary pause to scrap drives. Scrap collecting became as American as baseball and scout troops (incidentally, both of which provided drop-off locations for scrap). Movie theaters even began taking balls of aluminum foil in place of paying for a ticket. Scrap collection, once dismissed as a dirty nuisance, had been reframed to be unquestionably patriotic.

Businesses that had been in the scrap trade for decades publicly voiced enthusiasm for this new "cooperation." However, quietly, they held reservations about the gusto with which the government was moving into their industry. They predicted more regulation of prices and collection methods would accompany all the new federal interest in their trade. Another concern was that community drives would collect a significant amount of poor-quality materials.

In addition to being a sustainable method of managing materials, the recycling industry is a business, and recyclables are commodities. The items need to be of a certain quality to be marketable for purchase.

There must also be enough demand for these items to justify the effort it takes to collect them. This is why it's not enough to solely recycle our used goods; we must also mindfully purchase items to reflect those values. As consumers, we can flex our power to influence the market by choosing recyclable products *made with* recycled content, effectively completing the circle necessary for a functioning recycling system. Decisions we make every day drive demand, which ultimately shapes our entire society. What succeeds and fails in the market is often in flux, but the one necessity is a demand to exist and for it to be driven by a powerful force. During World War II, the demand for recovered materials was driven by the government. Harnessing community spirit through campaigns and calls for materials, the government may have created the demand for materials, but neighborhoods created their own moral incentives for participating in the drives. What kept the cycle from being completed was a lack of consumer demand for recycled-content products. This was not emphasized at the time, likely because recovered materials were meant to support the war effort and not to meet consumer needs for new products. Also, there were no labels used to advertise recycled content in products like we see today (more on this in later chapters).

Wastefulness was a problem that needed to be eradicated for the greater good. The pressure to conserve was contagious, and it helped expand the conservation mind-set throughout cities. One would see house window stickers touting the residents' sacrifices to the war, and this led to other homes trying to make similar changes to show their allegiance. We can see similar proclamations of stewardship today when people proudly use reusable bags, travel mugs, and their own Tupperware for leftovers and slap bumper stickers on any surface urging others to do the same. One person can truly make a difference, and when those individuals form united groups, incredible feats can be achieved. In this case, the reporter who wrote an article outlining material shortages was one person. And the article led to the great Nebraska scrap drive and then became a movement that rippled across the nation.

The widespread enthusiasm is important to consider, but we also need to analyze the ultimate impact the scrap drives had on the war effort. When moral incentives, like patriotism, are the driving force rather than a market demand for materials, there is a risk that the act is more of a symbolic gesture than one actually yielding results. There was no guarantee that the collected materials could satisfy what the industry needed during the war, neither in scale nor in quality. In *The Story of Scrap*, Edwin Barringer estimates nine million tons of scrap were collected during the U.S. involvement in the war, which dealers could not have acquired through normal collection.[7] When one tank would require eighteen tons of metal, nine million could certainly go a long way in helping out. More than one-third of all paper and paperboard products were recovered. Scrap drives brought in 6.4 million pounds of aluminum.[8] This made up 6.75 percent of all aluminum production made from old scrap. It has been argued that the scrap drives contributed more to boosting citizen morale than providing any real help in the war. While the practical effect of some collected materials was not considered extensive, the collected scrap did in fact provide assistance that otherwise would have been absent. The drives also provided a steady sense of purpose and were undeniably essential for maintaining community spirit in a challenging time.

However, it wasn't all smooth sailing and cheers for the scrap collection systems. In 1941, women were told that 10,000 tons of aluminum would build 4,000 fighter planes and promptly responded by collectively donating 70,000 tons of aluminum in the form of pots and pans.[9] It was learned later that brand-new aluminum was required for aircraft. The collected aluminum was eventually sold to scrap dealers and made into new pots and pans. This conceivably led to many women buying back the aluminum they had previously donated. While this could be described as a successful loop of recycling, the materials were not able to be used in the way participants had thought or intended. Criticisms of the federal government's directions on scrap collecting note it was asking too little (in volume and quality) and receiving too little in response. Things improved after 1942, yet we must ask, Can recycling succeed if key participants are not being asked to fulfill their roles in the best way possible?

When participants learn that the destination for their recyclables does not match their expectation, trust in the system can waver. If citizens during World War II were told that their scrap drives might not always help soldiers as much as they believed, it is possible that action on the home front would have become less passionate. At times, there were long delays in the collected scrap moving to refineries. People who had gathered these materials may have questioned the usefulness of their efforts, as they saw the piles sit and wait. In New York, a contributing factor to the delay was Mayor LaGuardia's decision to cut scrap dealers out of the system. Refineries wanted scrap that had been properly sorted—communities were collecting, but the key role of sorting was not being fulfilled.[10] This cautious feeling still exists today with recycling participants. In 2016, 33 percent of respondents of a Keep America Beautiful survey reported feeling skeptical that their recyclables are actually being recycled.[11]

The war era renewed and expanded other valuable habits beyond scrap drives, as conservation spilled over into other parts of daily life. By 1942, six million victory gardens were being cultivated by citizens around the nation. This inspired the secretary of agriculture to set the goal of eighteen million victory gardens, which the public quickly surpassed. In 1943, twenty million gardens, enough to fill the state of Rhode Island, successfully grew eight million tons of produce.[12] This was reportedly enough vegetables to exceed the "total commercial production for fresh sale for civilian and non-civilian use" and residents were urged, "Eat what you can, and can what you can't" to prevent food waste. Conservation habits were also motivated through necessity to comply with rationing directives from the government. By itself, recycling could not resolve material shortages—people were asked to make do with less of certain items. Historians report the rationing brought anxiety and fear, a stark contrast to the jubilant spirit of neighborhood scrap drives, since it feels more constricting to give up items we want or need rather than just our discarded ones.

Because this was soon after the Great Depression, people did not have to give up any excessive consumption habits to live more frugally; they were used to doing without. However, in the Depression, those who had private wealth could maintain a more privileged lifestyle; during the war, the government had first claim on resources.[13] Even the richest citizens could not maintain just any purchasing habits they pleased because the soldiers took priority. Despite the inconvenience and strain of it, citizens adhered to rationing to defeat the enemy.

Perhaps people were not as acutely aware of which materials touched every part of their lives until they were called on to gather it for the scrap drives. Americans were finding creative ways to use materials wisely, and this resourcefulness led to more self-sufficiency. Many people believed that the government did not need to be effective because the public could manage just fine on its own.[14] This kind of self-suffi-ciency, had it stuck, could have drastically altered the landscape of consumption. Imagine if today we constantly asked ourselves questions like, "How can I use less of X material?" and "How can I reuse this myself?" Our role as rampant consumers could shift toward being selective consumers, using our materials to their maximum potential before turning to disposal.

In World War II, there was an identifiable human enemy who stirred the anger and resolve of Americans. The threat arose from a specific source, and once it was eradicated, people celebrated. Collecting scrap, rationing goods, planting victory gardens, and living with less had all been rewarded with victory. When reflecting on the fervor for conservation during World War II, I wonder how to recharge that collective action for the sake of environmental stewardship. Urgency of the war created a time-sensitive pressure in which taking any action necessary to win was the obvious duty. It's possible that the call to urgency for the scrap drives was so strong that, while it spurred mass participation, it also came with an inherent sense of an end date. At some point, the war would end, and people could focus less on gardening and scrapping. But the monumental threat of climate change as we neglect to curb our greenhouse gas emissions does not strike a chord for such unified fervor to change our lifestyles.

Part of the challenge is the constant flow of information we absorb and how confusing it can be to figure out the most sustainable option when there are conflicting opinions cropping up with every internet search. You might have been recycling an item for years, thinking it was a good choice, only to learn (maybe even from this book) it was nonrecyclable and even creating issues within the system. It can be disheartening to do what we think is the right thing, only to learn a result of our choices could cause problems elsewhere. Sometimes this can mount into frustration and leave us disengaged from trying to do better, when we seem to constantly be told it's not enough. But we have a great opportunity to change course and build better habits for a greater good, like the citizens who answered the call to conserve in the war.

We contribute to the problem, yet we have the power to be part of the solution of addressing climate change. This willful omission of our role in fixing the problem is what keeps our society inactive on not just environmentalism but also a wide breadth of issues, and solutions can only be found if we face challenges with an open and ready mind. Most people have a strong urge to feel like they are a part of something bigger. We want to be part of a group that shares our values and rewards our efforts. The scrap drives and conservation of World War II tapped into this deep desire and mobilized people to devote their valuable time and energy into a cause beyond their individual selves. The country answered the call to reduce, reuse, and recycle. While there is some debate on the effectiveness of the scrap drives, there is absolute consensus that Americans changed their habits surrounding waste during this period.[15] However, once the urgent needs had been satisfied and the war was won, our country shed its prudent habits and ushered in the most rampant era of consumerism to date.

RISE OF A THROWAWAY CULTURE

The August 1955 cover of *Life* magazine depicted a family as they joyfully tossed disposable utensils and plates into the air, with the plainly stated headline "Throwaway Living."[16] During the postwar era of 1946 to 1956, national output for goods and services doubled, and two-thirds of the gross national product was directly from individual consumption.[17] Industries like television and plastics were born from this rapid uptake of consumer purchasing. The public was eager to spend, and companies jumped at the chance to oblige the itch for shopping sprees. Why were so many Americans ready to shed their habits of mindful consumption right away? For those who lived through the Depression era and then proceeded to a life of rationing for the war effort, perhaps they had been aching for the chance to purchase goods without constraint. When one goes an extended time without eating and finally has a meal, they may not notice the feeling of being satisfied, and end up with the discomfort of overeating to make up for the deficit of being hungry. Material consumption can be the same way. People were raring to purchase things because they finally could. After the war, the United States was ravenous for the rewards of prosperity, and with an increase in salaries and a booming economy, disposable goods became not only the norm but also a sign of luxury. The thinking became, why clean and reuse what could just be thrown away? It was modern and savvy to discard as you pleased, and the environment felt the consequences.

Recycling programs saw heavy decline during this period. Retailing analysts and economists concluded that, to have a productive economy, Americans must make consumption a way of life, and they strived to make buying goods as much of a ritual as possible. They decided that consumers needed to feel an actual spiritual reward in purchasing, using, and discarding to replace these things at an ever-accelerating rate.[18] And with this as the deeply flawed roadmap toward economic expansion, our country went from victory gardens and scrap drives to plastic plates and Styrofoam, and the model citizen's role went from conserver to consumer.

Shopping was on the rise because of personal desires; but, consumers were also incentivized to buy from another source. Have you ever heard "They don't make things like they used to in the good ol' days"? Well, they really don't, presuming the good ol' days are pre-1950. This refers to the rate at which products break and deteriorate compared to a previous time, when customers could rely on companies to make quality goods that were built to last. And if a product broke, it could be fixed by replacing its parts. Companies started sacrificing the integrity of their products to sell more volume more often. Planned obsolescence is a method of stimulating demand by producing goods that lose utility or style after a short amount of time. Think of clothing, disposable goods, technology, and even textbooks that are in one season and out the next. These items have baked within them an expiration date, a time in which they will be useless or simply outdated. Alfred P. Sloan Jr. was president of General Motors and in his autobiography noted, "The changes in the new model should be so novel and attractive as to create demand . . . and a certain amount of dissatisfaction with past models as compared with the new one."[19] Planned obsolescence refers to a intended loss of utility after a certain (usually very short) time, and perceived obsolescence is more about creating a social sense of disdain for an older model. These were key strategies used to stimulate the postwar economy and are still in heavy use today. You can see planned obsolescence when your smartphone gets sluggish after two years or when your favorite applications only work with a newer operating system or even when replacing parts in an older model costs significantly more than buying the new one. Perceived obsolescence is at work when a newer model has such significant excitement surrounding it simply because it's new that anyone using an older model is "behind the times," even if the older one still functions. Frustrating and inefficient, planned obsolescence trains us to not expect a product to last longer than a season or two.

France is leading an effort to reduce planned obsolescence through smart policy making. In 2015, it became the first country to demand manufacturers and vendors explicitly state a product's estimated life span.[20] All French manufacturers must inform vendors how long spare parts for a product will be produced, so that vendors are able to inform buyers. Failing to do this can result in a hefty fine. Additionally, France directs manufacturers to provide a two-year warranty for all sales. Mandatory warranties and product life-span transparency are believed to be good for competition in the marketplace by encouraging the production of better-quality materials. We as consumers expect cheap goods, so manufacturers use cheaper materials to generate a profit. We need to reframe our thinking on what we think goods should cost. By accepting and paying the true cost of goods, we can make high-quality, long-lasting products the norm again and extend fair wages to workers throughout supply chains. Ending planned obsolescence would result in a slight increase in product prices, but that can be offset by having a quality product for a longer period of time. As for the postwar era, the needs for industrial production had grown to satisfy necessities for the war, and afterward, these large factories were the perfect size for producing consumer goods—and a lot of them.[21]

The throw-away culture brought with it an apathy toward waste disposal. People casually tossed trash out of car windows and left garbage in public areas, and any instinct to recycle faded away. Children saw their caregivers littering and adopted the same habits. Regularly seeing litter on streets emboldens more people to litter with the subtle thought of "If they did it, why shouldn't I?"[22]

Eventually, the throw-anywhere culture elicited a response, although it was more for aesthetic reasons than environmental ones. Anti-littering campaigns used shame and guilt to keep people from tossing their trash all over by urging citizens to not be a "litterbug." In 1953, Keep America Beautiful was created and would launch a full-scale campaign in the coming years, complete with signs and brochures. Despite these efforts, littering continued to be prolific into the 1960s. Campaigns relying exclusively on shame as a vehicle to inspire change are rarely successful.[23] People are more likely to change after seeing responsible behavior and adopting it. If not littering is perceived as the norm, people will respond accordingly, regardless of any environmental impact. Citizen groups took on the challenge to defeat litter, like in Portland, Oregon. These Oregonians wanted to pluck the problem at its root and change public opinions on littering. They advocated for the automobile industry to be held accountable for the disposal of its products. Communities also supported increasing litter collection in national parks and other public lands and demanded more trash cans to be placed on roadsides. [24]

A fair criticism tied to some antilittering campaigns was how they placed all of the onus onto the consumer, letting companies selling wasteful items wiggle out of any responsibility, particularly when an ad campaign was born from many collaborators, including companies producing the very bottles and cans whose one-time-use products were driving the ease of littering. These companies were tired of seeing their logos on items strewn about public spaces, linking their brand to the trash. It's possible their aim was not to fix problems they were creating by taking action to change business practices but instead to shift responsibility elsewhere. Some campaigns have been cited for greenwashing, which is the attempt to mask unsustainable practices as green, often relying on the assumption that the public won't look into the claims. In this instance, what was being masked were the companies whose bottom line benefits when placing the blame for trash elsewhere—directly onto the consumer. Sales could continue going up, and the public would carry all the guilt for dirty public spaces. In 1965, less than 10 percent of soft drinks were sold in disposable containers, but by 1976, this would jump to 70 percent. [25]

But shouldn't part of the blame be assigned to the person who chooses to purchase wasteful goods? After all, we are the ones at fault for opting to use a disposable bottle instead of a reusable one. Personal accountability is important; however, when the systems we operate in are swaddled with incentives for us to buy these wasteful goods, either through lack of other options or planned obsolescence, we must not allow profiting companies to escape all blame. Remember the crying Native American commercial (later revealed to be performed by an Italian American actor) that circulated in the 1970s? An actor paddles his lone canoe through a polluted, trash-filled river and walks in moccasins along a littered highway, and his pain is displayed by a single tear. It states that people are the start of pollution and can choose to end it. In one staged tear, companies at the helm of this message hid themselves from the harmful effects of their products and assigned blame solely to the individual viewer.

While it was clearly memorable, the commercial was argued to be unproductive because it showed littering as a social norm by displaying the massive number of people who litter.[26] Social science tests suggest a more effective campaign would create and enforce a positive norm.[27] Robert Cialdini, author and psychology professor, advises instead of normalizing littering, a campaign should work to marginalize it. Communicating the idea that it just takes one person's litter to take away a park's beauty is more effective than saying "Look at all these people who are littering." The ad is credited for launching the environmental movement of the 1970s. Some have celebrated the ad for touching people who feel deep sorrow and guilt for the history of colonialism and its devastation, not only of the land but also of its original inhabitants. However, the message of this commercial is geared toward individual responsibility and does not question the larger systemic problems that directly cause pollution. What is productive about evoking feelings of guilt if no action to change the unjust and, in this case, wasteful systems occurs? Keep America Beautiful reports that, from 1969 to 2009, overall litter decreased by 61 percent and observed posting antilitter signs in littered spaces will most likely worsen the prevalence of litter instead of eradicating it.[28] Antilittering campaigns surely raised awareness of the issue and contributed to decreasing the habit, but producers of disposable goods were also successful in attempting to reframe the problem. Littering habits may have declined, but purchasing habits continued steadily upward.

From 1920 to 1970, municipal waste went up five times as quickly as the U.S. population due to a bolstered postwar economy, cheap goods, and planned obsolescence.[29] We were producing, consuming, and discarding products faster than ever. People had no problem throwing away items for the sake of convenience or status. But the *away* part of *throw away* is a serious inaccuracy that perpetuates wasteful behavior. Once we've used something, even just for mere minutes, we can toss it into a can and know it will be carted off somewhere else. "Away" is not a real destination for our trash. It might be away from our immediate person, but it still has to go somewhere. Also, one person's "away" might be in another person's community. A common reaction to trash is, once thrown away, it becomes someone else's problem. The physical transport of it may depend on someone else; however, it remains our collective problem, as the trash piles up, and we continue to think it went "away."

In 1962, a soft-spoken scientist with a strong message shook the nation with her evidence that, in the case of harsh pesticides, *away* is a misnomer. Through a steady determination and relentless research, Rachel Carson exposed the dangers of pesticide use through her eruptive work *Silent Spring*. Carson explained how nature suffered under pesticides like DDT and how we would suffer in return due to interconnected systems like food chains. She drew national attention and sparked policy debates surrounding the issue, and shortly after its publication, President John F. Kennedy cited her work and created a committee meant to analyze pesticide use and effects. Ten years later, DDT would be banned from production in the United States. Carson's writing helped the public realize that caring for human health meant caring for the environment and vice versa.[30] Her succinct evidence and moving eloquence reminded people how the functions of industry are not separate from the rest of our lives. As technology shoots forward at breakneck speed, *Silent Spring* was an unwavering sign urging us to pause and deeply consider how we are advancing and at what costs and advising us to find a balance with nature. As Carson writes, "How could intelligent beings seek to control a few unwanted species by a method that contaminated the entire environment and brought the threat of disease and death even to their own kind?"[31] While this references practices to eradicate pests and weeds, it can also apply to our demand to get trash out of sight so we can put it out of mind, regardless of where it goes and who else it harms. *Silent Spring* was extremely effective at sounding an alarm for the dangers of pesticide use, but its larger achievement was in changing how people viewed our relationship with nature. The interconnectedness that flows throughout Carson's work is a sobering reminder of why we must approach problems through a systems-thinking lens. We can't expect long-lasting, thoughtful solutions when we consider only one piece of a much larger, multifaceted system.

And so, what happened with recycling during this postwar period? The scrap industry actually expanded, but not to satisfy any environmental aims. Americans were buying and tossing at such a fast rate that the scrap companies reclaimed all they could just to keep up. Goods that were in vogue during this period were becoming more complex because they were made with a variety of materials, like mixtures of steel, glass, rubber, and plastic. This made recycling more difficult because materials needed to be recycled with like materials. Scrap firms that could adapt to these changes grew, and smaller companies who could not meet new demand closed their doors. Steel was the main material keeping the scrapping industry busy, with an 88 percent recycling rate by 1969. Cars were in fashion one year but then quickly replaced by newer models, sometimes within mere months, and this left mountains of materials strewn across the country. It's estimated that 25,000 junkyards were devoted to automobiles in 1951, with more than 8 million vehicles awaiting the scrap process throughout the 1960s.[32] With heavy littering and abandoned appliances and automobiles, the government began to push regulations onto scrap firms, which led to scrap yards being relocated into underserved neighborhoods with less political power to push back against them. Plastic was becoming more commonly used, and it complicated the recycling routine. Plastics were appealing due to their lightness and durability. Using it in packaging made transportation easier and allowed customers to carry beverages without breaking glass or as much weight. But when it came time to dispose of plastic items, challenges arose for companies now faced with a complex mix of polymers that differed among products.

Throughout the subsequent years, social norms were scrutinized and challenged through a collective force. The counterculture movement sought to question and change what had become widely acceptable in society, including reckless environmental pollution. The start of the 1970s brought not only the first Earth Day in our country but also a renewed excitement for recycling and other conservation efforts that had faded away after the war. Activists dumped disposable items on the front steps of major companies producing the goods and publicly shifted the blame back onto industry, pushing back against the antilittering campaigns that had put all accountability onto consumers.[33] Although companies prepared for such demonstrations and met the protesters with polished speeches and wide smiles, the fact that they felt the need to react at all showed that the movement was striking a nerve through corporate America. The public's attitude toward waste and litter evolved throughout the decade, as people organized and demanded a cleaner future. As a result of activist pressure, Coca-Cola began offering a five-cent bottle deposit in 1971, a new strategy to force companies to share responsibility for the goods they sold.[34] Recycling wasn't necessarily seen as patriotic as it had been during the war, but it was becoming a quality of a "good person" and an active steward. The incentives were simply moral, and that was enough to bring recycling back from the low priority where it had idly sat since the war ended.

The scrap industry redefined its reputation and embraced the sweeping tides of environmentalism starting to engulf the country. Scrap trade groups staked their claims as pivotal to the movement by calling themselves the "original recyclers" to prove they were reclaiming old materials for new before it was cool. Organizations rebranded and emerged, incorporating the word *recycling* into their moniker, signaling they assumed the habit was here to stay. People still wanted to buy things and have their disposables carted "away," but they felt much better about which "away" they were taken to.

3

RUNNING OUT OF ROOM

In spring of 1970, fifty activists marched through California's Central Valley on a six-week-long journey from Sacramento to Los Angeles. The five-hundred-mile "Survival Walk" was led by Ecology Action to raise awareness about human impacts on the environment and to highlight solutions to live less wastefully.[1] While walking through Modesto, founders Mary and Cliff Humphrey saw the potential for newspaper and glass recovery and decided the area could be transformed into a "model of ecological sanity." The efforts resulted in Modesto becoming the first city in the country to offer free and voluntary curbside recycling pickup two years later.[2] The activists created a recycling service that was efficient and easy for residents to use. Despite opposition from a few of the more conservative community members and discouragement from some city officials, Cliff Humphrey persevered to establish this vision, affirming that, if they could make recycling work there, it would work anywhere.

A residential curbside recycling program was not some fun and easy project for a few plucky environmentalists—it was hard work with no guaranteed return. Outside of the daunting logistics of collecting recyclables, there was the huge gamble of relying on public participation to make this idea work. Commercial recycling was one thing; materials could be picked up in bulk from a handful of sites with reliable volume and more controllable quality. Introducing curbside service meant bringing another source of material to the recycling stream, and although it would give people easier access than the drop-off centers they had been using, it would also mean there was less control in the amount and quality of the materials collected. The extra effort of scooping up recyclables from house to house might not even be rewarded. The idea of people changing their habits to recycle and sort out materials was far-fetched at best. Despite the numerous odds and causes for doubt, Ecology Action used secondhand trucks to provide Modesto residents with simple curbside services. The local government permitted this DIY-style waste collection with a slightly raised eyebrow, awaiting the activists to get burned out or bored and this experiment to run its course. But the course continued, as the presumed impossible became possible. People kept putting their recyclables out at the curb, week after week. What occurred in Modesto was the result of activists who wanted to see tangible results of putting their environmental values into practice. They wanted to build something on hope and optimism that was also deeply pragmatic and functional, something that could both serve the community and offer citizens a method of acting to help solve environmental problems. The practice became integral to the city's identity; its residents accepted the habit with enthusiasm, and the curbside pilot program started a movement of towns throughout the country following its footsteps.

Social habits were not the only sphere of environmental change of the era. Concerns surrounding environmental impact and efficient use of resources were amplifying, along with the mounting connections to waste disposal and public health. The rising public outcry, coupled with research confirming the threats of greenhouse gases and ozone depletion, gave ample cause for the government to act. It responded with such solutions as establishing the Environmental Protection Agency (EPA) and passing the Clean Water and Clean Air Acts. State and local governments acted to curb wasteful behavior, too. A landmark was Oregon's 1971 statewide beverage container deposit law, the first state to do so. Bottle bills require companies to include a refund in each purchase that equals the value of the bottle, so just a few cents per container. The customer can take the container back to a store or some drop-off location or machine to receive that monetary deposit back. (Today, states with similar bottle bills have a 70 percent recycling rate on average.[3])

Recycling was becoming more complex and had to navigate an influx of appliances made from varied materials arriving at scrap dealers. For example, air conditioners and refrigerators used Freon and CFCs that could be carcinogenic, which marked the units as hazardous for disposal.[4] In 1976, the Resource Conservation and Recovery Act (RCRA) was established, empowering the EPA to control hazardous waste management from its creation to its disposal. The act also implemented a framework for nonhazardous waste sites, including municipal landfills and incinerators.[5] For the sake of human and environmental health, regulations would ensure landfills were better operated or forced to close. As consumption continued to grow, the United States began to fear a shortage of landfills. We seemed to be running out of "away" places to send our trash.

HOW A LANDFILL CRISIS RAMPED UP RECYCLING

For years, residents living anywhere near the Staten Island Fresh Kills landfill could not open their windows during the summer. Harsh odors of garbage cooking in the sun would waft into nearby neighborhoods, as seagull flocks circled above the 2,200-acre dump. This was the first U.S. landfill to cover garbage with incinerator ash and a layer of dirt to keep the smell down. Fresh Kills began operation in 1947 and was intended to be a twenty-year project. However, the closing date continued to be pushed back by the city, and just eight years after opening, it was the world's largest landfill, taking in 13,000 tons of refuse a day.[6] In 1979, the United States had more than 16,000 landfills; however, in less than a decade, that number declined to 7,900.[7] The closures were caused by a variety of factors, including policy like RCRA, demanding safeguards be put into place to protect communities. But there were still enough operating landfills and more being built in compliance with new regulations. Regardless, the landfill closures were heavily reported by media outlets, giving a platform for the public to fear that the United States was trundling toward a grave landfill shortage. Despite the construction of new, larger landfills with the capacity to take in more volume, concern of a shortage persisted.

There was a change happening in the waste industry, where smaller dumps were closed because they couldn't comply with linings to protect groundwater. This opened the window for larger regional landfills to take on waste of municipalities previously served by these smaller companies, and trucking waste from across county and state lines became routine. Disagreements about whether the landfill crisis was even real ricocheted from all sides of the issue. Many people, from governmental and industry sectors as well as environmentalists, believed there was, in fact, a nationwide crisis, whereas others thought these worries were overblown. What most everyone agreed on was that larger urban areas had cause for concern with capacity due to the higher-density areas turning out so much waste. This era also saw jumps in landfill tipping fees in certain parts of the country, making it all the more costly to not find alternatives.[8] The public was demanding more environmentally friendly options for waste while still consuming stuff at high rates, and so decision makers began to reconsider incineration.

Burning waste has had a tumultuous history in the United States. Governor's Island, New York was the site of the nation's first incinerator in 1885.[9] By the late 1960s, 10 percent of solid waste was being burned. Then in 1970, the Clean Air Act put new standards on incinerators, and many were found to be environmentally inadequate at the time. Coinciding with what was to become the environmental movement, incineration met pushback from people concerned with its effects on communities. The industry began referring to the practice as "waste-to-energy" (WTE) and "resource recovery," attempts to distance itself from previous negative reputations, and to raise attention that utilities could purchase electricity generated from incineration. Nothing got state and municipal officials excited quite like the promise of reducing trash volume by 90 percent along with a byproduct of some useful energy.

There are two types of incineration. There's mass-burn incineration, where only large and noncombustible pieces are removed before the remaining trash is burned at high temperatures. The heat converts water to steam, which is sent to type of generator to make electricity. The ash is then taken to a landfill to be buried. There is also the refuse-derived fuel model, where recyclable goods are separated out and then the rest is shredded into pellets before being incinerated.[10] At the time, these processes showed trace emissions of chemicals and metals, including furans, dioxins, lead, mercury, and sulfur dioxide. Measures have been taken to remove toxins from incineration emissions, but opponents have pointed out this redistributes the problem to one of ash disposal. Like a backyard bonfire, anything that is burned leaves ash in its place. In the case of incineration, toxic ash is the stuff that gets left behind. Unfortunately, the better a plant is at preventing unhealthy emissions going out into the air, the more toxic the residual ash is because the toxins have to go somewhere; if they aren't flowing directly into the air, then they're "trapped" in the ash.[11] If the ash is disposed of improperly or in a defective landfill, then the ash can leach into groundwater and become airborne, allowing toxins to be ingested through inhalation or food crops.

There's also the loss in potential resources if you're sending more goods to a WTE plant rather than recycling. Critics of incineration noted that contracts for new facilities could require a set amount to burn per day, and this may take precedence over recycling efforts to ensure the agreements were met.[12] We would miss out on the new products those used materials could make and take away from the supply of recovered materials. This deficit would be filled through the extraction and production of virgin materials, processes that require more resources and emit more environmentally damaging emissions. By the early 1980s, with many government officials onboard, companies were poised to receive a deluge of new WTE facility construction projects. However, communities showed opposition and resistance with a momentum unanticipated by WTE interests. A new movement was rumbling under the ground of what many companies had previously assumed was a sure thing, and the cracks were enough for new and renewed solutions to grow through.

With the public unwilling to change high consumption rates, municipalities attempted to plan for new waste-deposit sites. Some residents found themselves facing plans for new landfills or incinerators, both of which caused unease over health and quality-of-life concerns, spurring actions to push back. Residents worried about the effect of nearby incinerators became known as "NIMBYs," or "Not in My Backyard." Some NIMBYs didn't want incinerators at all, whereas others wanted them out of sight and out of mind, but what really differentiated the NIMBYs came down to access to power. Affluent residents with the time and political means could push back against hazardous waste, incinerators, landfills, and power plants being located near their neighborhoods. This put municipalities in a tough spot to cost-effectively meet waste demands without encumbering residents with new facilities. Affirming "I don't want it in *my* backyard" implies that it should go in someone else's backyard. As Dr. Robert Bullard points out in *Dumping in Dixie*, the backyards often chosen are those of underserved and politically underrepresented communities of color.

In 1982, a depository site for soil contaminated with polychlorinated biphenyls (PCBs) was set for the Afton community in Warren County, North Carolina. This community had the highest percentage of black residents and was one of the poorest counties in the state. With a shallow water table and the community relying on well water, the area was an illogical location for a disposal site that would certainly leak the highly toxic PCBs into drinking water. This plan was met with a force of protests and demonstrations by community members, resulting in more than four hundred arrests. Unfortunately, despite the powerful mobilization of community members and other activists, as well as support from EPA officials and the Congressional Black Caucus, the six thousand truckloads still came, and the waste was dumped in Afton.

This example of environmental racism was pivotal for the environmental justice movement. Environmental racism is racial discrimination in environmental policies. It is the calculated, intentional placement of landfills and incinerators within marginalized communities and the blatant disregard for the health of those citizens when officials turn a blind eye to dangerous toxins in neighborhood water and air. The injustice of Warren County commenced a study of hazardous-waste landfill placement which "observed a strong relationship between the siting of offsite hazardous-waste landfills and race and socioeconomic status of surrounding communities." As Dr. Bullard observes in *Dumping in Dixie*, social activists began shifting environmentalism to the left to tackle such inequities as waste-disposal placement, and "although ecological sustainability and socioeconomic equality have not been fully achieved, there is clear evidence that the 1980s ushered in a new era of cooperation between environmental and social justice groups."[13]

Due to lack of political support or resources, some residents have had to oppose waste-deposit site plans while also pushing for solutions that can help tackle the trash. Community recycling centers have been places in which people can gain opportunity and self-sufficiency, like the Resource Center based in Chicago. This facility was opened under Ken Dunn's leadership in 1975, offering collection services to neighborhoods and providing cash to lower-income people bringing in recyclables. It has since grown to a full operation, with hauling trucks depositing materials every half-hour to be sorted at the drop-off location. In the '80s, the center expanded to developing some of the 70,000 vacant lots in the city into parks and gardens. These land projects used construction materials from abandoned structures, keeping the entire operation true to its cyclical, recycling values while holding community growth and renewal at its core.[14]

By the late 1980s, organizers throughout the country were working tirelessly to prevent new landfills and incineration facilities from being built. Municipalities were still anxious about landfills reaching capacity and took measures into their own hands through legislation, like Illinois's Retail Rate Law in 1987, which offered subsidies to incinerator companies. This ushered in the construction or permitting of nine additional incinerators in the state, most of which were in black neighborhoods. There was some support of these projects, providing the hope of new jobs and economic growth for community members. Unfortunately, based on the records of one planned facility, most of the jobs available to local residents would be low-wage and hazardous, whereas the white-collar jobs would be offered up to residents outside of the community. This hotly disputed facility set for the Robbins community would cost $730 million to build, funding that some suggested could better expand and strengthen existing recycling programs and provide jobs. The EPA gave approval to the facility, but the opposition group pushed on, and began arguing to repeal the Retail Rate Law to remove economic incentive for companies to build. Once the facility was built and began operations, the incinerator was proven to violate the Clean Air Act and remained the focus of many environmental opposition groups. (The Retail Rate Law would late be repealed in 1997 and the facility closed its doors in 2000.)[15]

In 1987, New Jersey became one of the first states in the United Stateas to pass mandatory recycling and set aggressive goals for material recovery.[16] During the same year, the nation was captivated by a barge full of New York City's trash meandering down the coast, looking for a place where it could be dumped. The Mobro 4000 was a floating pile of city garbage that couldn't be deposited in the local landfill because it lacked sufficient capacity. In an unsuccessful experiment to try depositing the metropolis's waste in the South, it was turned away from its original destination in North Carolina because of public outcry against it. The barge then toted its six million tons of trash to ports from New

Orleans to Mexico and all the way to Central America, trying to find a place to dump but denied at every port. It would return to New York after six thousand miles of meandering to have its waste disposed on Long Island, where it had originally been rejected, but state regulators had approved the landfill being expanded.[17] The trash was burned in a Brooklyn incinerator before going to its burial in Islip, Long Island. During the six months the Mobro was looking for a port to take it in, the images of floating garbage captivated people across the country, and many came to the startling realization that there's no real "away" when we throw something away. This barge's journey was a turning point in how Americans think about waste and served to jumpstart the most significant period of growth our recycling system had experienced yet.

A BOOM ERA FOR RECYCLING

If the zeal for recycling was revived in the 1970s, it was the 1990s when it became more widely entrenched in routines as its popularity grew, with more than four thousand communities implementing curbside programs. By the dawn of the '90s, 17 cities and rural areas recycled more than 25 percent of their waste and 15 jurisdictions had recycling rates between 40 and 60 percent.[18] Additionally, more than ten thousand drop-off centers were in operation throughout the country.[19] By 1996, the U.S. recycling rate was 25 percent, a huge increase from 16 percent seen at the start of the decade.[20] Kids who grew up in the '90s were instructed (in schools and through various media like TV) to not litter and to recycle, the two activities we could do to help "save the world." I was one of those kids who took the recycling lessons to heart and would scold anyone in my family who didn't recycle, even though our neighborhood did not have any residential program. I was a tad annoying but hardly alone in my enthusiasm. Recycling was impressed upon people as a moral imperative and the most basic thing we could do to protect the planet.

It might not have occured to most kids of this era that residents and organizations had worked very hard in prior years for recycling to be as customary as it had become for us. Talking about trash became a part of many school curriculums, with suggested lesson plans put out by the EPA because it was an environmental issue students could relate to and conceptualize. Ads flitted across screens, with celebrities making the practice cool and hip, not only advocating for recycling participation but also stirring a call for civic engagement to demand that cities provide curbside service. The 3 Rs became rudimentary, and there were even songs produced to encourage the habits, making the alliterative message even catchier. It was gaining traction outside of classrooms and kids' TV shows, too. Curbside recycling grew by 250 percent from 1988 to 1991, and the EPA set a new goal of a 35-percent recycling rate for the nation.[21] People were making the decision to incorporate sorting recyclable goods into their daily routine, reminiscent of war-era conservation efforts. But, not everyone was quite so eager to alter habits for an environmental cause. Opponents to recycling used op-ed columns to cite problems with the practice and call for its demise. But there were swift responses to these claims, presenting the gaping holes in arguments against it. These rebuttals also noted many recycling critics had connections to trade groups and companies in the packaging and waste management industries who benefit from landfilling fees.[22]

As public enthusiasm grew throughout the 1990s, companies were met with the task of accessing and incorporating recycled materials. Navigating the dysfunctions of the industry did not inspire confidence in everyone. It was theorized that the Reagan and Bush White House administrations had minimized the federal government's role and this was affecting recycling. More of the role coordinating the system was put onto state and local governments, and this included diffusing the opportunity of developing nationwide mandates for recycling programs. Our rates of consumption of goods and packaging showed that there was ample supply of potential recyclables for manufacturers to use; however, the flows from supply to demand were not connected. Manufacturers might have had an interest in using recycled materials but were concerned about an unstable supply if there was not adequate collection of recyclables. Vice versa, companies were hesitant to invest in collection if there was not a guaranteed demand from manufacturers. There was plenty of skepticism from each of the system's stakeholders about participation from the others, which kept the entire system moving slower than the public's enthusiasm for it.[23]

Companies were increasingly choosing plastic over other packaging materials but had concerns of a dwindling recycled plastic supply. Simultaneously, fears reverberated among manufacturers, who ques-

tioned making the necessary technology investments to process recovered materials in the face of an uncertain level of demand. What was
(and still is) needed for the recycling system to flourish was regular
communication between all the parties involved. This would seem to be
a natural role for the federal government to fill. However, after administrations sought to shrink influence over such an economic system, this
role remained unfulfilled.

In 1997, the President's Council on Sustainable Development
ushered in a new commitment for the United States on building sustainable communities. This report laid out a vision for places where
people worked collaboratively to keep communities healthy and thriving. The vision also kept natural resources preserved, jobs plentiful, and
sprawl contained. In short, communities should be developed with
keeping the "three Es" balanced: economic opportunity, social equity,
and the environment.[24] Supporters of this vision were then tasked with
the challenge of achieving a prosperous local economy in struggling
communities while raising the quality of life for residents through many
social systems and maintaining ecological integrity—a tall order, considering there were groups who favored one of the three areas over the
others and may have considered it necessary to sacrifice the others to
achieve success in one. These debates and tensions of how to make
prudent choices to achieve a thriving community still exist today, and
with an influx of younger generations desiring life in cities again, challenges of capacity and gentrification are also on the rise.

Given its many benefits in these areas, recycling was naturally a key
part of the portfolio for a sustainable city. It's one activity that delivers
on balancing the three Es when the system functions as it should. It was
a solution to the social pushbacks against new landfills and incinerators,
as well as an environmentally sound way to handle waste, generate
some revenue for the city, and reduce its costs of garbage disposal. To
achieve this, cities would need to make investments in infrastructure,
such as contracting with material haulers and building sorting facilities.

In the past, community-based programs were the source of recycling
at drop-off centers fueled by volunteer efforts and citizens who took it
upon themselves to facilitate this triple-win solution. Detroit is an example of a city that has weathered economic challenges through the
collapse of key industry. What is less often recognized are the resourceful and determined residents who seem to have a keen understanding

of the adage "If you want something done right, better do it yourself."
In 1990, a resident named Margaret Weber decided to provide something Detroit was lacking. She organized Rosedale Recycles, a monthly
drop-off location where residents could bring materials. Many were
parents of kids who had learned about the importance of recycling in
school and urged their families to keep items until the third Saturday of
the month, when they could leave it with Weber and her team. The
organization was created in response to the existence of an incinerator
which burned all municipal waste. *Rosedale Recycles* provided recycling
options where there had previously been none. Margaret Weber and
volunteers maintained the monthly drop-off collection for nearly 25
years. Community participation demonstrated the desire of residents
for recycling and kept the issue alive in public discourse.[25]

Toward the end of the century, the United States was getting closer
to a 30 percent recycling rate, and the Worldwatch Institute predicted
that, by 2030, recycling will have nearly replaced landfills.[26] One challenge of the soaring popularity of the practice was that recycling had
become less economically feasible, even with more participation from
the public. Supply was up, but demand for the collected materials was
low. People were recycling more but still consuming at increasing rates
and giving no market signals to manufacturers to prioritize using recycled content. In 1988, Susan Kinsella, executive director of Conservatree, observed this disconnect in the system and pointed out, "If you're
not buying recycled products, you're not recycling."[27] Ten years later, in
1998, EPA broadcast this theme for America Recycles Day. The agency
affirmed in a press release that true recycling also involves purchasing
goods made from recycled materials. It explained within the Mobius
Loop symbol, the three arrows chasing each other to make the familiar
triangle, each arrow represents a different part of the recycling system.
The first arrow represents gathering the used recycled items, the second represents processing and manufacturing these into new products,
and the third symbolizes the new products being purchased again by
consumers. Once again, we saw the government make a call to action,
and states responded accordingly by urging their citizens to do their
part—only in this instance, doing their part was not specifically planting
victory gardens or doing more with less; it was pledging to increase the
demand for recycled products. There were weeks of promoting the
pledge everywhere, from movie theater previews to printing the slogan

on grocery bags, and in the end, hundreds of thousands of people pledged to buy recycled. Whether it was the compelling call to close the recycling loop or the tantalizing prizes promised to lucky pledge takers, we can't know for certain. But as the twenty-first century was beginning, it seemed recycling was a national fixture that was here to stay. Once again, Americans were excited to collect and send their used items off to become new products. Only now it was not an action popularized to win the war effort but to protect the entire planet. The concept itself had been recycled, and an old process was now wrapped in a fresh and hopeful package for a new generation.

The pounding of determined feet racing across a park outside of New York City tread over decades of forgotten garbage, although not so soon forgotten by the neighbors who call the area home. Smells of acrid trash baking in the sun and the circling seagulls have vanished, as what was once Fresh Kills landfill now serves as a 2,200-acre park of grassy knolls, an expanse three times the size of Central Park.[28] Already the setting of annual 5K runs, photography, and kayaking excursions, the Freshkills Park has its sights set on providing playgrounds, horseback-riding trails, massive art installations, ecological restoration projects, and more to the community it once compromised. Different areas of the park will be opening in phases and will be completed in 2036, as converting the legendary dump to a safe park takes considerable time and effort, including six layers of barrier protection covering the garbage below.[29] What was a symbol of consumption and waste, of disposable goods building the world's largest landfill, will now stand as a living, breathing monument for renewed possibility in a society living more harmoniously with the natural environment. It will be a testament to how humans make significant impacts on the planet through our choices, sometimes with consequences that plague our air and water for years, a reminder of how destruction screeching from our collective waste has the potential to amount to far beyond what any living species should produce to maintain a balance. And yet it will tell a second part to that story: that we also have the ability to alter those decisions and move away from using so many disposable goods, avoiding falling into the costly traps of planned obsolescence. We can instead grow toward a balance of sustainability, even with the history of rampant consumption seemingly sewn into the fabric of our society. It's possible for people like us to make the choice to cut those threads and weave a new plan of needing less stuff to throw away and receiving more experiences that bring communities together. While the distant smokestacks dotting the skyline are a sign of the region's past, the land-reclamation project is truly an impressive feat achieved through community efforts and the local government.

Since the closure of the landfill, nearby Staten Island residents can breathe easier and let their kids play outside. The smells have subsided, and the promise of a new park sits atop decades of old trash. Unfortunately, this transformation does not mean the problems of the waste have been eradicated—they've simply moved elsewhere. Consumption still occurs, and the discarded packages and food scraps have another "away" to which they're delivered. This one part of a system may be better, cleaner, and on a positive path toward land recovery, yet we cannot ignore the other parts of our waste system that now host additional problems. Recycling is not simply a method of disposal, like landfilling or incineration. It is an overall reduction in our need for both of these things. Recycling is managing materials to extend their usefulness and reduce our environmental impact. It has wide-reaching benefits, some of which are obvious and some less so. As we've observed, the modern history of our consumption and waste disposal has evolved and escalated since those war-era days spent scrapping and conserving resources. Now let's dive further into the recycling system, beginning with essential steps to take before recycling something at all.

4

WHY REDUCE AND REUSE COME FIRST

I once wrote a blog about reducing waste around the holidays, and within it was a suggestion to reduce the number of cards we send or use alternatives to traditional paper mail. After receiving a few responses defending paper cards and advising me to be less of a Grinch, I observed two things: 1) people are far more passionate about holiday cards than I had realized, and 2) people are more open to compromising on practices rather than being directed not to do a specific action. For instance, if you can't imagine not sending cards, then do less in another area, like replacing wasteful disposable wrapping paper with reusable fabrics. Using cloth folding methods instead of paper and tape can make reusable wrapping both functional and beautiful (search for the Japanese Furoshiki fabric wrapping technique for examples). Striving to find a balanced way to green your habits means they are more likely to become lifelong practices. This is more effective than wanting to be more sustainable and feeling discouraged by some person trying to take away your holiday cards. We all have countless opportunities to insert more responsible habits into our lives, and we can begin by acknowledging the ways we can do with less and stick to it.

Reducing our consumption is the number 1 way to decrease our waste. The memorable phrase "reduce, reuse, recycle" is more than a catchy saying; it's a hierarchy of steps designed to increase sustainability. The full waste-management hierarchy (see figure 5.1) shows our options for disposing waste and goes from greatest environmental benefit to lowest. The top tier is source reduction and is what we should strive to do most often. Landfilling and incineration fall at the bottom to emphasize that we should avoid these due to their lack of environmental benefits. Some view landfilling to be worse for the environment than incineration, while others affirm it to be the opposite. The EPA's Waste Management Hierarchy considers incineration as resource recovery and places it above landfilling, but communities concerned with dangerous air pollutants from incineration may disagree. What burying and burning waste have in common is the loss of extended potential for using materials again. In both these disposal methods, the future usefulness of materials is cut short. We need to strive to use the top three tiers the most, beginning with reducing waste altogether.

> **Source Reduction (a.k.a., "reduce"):** Waste is eliminated at the very source from which it comes. A key part of this is refusing to take an item in the first place, like saying no to a plastic straw. Another aspect of reducing is to find solutions to disposable items you regularly use. This can include having a home garden, since you'll use less packaging by not buying those foods at the store. Another example is going to your local library and borrowing tools from neighbors instead of buying new. Source reduction can also be practiced at the manufacturing level when a company switches to use more-efficient packaging with less materials or redesigns products to be less wasteful or limit pollutants from its production.
>
> **Reuse:** This can be a subcategory of "reduce" because reusing old items reduces the need to purchase new ones. Examples of reuse include shopping secondhand for your clothes or housewares and repairing items rather than disposing and buying new ones.
>
> **Recycle/Compost:** This is collecting used items, sorting them, processing them into new materials, and then using those to manufacture new goods. This tier also includes composting organic waste like food scraps that can't be used or saved for later use. The composted soil can be used for planting new food and other landscaping needs. To contribute to this tier, know the local recycling rules and best practices (which I expand on later), and either do your own composting or participate in a city program or company that picks up your compost and transports it to a facility.
>
> **Landfill:** Modern sanitary landfills in compliance with regulations are shown to be less damaging than older open air dumps. How-

ever, it's important to divert usable waste from landfills to reduce the need to make virgin materials, as well as to keep landfill sizes low.

Incineration/Waste-to-Energy: Waste is converted into heat, electricity, or fuel through processes like combustion or gasification. This method has a range of views. Some consider it above landfilling because the waste is used to make energy rather than buried, however there have been powerful community-driven movements in response to the potential for toxic air pollution. Incineration still relies on landfills in part, as the EPA estimates that 10 percent of the volume remains as ash to be disposed of in a landfill.[1]

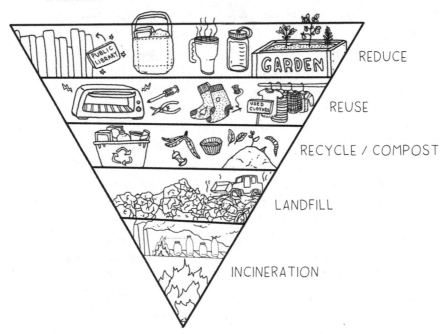

Figure 4.1.   Waste Management Hierarchy Pyramid. Iris Gottlieb

THE FIRST R: REDUCE

In the shortened hierarchy of just the Rs, recycling is the last option of the three that we should turn to as a solution. The importance of reducing what we consume cannot be overstated. The average American

produces more than four pounds of waste every single day,[2] from disposable coffee cups and food containers to the paper napkins and receipts we casually toss into the trash. Each purchase we make or don't
make is more than a mere symbolic gesture of our values. Our everyday
purchases from small to large directly shape the world we live in. Green
America has been urging citizens to vote with their dollars for more
than thirty-five years. The national nonprofit organization asserts that
we can wield more power than we may realize through how we spend
money and how we save it. It shares green businesses we can support
that have strong environmental and social practices and also helps people seek out community banks or credit unions that prioritize investing
in services that benefit our neighborhoods rather than enrich a few
high-level CEOs. Through Green America's work and resources, we are
reminded of the ways we communicate through these daily decisions.
Buying from a local business shouts an allegiance to your community
instead of a big-box store. Choosing to patronize a business owned by
women and people of color builds a more inclusive economy. And of
course, every dollar not spent affirms we won't be seduced by mountains of stuff we don't need to have a high quality of life.[3] Regardless of
the methods of responsible waste disposal, the singularly most important question we can all ask ourselves is, Do I really need this? The next
essential step is answering with honesty and behaving accordingly.

The ways in which we spend our money communicates to industries
and urges them to look more closely at what they are producing and
how. It's wise for companies to practice source reduction by using
more-efficient packaging for products and finding strategic ways to produce goods or offer services using less resources from the "cradle."
Source reduction focuses on not producing the waste in the first place,
and this is more than just the act of not buying something sitting on a
shelf. Instead, it focuses on preventing the item from ever being made.
It asks the questions recycling doesn't, namely, Why is this even produced? And it provides an opportunity to alter consumption habits at
the beginning.[4]

Companies control this aspect by electing to produce an item, but
we also have a direct influence through our demand and purchasing
habits. We can validate a company's choice by continuing to purchase
their product, but unfortunately, even if we verbalize our wish for a
more sustainable product, what speaks the loudest is what we actually

do. I've seen representatives from industries nod in agreement that customers don't seem to care about recycled content being used in their products, based solely on our purchasing habits. Industry will adhere most strongly to the money it generates, dismissing any surveys in which people affirm their sustainable values as an example of people saying one thing but doing another. However, the labeling of environmentally preferable products can be confusing (I address this more later). If an individual recycles diligently, then they may assume there is high recycled content in most products because where else would it be going? Of course, customers also value convenience and cost, but reducing consumption can serve these priorities, too. We can save money by avoiding unnecessary shopping trips and find added convenience in reducing our consumption to focus on what we truly need.

I have heard (and contributed to) the mountain of complaints about unnecessary amounts of packaging in the mail. It feels absurd to receive endless tissue paper and plastic wrapping for that one small item you ordered online, and in some cases, this frustration is spot on. Packaging and containers are the largest segment of municipal solid waste by product category.[5] Industry experts have suggested that proper packaging can have environmental benefits, such as curbing wasted food each year. One-third of food produced for human consumption worldwide is wasted, and this not only is a waste of the food itself but also all the energy and resources that went into growing and making it.[6]

As for online shopping orders, there are claims that excessive packaging is environmentally beneficial because it protects an object through delivery. By preventing any damage to what you've purchased, it's argued that more packaging can curb additional emissions because a broken delivery means added transportation to ship it back and the emissions send out a new one. Companies may think extra packaging is more cost effective than replacing broken items, but simply using more does not solve the problem.[7] Using a giant box for one small item is a waste of cardboard and a company's budget. The key is to pack efficiently and use appropriate cushioning materials that are easily recycled. Additionally, we have a tendency to fixate on the amount of packaging used rather than the environmental impacts of the objects we've purchased. We must urge companies to maximize recycled content in various materials and to pack smarter and more efficiently, but it's just as important for us to question if we truly need to make the purchase in the first place.

Zero landfill goals focus on diverting as much volume as possible away from the landfill; and zero-waste goals seemingly do the same. But, "zero landfill" does not necessarily include reduction and maximizing use of recycling, but instead can rely on incineration as a landfill alternative. Zero waste brings back the idea of source reduction as a key component. It strives to reduce impacts from extraction, production, use, and disposal. Zero landfill, however, only focuses on disposal or "end-of-life" and rerouting from landfills to other options. The zero-waste movement has struck a chord, from individuals to companies to municipalities, who are all enthusiastically looking for ways to use less stuff and, in turn, discard less stuff. Many participants in the movement have popularized the goal of fitting everything you'd send to the landfill in one year into one mason jar. The internet holds endless do-it-yourself recipes and tips to help you achieve that goal. This is an admirable idea, but there's still waste that doesn't get added to the jar because the individual doesn't touch it. From the packages used in a kitchen to prepare your food at a restaurant or the waste from the production of goods you consume, even if you recycle or compost the end result, none of these bits of refuse take up physical space in the jar. This is why "zero waste" is not actually about arriving at zero, since living in our society means making some amount of waste. It means striving to lower our waste, which is an excellent goal. But, as someone who has done this, it can be all too easy to be swept away by well-intentioned articles laying out steps to consume less and not put them into action. If browsing those articles is the only step we take, then all we've done is create a pathway for guilt and shame for later when we realize how we've failed to adopt all those habits. Betty Shelley, an Oregon native who teaches classes on reducing household waste, advises starting immediately with what's right in front of you.[8] Walk over to your garbage can and your recycling bin. Look inside, and note the items you are throwing out. Make a decision about which item you will not have in that bin next week. It could be the empty rice bag that you can replace with a reusable bag and a trip to a grocery store offering loose or bulk grains that you measure yourself. Maybe it's junk mail from a company you can call or email to request removal from their mailing list (or use services like PaperKarma and Catalog Choice to stop the junk mailings). By committing to reducing an item every couple of weeks, you will build environmental habits in a manageable way, and you'll be reducing your negative impact.

Thanks to the growing "zero-waste" trend, I've had the chance to dabble in many of the suggested tips, like using homemade deodorant and moisturizers. I've learned that coconut oil is a staple used in dozens of do-it-yourself (DIY) concoctions. I've strategized ways to get around buying food packaged in plastic, sometimes successful and sometimes less so. But it's worth noting that these DIY solutions still have some waste associated, like the jar for coconut oil. It's less waste and allows me to find the right mixture of ingredients that works best for me, but there's still an impact. Zero waste is more of a journey than a strict destination. It's an aspirational journey, where we take a closer look at the things we buy, the frequency we buy them, and the amount of waste we generate.

Striving for less waste is a noble goal; however, it can be easy to fall into the cycle of purchasing new items to help in your efforts to go zero waste. The resolution might bring you to buy a reusable item (or lots of them), but sometimes people stall at simply owning the reusable item and not weaving it into their daily lives. It then sits on a shelf as a once-promising idea, but because its purpose was never fully achieved, it becomes a waste. A common example is the reusable grocery bag. Tote bags have long been a staple of reducing our waste, as it targets an item that ends up in landfills and waterways. Five trillion plastic bags are created every year, enough to circle the globe *seven times*. Due to its painfully slow one-thousand-year decomposition rate, every plastic bag that has been created to this point still exists somewhere in the world.

The solution is a reusable bag; but many companies latched onto this idea as a great way to show their environmental aims and also further their brand by customers carrying an item with their logo. Stores often showcase their reusable totes at the checkout counter, so if you forgot yours in your house or car, no problem! Just buy another to avoid that dreaded plastic bag! Unfortunately, we now see a plethora of (in some cases very poorly made) reusable grocery bags throughout the country. Reusable bags are clearly a great way to curb plastic bag waste, but to achieve the full benefit, we must use them consistently and own the amount we typically need. A sturdy, long-lasting and locally made tote is a stronger environmental choice than a flimsier bag made overseas, even if it's made of recycled polypropylene.[9] Because the goal is to reuse the bag over and over, durability is a central quality to look for, and buying locally made items lessens transportation emissions. The first question to ask when acquiring another reusable bag is, Does my home need this, or do I need to just use the bags I already have more often? And if you do need the bag, then ask yourself if this bag built to last. I've had the best results with cloth reusable totes because they are sturdier than some of the wispy bag options and easier to wash (just toss them in with your linens). It's hard to resist the urge to buy more, but we need to remind ourselves that stockpiling charming tote bags defeats the whole purpose of using less, so we can strive to stick with what we need for shopping.

The zero-waste movement may seem daunting, particularly if you are someone with limited time to research DIY experiments because of the other demands in your life. Or perhaps the logistics present another barrier; for example, a store that sells fresh foods in bulk so you can bring reusable packaging for your groceries might not be accessible to your household due to distance or cost. People have very valid concerns about adopting more zero-waste or general environmental habits, but there are ways to use less and remove or work around any barriers you may encounter. It doesn't take a lot of extra time or added cost to say no thanks to a plastic straw or extra paper napkins, if you're able to do without them. Once you have a reusable tote, you can pass on the plastic or paper bags at the grocery store (and if you're in a town with a bag tax, you'll even save a few cents by using your own). Avoiding accumulating things we don't need is better for our wallets and cuts down on the clutter in our homes, so we save some cleaning time with less stuff to shuffle around. You can scope out any low- or no-packaged foods at your local market, and if you have a spare moment, you can ask for more options like those. Business owners want to keep their regular customers coming back, so sharing your preferences could bring about a positive change in the store. You can also find free ideas for less-wasteful projects by checking out DIY books or going online at your library. Turning off water or lights when you aren't using them are common habits we develop to use less and save money on bills. By observing the items you use throughout the day, you can make small changes without spending a lot of time or money, and you can even save both of these things in the long run. The important thing is to be aware of and strive to do what you can within your life, try to lead by example, and don't get bogged down in shaming yourself when it feels like you aren't doing enough.

When we're asked if we need something rather than just being handed it, we're more likely to actually consider if we do need it or not. If you are an employee, you can ask customers if they need a bag or receipt or a straw. You can also approach your employer about incorporating this into training new employees who interact with customers so it becomes a company-wide practice. You might also propose a modest discount for customers who bring their own reusable items, like mugs. Changing habits isn't easy, but when social norms are put into place to help us to confront our consumption in a positive way, movement towards producing less waste as society can occur.

Do you have an item that you regularly buy but fume a bit each time at the wasteful packaging? An item that always frustrates me is the disposable razor. I got angry each time I tossed out the plastic razor heads or handles or the rigid packaging. I blamed the razor company for making me buy unsustainable garbage rather than letting my frustration incentivize me to find a better method. I let this bother me for too many years before turning to the readily available, cheaper, low-waste option: safety razors. They're made to last for a long time, as opposed to the planned obsolescence delivered with disposable razors. Instead of spending money on new plastic razors and cartridges from year to year, I can buy bulk blades that are recyclable (not curbside, for safety reasons), packaged efficiently, and extremely affordable. Adapting to a new process was slightly intimidating, but there are tons of videos and tips people have shared to adjust. It helped me realize that, if all these people had successfully switched to a new routine, then maybe I could do it, too.

Think about an item you buy that causes you to curse its packaging or waste while grumpily escorting it to the checkout counter. Search online or ask friends if they've come across an alternative, less wasteful version of that product, maybe even something you can make at home (there's a surprising number of products you can concoct from supplies you might have sitting in your kitchen right now). If we peer into our garbage, we could see a lot of depressing, possibly smelly lessons in the amount of stuff we throw away. But as we become aware, we are also empowered to find solutions and make better decisions.

THE SECOND R: REUSE

Second in the three Rs is *reuse*, the practice of using what you already have more creatively, or repairing things instead of buying something new. Many people have brought this into their communities through Little Free Libraries, tool- and equipment-sharing systems, and clothing swaps among friends and coworkers. Since 2009, community hubs called Repair Cafés have sprouted up throughout Amsterdam and beyond. These centralized locations host neighbors coming together to fix their broken possessions. A wide range of hand tools, sewing machines, discarded fabric, and other odds and ends await visitors' use at the cafés. You can find DIY books and perhaps a cozy nook with coffee, perfect for scouring new ideas for old items lying around your house. The only thing keeping these items from the landfill is you. If you equip yourself with the right tools, a plan, and even an imagination, then you can give life to goods whose imposed end date has already passed. Planned obsolescence says your shoes can only make it through one winter, while Repair Cafés beg to differ.

The Netherlands has a municipal solid-waste recycling rate of more than 65 percent,[10] but it also relies heavily on the waste-disposal hierarchy, emphasizing waste reduction and product reuse (and repair).[11] In only two years, with a grant from the Dutch government and donations from individuals, Martine Postma's idea to reduce waste had grown to thirty Repair Cafés across the Netherlands. She was inspired after the birth of her second child to do something to address waste and resources. After seeing an art exhibit on reusing materials, Postma decided to create a place for sustainability, where people can take action to help the environment and themselves. People show up to Repair Cafés with their malfunctioning appliances and work with volunteer fixers to problem-solve their way to a "good as new" product. There's no reason to feel ashamed for needing help, and having a friendly neighbor help you learn allows for greater self-sufficiency. None of us were born knowing how to sew on a button, but we can ask for help to learn. The Repair Café Foundation has made waves in more than a dozen U.S. states, and each location organizer maintains communications with other nearby cafés. In less than a decade, nearly 1,600 Repair Cafés can be visited in thirty-three countries throughout the world.[12]

Resolving problems allows us to feel a sense of pride and accomplishment. Psychologists even say that self-sufficiency gives us a stronger internal "locus of control," meaning we feel empowered to make our own decisions and trust our instincts.[13] By strengthening our locus of control, we can resist marketing ploys designed to nudge into unnecessary overconsumption. Learning how to fix our broken household items and developing these skills not only benefits the environment through less waste, but it also leads to stronger sense of self.

Living in our society means consuming some things more regularly than others, like food and clothing. Undeniably, we need to consume food every day (plus it's delicious), and we need clothes to deal with the elements (plus it's required by law). We can reduce packaging through growing fresh food and taking reusable jars and bags to the grocery store. As for clothes, the best option is to buy secondhand. It can be tempting to shop at thrift stores and buy tons of clothing we don't need because the goods are less expensive than their new counterparts. Buying used also feels guilt-free, especially when you can just donate the clothes back where you found them, if you determine they aren't the right style or size. Buying secondhand is always better than buying brand new clothing, but we can't forget that it also has an impact, so it's important to still mindfully purchase all items.

Our donated clothing goes on a journey of its own, as opposed to the 13 million tons of textiles the U.S. sends to the dump every year.[14] Donations are often shipped overseas or to secondhand garment markets in the Global South. Almost half of donated clothes that remain in the states will be worn again; the other half will go into a recycling system.[15] Goodwill Industries International is a nonprofit that provides job training and other community-based programs which are funded by its retail thrift stores. Its goal is to keep as much as possible out of the landfill, and they give the public ample opportunity to purchase these secondhand goods. But there's only so much space on the shelves and racks, and eventually the products have to be moved elsewhere. Clothing that doesn't sell from a Goodwill storefront is moved to an outlet store to be sold for even cheaper prices (sometimes a dollar per pound) in these bin outlets. What doesn't sell then gets sent to a textile-recycling facility, and almost half of what is sent to the facility is successfully resold to the clothing industry or overseas.[16] Up to 80 percent of all clothing donated to charity thrift stores ends up in textile recycling.[17]

According to the trade group S.M.A.R.T. (Secondhand Materials and Recycled Textiles), there's only a 20 percent chance that an article of clothing you have donated is still being used by someone else in your community.[18] Of the items not resold, the rest are typically stripped into rags or used for projects like home insulation. Secondhand companies report only sending 5 percent of donated clothes to the landfill when they are found in unusable conditions, such as arriving moldy and wet. This amount is dwarfed by the mountainous pile of landfilled clothes that don't travel the journey of being donated or recycled. Fast fashion is clothing that many consider disposable due to its low quality and cost. It's made in swift methods to keep up with trends and to feed perceived obsolescence habits. We buy it, wear it a handful of times, and then toss it out. But this breezy process has substantial consequences.

The United States produces 25 billion pounds of new textiles every single year, and of that, 85 percent ends up in landfills.[19] The rest are sent to secondhand stores to either be bought or begin the process I just discussed. In ten years, we've increased our textile production 40 percent and hardly upped our rates of keeping those discarded items from the dump. We easily buy and toss clothes because they have become incredibly cheap. With decades of increased international trade and poor labor practices, we can snag a new shirt for $5.99 and give it little thought when the cheap fabric rips and we toss it out. Americans are buying five times the clothing that they did in 1980, and the surge in consumption of fast fashion comes with a price tag of not only environmental problems but also poor labor practices.

In 2013, a devastating collapse of a garment factory building in Bangladesh was a sobering moment for many consumers on the real costs of inexpensive clothing. The Rana Plaza building hosted multiple factories producing clothing for European and American consumers. It had been constructed poorly and illegally, and many floors had been built without permits. There were 1,127 deaths as a result of negligence and unsafe working conditions. Although there was evidence the building was unfit prior to the collapse, company owners urged workers to continue as normal in order to not let profits slide[20] The collapse was a culmination of the poor construction; cracks appearing in the building; and, finally, generators that had previously shaken the building during operation and triggered the tragedy. Bangladesh became the second-highest producer of clothing exports (China is first), with thousands of garment factories in operation, and has achieved this level of production due to low costs, meaning workers are grossly undercompensated and also clearly at risk of fatally unsafe working conditions as companies, cut corners to build and maintain factories. Workers are expected to engage in brutally long hours of producing garments we buy for a few bucks and in turn often make insufficient money to even provide their families with basic human necessities.[21]

Among those workers are children, as an estimated 152 million children are engaged in child labor, many in the fashion industry.[22] The collapse of Rana Plaza brought more awareness to the very prevalent issue of unsafe and unfair labor conditions around the world, and people have called on companies to practice more sustainable and fair practices. However, the challenging truth is that companies in Europe and the United States often have little to no idea where their products are coming from. With multiple tiers to every supply chain, companies often are familiar with their first suppliers but are confused or in the dark completely about other suppliers working more closely to the extraction and construction of their products.[23]

I don't share this to make you feel terribly guilty for buying a new pair of pants. My intent is for us to strive to consider the impacts of what we buy from production to disposal, and the people and environments affected at each stage. Every item we purchase has within it a suite of impacts and some choices have fewer or better impacts than others. It isn't our fault that some companies don't do their diligence in maintaining a responsible supply chain, but it can be our role to seek out better companies and more sustainable products to communicate that we demand these practices become the new normal. Not all businesses prop up sweatshops, and many operate with strong labor practices that support workers. Just because an item was made overseas doesn't mean it began in a sweatshop. A way to distinguish responsible labor practices is by certification, such as fair trade or union made, which are systems that honor workers, producers, communities, consumers, and the environment.[24] You can also speak with businesses you patronize about where their products come from and assert your commitment to support companies that prioritize safe working conditions and fair wages for employees and environmental sustainability. When you purchase a fair-trade product, make sure to tell the company you purchased it because of the way it was produced; it's important not only to call out unsustainable behavior but also to affirm good practices (and thanks to social media, it's easier than ever to submit a comment to a business). And of course, reducing our consumption and reusing through secondhand shops is essential.[25] These unjust labor practices continue so companies can turn a profit while creating a supply to meet demand, which ultimately comes from each of us. Making thrift-store and used choices is a great way to make sure to reuse items, but second-hand always comes second place to reduce. Elizabeth Cline, author of *Overdressed: The Shockingly High Cost of Cheap Fashion*, explains that ultimately our view of clothing must shift from seeing it as a disposable good. As she says, "Clothing has a life cycle and we have to take responsibility for it."[26]

Developing a better understanding of the ripple effect caused by every purchase we make allows us all to become more mindful individuals. We can ask ourselves if we truly need to purchase something. If the answer is unequivocally yes, we can select a long-lasting option made with recycled materials from a company committed to sustainable business; or at least, choose a product that checks one of those boxes. We can strive to reuse and repair our possessions, making the most of our purchases and improving our lives through greater self-sufficiency. Consumption is part of existence and even in the forest, resources are used and disposed of once their purpose has been completed. The key is being strategic and mindful with how we consume, as well as have a plan to responsibly dispose of our materials, leading us to the final "R," recycling.

5

WHAT'S THE POINT OF RECYCLING?

After all the adaptations and advancements our recycling system has been through, it comes back to natural ecosystems. While the branches of it are wound through industrial and economic systems, the roots of this concept will always be found on the forest floor, where debris is recycled back into useful nutrients. Its intertwined history with social movements connects humans to that natural process. As the journey of recycled goods is cyclical, our respective roles in it are unending. People are often hesitant to take part in a perennial task if we aren't certain on the return of our time investment. It's beneficial to understand how the system works in order to really conceptualize the process so we can see the value of it and how to best fill our role.

But before delving into the how recycling works, I want to clarify its purpose. The point of recycling in the 1930s and 1940s was due to economic pressures and to contribute to the World War II effort. The 1970s brought a renewed enthusiasm for recycling to reduce litter and our impact on the environment. The 1980s experienced fears of landfill shortages, so recycling programs were accelerated by communities to avoid building new trash-burning incinerators near their homes. This leads us to the present era of recycling and the system's multiple goals and complexities. There are victories to celebrate, such as an increase in recovery for recycling from 5.6 million tons of materials in 1960 to 87 million tons in 2013.[1] However, when you consider that, during the same time period, the population size doubled and total municipal solid waste generation tripled, it's clear we still have a long way to go.

TODAY'S LANDFILLS AREN'T YESTERDAY'S DUMPS

When we think of a landfill, we likely imagine a giant pile of garbage, complete with rotting smells, scavenging animals running rampant, and all sorts of volatile liquids oozing out and sneaking down to our groundwater. While this image was once a spot-on visualization, the landfills of today are not the dumps of yesteryear. When Congress amended the RCRA in 1984, it granted the EPA regulatory authority over all landfills and directed it to determine landfill criteria, which would then be adopted by every state. It encompassed a half-century of data, provided by individuals, organizations, researchers, solid-waste management companies, landfills, and the agency's work from hazardous-waste sites. The EPA laid out requirements on municipal landfills to make the sites more sanitary and less harmful to human health. It provided state agencies with guidance and policy support to help states use better options for waste, including specific design criteria for landfills to keep pollution and health hazards down.[2]

A common response to "Why recycle?" is a passionate call to keep goods out of landfills, and based on these responses, you may think this is the main reason to recycle. There is truth in this because in the United States, we deposit more than 169 million tons of trash, or the weight of more than 2.5 million semitrucks, into landfills every year. Our current recycling and composting efforts keep more than 80 million tons from being added to that heap, but we could be doing significantly better.[3] While there is no doubt we need to divert useful items from ending up in these hills of lost material potential, there are some misconceptions surrounding landfills to clear up.

Upon arriving for a tour at the Prince George's County Landfill and Resource Recovery Facility in Maryland, my guide Bruce O'Dell kindly corrected me when I asked a question by adding *sanitary* before *landfill* to emphasize how the practice has changed.[4] The land consists of two large areas, the active landfill and the closed one, spanning a total of nearly three hundred acres. The entire facility opened in 1968 and was taking in between twelve and two hundred tons of refuse per day. Fast forward a few decades, and it was accepting 2,500 tons per day. Now, thanks to waste-diversion efforts, it takes in one thousand tons each day. Although the landfill generates money from the amount it accepts, Bruce noted the need to reduce volume brought in to increase the life of the facility. One plot of land cannot operate in perpetuity, so Prince George's first landfill was closed in 1992, coinciding with the current active landfill's opening. The mounds are situated right next to each other, but the difference in appearance is striking. We bounded up the closed landfill in a truck, bumping over the ground's imperfections beneath a bright green sheath of grass. Perched on 17.5 million tons of waste, the result from decades of changing trends and disposable goods, we could peer across to the active landfill. Swarms of seagulls circled above the trucks as they compacted the trash into the ground. Our truck then careened down the path to observe the working landfill more closely, following our noses and the overpowering stench of consumption.

Giant trucks with five-foot-tall wheels crunch down garbage in its tracks, compacting it into the ground. The facility uses GIS (geographic information system) mapping technology to track compaction, and the aim is to squeeze in 1,400 pounds of waste per cubic foot. It's an important component to the process because it provides more air space and extends the landfill capacity. At the end of every day, the compacted waste is covered by six inches of soil, and the next morning garbage is spread, and the compactor trucks roll again.

There are by-products from the landfill that must be dealt with to keep it at a sanitary standard, one of which is leachate, the result of many liquids coming together from dumped items as they are crushed into the landfill. Bruce explained the leachate process using a metaphor of brewing coffee. As a coffee maker brews, liquid running through the grounds (the trash in the landfill) ends up in the pot (in this metaphor, the collection system). The result is the coffee, or in this case the leachate; the two liquid products even share a similar hue (although the best part of waking up would never be leachate in your cup). Leachate is then treated on site until it shows a lighter shade, more of a tealike transparency, and then is sent to a facility to be treated until the liquid is completely clear and passes environmental quality tests before being released into a nearby waterway.[5] But leachate that seeps into groundwater before being treated can pollute water quality. While there have been safeguards in place to reduce leachate effects on nearby communities, any leaking can be detrimental to human health. The 1976 RCRA required landfills be lined with plastic or clay liners that collect leachate (like the coffee pot) so it can be delivered to a sewage treatment plant.[6] The Prince George's facility also has catchment in place to divert storm water before it becomes leachate. However, this system is not without its flaws. Poorly constructed pipes in a facility can become crushed or clogged as land settles over time, preventing them from working correctly.[7]

Trash is not necessarily meant to break down in a landfill but is only meant to be buried and stored (unlike a composting process, which involves aeration of the materials to encourage decomposition). Garbage does decompose at a slower rate, and without adequate oxygen, what results is methane, a greenhouse gas with eighty-six times the heat-trapping power of carbon dioxide over the course two decades.[8] It is shorter lived in the atmosphere, averaging just over a decade, whereas carbon dioxide remains an influence on the atmosphere's chemistry for a century. Because of its heat-trapping efficiency, methane has a considerable impact on the climate by controlling how fast warming occurs. Methane makes up roughly 10 percent of all global greenhouse gases,[9] and more than half of its emissions come from human activities. During its shorter gig, methane delivers long-lasting impacts on the climate, and we need to address the sources of methane. Landfills account for the third-largest source of the gas in the United States (after natural gas production and agriculture), and if the methane is untended in these trash mounds, it can also become flammable and very dangerous.

A clear solution is diverting more useful materials into the recycling stream so that less decompose in landfills and the associated methane emissions are reduced. Many landfill operators are working to capture methane and generate some revenue (the other option is to leak the gas into the air to prevent flammable hazards). If you go to a sanitary landfill, you might notice tops of wells dotting the mounds where garbage is buried. These wells connect to a city of pipes below, stretching through the layers of garbage and soil to vacuum up methane gas during its release from our discarded items. The methane is then directed to a facility (either on site or off) to be burned into electricity, which landfill owners can sell directly to power a specific location or into the grid. There can be hundreds of wells used, and even landfills no longer taking in trash have wells still working to capture methane from the decades of decomposing yet to occur. Landfill companies might save millions of dollars on this process from avoided electricity costs, but the revenue generated from the sale doesn't go as far as one might think. Revenue from methane capture wouldn't solely cover the costs of investing in the technology, so facilities rely on subsidies to make their gas-to-electricity product cost competitive with other fuels.[10]

Methane is accompanied by carbon dioxide as the other main gas emitted from landfills, as well as smaller concentrations of odor-causing ammonia, hydrogen sulfide, and nitrogen.[11] The kind of waste present, the temperature, and the level of moisture at the landfill influences the amount of gases emitted (high temperatures and more moisture means more gas production). While improvements have been made to landfill practices, there are still environmental impacts associated with them. Companies have pioneered some solutions, like methane capture and even using closed landfill space for solar panel projects, but we still need to reduce the amount of materials being discarded.[12]

What separates old dumps from newer sanitary landfills are federal regulations and waste-diversion goals. The Prince George's facility is an avid participant in the diversion goals set by the state and the county's Department of Environment. Bruce explained that the local recycling facility and the landfill are on the same team, working together to achieve more waste diversion. The county boasts an impressive 65 percent diversion rate (the amount of municipal solid waste going into composting and recycling instead of the landfill), putting it near the ranks of San Francisco and Seattle (with 80 percent and 72 percent diversion rates, respectfully).[13,14] However, vast improvements can still be made to increase diversion. Bruce says roughly 75 percent of all the waste coming in is actually recyclable, and they do their best to hand-pull items to put back into the recycling stream; specifically, they rescue metals, rigid plastics, and cardboard. Unfortunately, with staffing capacity and the huge volume they receive, it's impossible to save all the useful materials, so the ultimate solution comes from more residents better using the recycling program.

IMPACTS OF NEW MATERIAL PRODUCTION

Landfills must be run in efficient, smart ways to reduce environmental impact, but focusing solely on landfill capacity as the main reason to recycle misses a much bigger incentive. On its own, recycling is a valuable process and not just an alternative to the landfill. Disposal is only part of the impact our goods make on the planet, and the reason we need to recycle is to reduce raw material extraction and production. Even if we could begin recycling every bit of our used stuff immediately, the impacts of new production would still exist if we neglect to close the loop. The production of new materials requires resources, including energy and water, and creates solid waste before a new product even gets to the store shelves. Roughly 3 percent of global greenhouse gas (GHG) emissions come from landfills,[15] but emissions from new material production are even more prolific. Energy use emits 73 percent of global GHGs,[16] and the biggest user of energy continues to be the industrial sector. This sector is comprised of energy-intensive manufacturing (like food and beverage products, paper, chemicals, iron and steel, and aluminum), nonenergy-intensive manufacturing (pharmaceuticals, paints, detergents, and electronic devices), and nonmanufacturing (agriculture, forestry, mining, and construction).[17] The extraction and production of the new goods we demand contributes significantly to our global energy usage and, by extension, climate change.

We can lessen these emissions by reducing our overall consumption and using recycled materials instead of virgin ones.[18] Taking a systems-thinking approach to our waste means considering the extraction and production of goods (the "upstream" impacts) as well as the practices for end-of-life disposal (the "downstream"). Across the board, making something from recycled materials emits fewer greenhouse gases than using newly extracted content, or virgin materials. You've probably been urged to "save trees by going paperless" before, so it's easy to think of the forests affected when confronted with a new paper product. Perhaps less common is our thinking of the petroleum used in new plastics or bauxite needed for new aluminum. The extraction of raw materials not only results in higher greenhouse gas emissions but also affects nearby communities.

Residents whose homes are located near working forests and paper mills have felt the brunt of production in the past when mills were run without safeguards for curbing air and water pollutants. Toxic solvents and chlorine have been used to bleach wood pulp to make those sheets of bright white paper and other products. When these substances are released into waterways (a common practice to flush out wastewater), it can result in damage to the water the communities depend on. Regulations have required mills to adjust their discharge process to eliminate the pollution, and these can be effective, if regular monitoring occurs and confirms compliance with those rules. A machine malfunction can cause thousands of gallons of untreated wastewater to be released into rivers. A company's negligence and refusal to adapt waste-treatment processes can curse nearby residents with noxious odors and corrosive liquid waste. There have been cases of paper mills irresponsibly disposing of waste and inflicting damage on communities. In 2016, for example, a contractor said he was required by a Georgia-Pacific paper mill to bury ash from production dozens of feet deep and cover it with a few inches of dirt to give the appearance of normal land.[19] Irresponsible disposal methods have been linked to severe health issues for employees at the plants and unusually high rates of cancer in communities. Air pollution has also been a product of virgin paper production, with carbon dioxide, sulfur dioxides, and other particulate matter released from mills. This is particularly an issue from larger mills, which often have on-site coal-fired power plants that emit even more pollutants into the air.[20]

Unjust logging ventures, as well as large-scale agribusiness and mining, have a history of taking land from indigenous peoples without their consent. In 2014, the Palangkaraya Declaration on Deforestation and the Rights of Forest Peoples declared that even laws that recognize indigenous land rights were all too often disregarded by industry. The declaration asserts that indigenous peoples know how to protect forests, and their unique understanding of how to both develop economic livelihoods and food while allowing the forest to thrive should be empowered rather than ignored.[21] Indigenous peoples also manage 24 percent of all above-ground carbon sequestered in the tropical forests in which they live, and because many of these areas have been underrepresented on maps, this number could be even higher.[22] Many of these communities have lived sustainably for generations, operating within nature as opposed to separating from and exploiting it to degradation. These ways of life have allowed both communities and the ecosystems in which they live to sustain a harmonious balance that does not deplete natural resources. This perspective and experience is essential in global governance of the environment, specifically forests. Unfortunately, indigenous peoples and local communities legally own a mere 10 percent of the lands they customarily claim. By improving the protection of customary rights, these communities could be recognized by all governments as the stewards of their forests and leaders in the fight against climate change rather than victims of it.[23]

Forest loss translates into human loss of essential services, like carbon absorption, biodiversity, regulation of storm water, and oxygen. These benefits from forests are difficult to attach a dollar amount to, meaning defending the necessity of natural forests has proved challenging over the years. Business comes equipped with a set price tag for the value of cutting down a forest, but it's trickier to convey the vast health and environmental benefits we receive by keeping a forest in the ground. Converting natural forest ecosystems to single-species tree plantations for paper and wood products reduces the opportunity for efficient carbon sequestration (a forest's ability to absorb greenhouse gas through its trees, plants, and soil). Recent studies show forests with a variety of species are more productive in tree growth and carbon sequestration than monoculture forests made up of one species of the same age for harvest. These same-species tree plantations are also prone to fire, disease, and insect infestation. This underscores the importance of leaving natural forests intact and reducing the pressure that our demand for wood and paper products places on forests. We can do this by choosing paper products with recycled content and recycling our used paper.[24]

Positive changes will continue to be made through regulations, community pressure, the influence of environmental organizations, and customer demands, as well as individuals within the industry pushing for improvements. Regulations and company commitments can spur the retrofitting of old mills to stop polluting our water and air with harsh contaminants.[25] It is possible to obtain paper and wood products made with fiber from responsibly managed certified forests, but only if we keep demanding it.

Managing forests responsibly is vital to keep the ecosystem healthy and promote longevity of the soil. However, it still requires more energy and emits more greenhouse gases to make paper products from virgin wood than recovered fiber. For a simplified example of the pulping process, imagine a kid making a spitball to shoot across a classroom to stir things up. If that student were to scrape off the bark from a tree branch and chew it into a spitball, a greater amount of energy and saliva would be necessary to break down the wood fiber into its final product.

If the spitball maker uses a strip of paper, though, less is needed to repulp it because it has already been pulped into its current state.[26] Producing one ton of 100 percent recycled copy paper requires 40 percent less energy and produces 55 percent fewer greenhouse gases than the same amount made with virgin fiber. It also saves 53 percent of the water; and, of course, saves 100 percent of the wood fiber needed for virgin production.[27]

There are many grades of paper products, including printing and writing paper (used for magazines and office paper), paperboard (cereal boxes), corrugated cardboard, and tissue, to name a few. Given our increasingly digital communication methods, printing and writing paper is a sector commonly assumed to be dying out. While it's true that we are using less paper due to email, the impact of this sector on the environment still proves to be significant. It's the most intensive paper grade to produce, and it makes up one-quarter of all paper produced worldwide but unfortunately has a global average of just 8 percent recycled content.[28,29] This small number shows multiple challenges in the system that need attention, including the lack of printing and writing paper mills with recycling capacity. When mills do not have the capability to process deinked, recycled pulp, this limits the chances for that collected pulp to be used in new products. The eight percent also signals that companies and consumers are not demanding recycled content products enough, so virgin fiber continues to be used at high rates. And it shows a system fraught with contamination is not churning out enough quality fiber. Chapter nine will list action steps to address these problems, including ways we can signal demand through purchases and requests to companies.

Where paper fibers can be recycled around seven times, aluminum is an infinitely recyclable material.[30] However, producing new aluminum has damaging effects on the environment and nearby communities. This material is used in many products we encounter daily, including common detergents, medicines, beverage cans, foil wrap, some makeups and toothpastes, and vehicles. Making new aluminum necessitates mining an ore called bauxite, which is a collection of aluminous materials, and smelting it into the foil we use to wrap our leftovers, among other products. It takes four tons of mined bauxite to produce one ton of aluminum.[31] The material is found in tropical and subtropical parts of the world, and while reserves of bauxite are projected to be available to us for centuries to come, the process of extracting it delivers immediate impacts. The intensity of the effects is site specific, but communities with heavy bauxite extraction must contend with pollution from dust and truck transport affecting the air quality, vegetation, biodiversity, forests, and water.

The Pahang state of Malaysia has quickly become a heavy producer of bauxite ore in recent years.[32] After Indonesia (a previous exporter of bauxite to China) essentially closed its doors, Malaysia became a main source of bauxite for the country. Nearly half of the bauxite being imported to China was coming from Malaysia in 2015 as extraction skyrocketed in the region, peaking at 3.5 million tons exported per month. Many of the operations did so without a license, and what followed was a drastic change in landscape, with congested roads ill fit for transporting the demanded ore to ports. The sediment from the strip-mining methods has turned rivers red, and the Malaysian health minister advised against direct contact with river water, stating that not even boiling it would make the water safe.[33] Residents saw thick red dust coating their homes, and some noticed the trees along the transport roads had begun to die. After such a drastic effect, the government halted any mining in 2016 to mull over regulations for the process; however, it allowed exports to continue for the existing stockpiles of the material waiting at ports. Months after the ban began, the stockpile heights were reportedly unchanged, yet Malaysia had continued exporting millions of tons of bauxite to China.[34] Residents living along transportation routes note hundreds of truck deliveries every day from the mining sites, signaling that the ban has not been effectively enforced. Demand from China speaks louder than the environmental and health concerns, and because the demand for the resource continues, the mining has continued. Policy makers shift from one foot to the other as they debate the harsh impacts of the extraction with the economic benefits and job opportunities. But, the mining has had consequences to local economy, too. Agriculture has already been drastically affected by the toxic red dust settling on crops, making them unfit for sale, to the point of inciting a two-week-long march of farmers to demand stricter regulations on the practice.[35] Regardless, the dust from the boom in extraction will not settle for years to come. Slashing trees to burn, forever changing the soil and landscape, and the energy and water required to create aluminum out of the bauxite will all take its toll on the planet. In stark contrast, using recycled aluminum reduces the need for mining bauxite, saves 95 percent of the energy, and produces 95 percent fewer greenhouse gases than new aluminum production.[36]

When the forest decomposes its waste, the usefulness comes from the waste feeding back into the productivity of the whole ecosystem. Decomposition is not simply the end of a cycle but is, in fact, the beginning. The connectivity is what makes this process valuable, just as the loop of our use, disposal, and reuse of materials is how our recycling system best serves the environment and our economy. It's important for the forest to decompose waste to keep refuse from building up on the ground, just as we must consider landfill capacity when choosing to divert our waste. But what makes this cycle so essential is that the decomposed materials have a purpose to serve in keeping the forest productive and healthy, and the nutrients will loop back to serve the ecosystem without interruption. Our recyclables have more life to offer in new products, and if we send them off to the landfill or the incinerator, then we lose that potential in those objects forever. Placing correct items into recycling bins is a key part of the loop, but the cycle is connected when we choose new products made with recycled content. When we demand not only the access to recycle, but also the use of our recyclables in manufacturing, we can then renew materials like the forest cycles nutrients. To receive the full benefits of recycling, it's essential for all of us to adhere to our local recycling rules. We might question why some materials are accepted in municipal recycling and some are not. Knowing what happens to recyclables when they leave our homes and the processes they go through can help us see the purpose of local rules and allow us to see the ways our actions affect the larger system.

6

WHERE YOUR RECYCLABLES GO

"I could've sworn I saw them toss our recycling into the garbage truck with our trash."

"How do they separate all this stuff? It doesn't make sense to me."

"I recycle, but it's kind of something I do and hope it makes a difference because how can we really know?"

These are just a few examples of what people muse about when discussing their recycling habits. It's less common to meet someone with a deep curiosity about where their garbage goes and how it's handled. But many people have questions about the fate of their recyclables and whether they really do end up back on our shelves as new products or not. People seem to feel a deeper sense of investment in recycling and are intrigued to see a return on it.

It's tough to enthusiastically participate in a process when you don't really know if good results will come from your efforts. And in recycling, the willingness to participate from people like you and me is essential. The single-stream method of tossing all recyclables into one bin (ideally) removes all the guesswork of sorting so more people participate. After all, if recycling is as easy as tossing something into the trash, who wouldn't do it? Single-stream originated in California in the 1990s and has since spread through most major cities throughout the country, and many have greeted its popularization.[1]

A community I lived in years ago was extremely excited when we started receiving large ninety-five-gallon blue recycling bins with wheels to practice single-stream. The new recycling bins rivaled our trash cans in size, and we thought accommodating a higher volume would result in more recyclables and increase the supply of materials for new recycled goods. These larger bins boosted recycling, but in some cases, when residents are given more space, they fill it with incorrect items. Extra space also encourages people to toss in large items that might not be recyclable, like huge old garden hoses. Large, cushy bins can leave residents less likely to break down their cardboard boxes, a necessary step for collection and sorting of items. Using larger bins offers many upsides to communities but also allow us to further develop unhelpful habits. Once you know the journey recyclables go on after they leave our homes, it's easier to foresee problems of putting incorrect items in the bin, despite our good intentions and the extra bin space we might be eager to fill.

An estimated 94 percent of Americans have access to a recycling program, 73 percent of whom can put it right on their curb.[2] The remaining 21 percent of the country relies solely on drop-off centers and to participate must load refuse into a personal vehicle and transport it to these centers, where they typically find large dumpsters to deposit their various materials. Best practices suggest positioning one drop-off location for every 3,000 to 3,500 people.[3] Depending how the location operates, if you swing by during the center's open hours, there will likely be some helpful workers to guide you through the process or simply take the materials off your hands. In rural areas and smaller towns, these centers might be the sole opportunity to recycle. However, drop-offs can also exist in larger cities that offer curbside collection and will often help you dispose of hazardous materials and other tricky items not accepted through curbside, like textiles, electronics, paint, car parts, or old appliances like refrigerators. They're also helpful for households or buildings generating more recyclables than they can move out in weekly or biweekly curbside services. Municipalities offering drop-off centers have touted greater success in participation because it becomes a central spot for residents looking to dispose a variety of unwanted materials, and it can reduce costs of collection associated with curbside services. Sometimes a city might even use a drop-off program to test the waters and see what participation levels are like before investing in a full curbside program. This allows a city to see not only how many residents are willing to recycle but also the volume and type of items they can expect to receive and to determine what the markets are like for those materials.[4]

Most people (almost 90 percent) with curbside service don't have to sort their recycling because they are now using single-stream collection.[5] Another option is dual-stream recycling, where one item, like paper, is sorted by the resident. Single-stream takes the task of sorting materials off the resident and puts it on the material recovery facility (MRF; rhymes with *Smurf*). There are nearly one thousand MRFs in the country run by different companies.[6] The first destination of the recyclables' journey is being sorted by employees and a series of machines at the MRF before being baled and sold to facilities that break materials down to their raw states, process them, and sell to manufacturers.

RECYCLABLES IN THE STREAMS

The MRFs' role is to sort out the junk, put like materials together, and ship off to each commodity's respective processing plant. There must be a market for these materials to keep this system going and create incentive to collect and sort specific items, and there is not much of a demand for flawed materials. The recycling industry lists low-quality materials or incorrect items from residential bins as a substantial problem. Contamination is one of the main barriers keeping our recycling system from its full potential. It occurs when materials are dirtied or rendered useless due to the contact with other items unfit for recycling or when recyclable items aren't put in the bin correctly to be adequately sorted. Recall the example of tossing a used container with some lingering food or liquid into a recycling bin along with old newspapers or magazines. This residue can easily find its way to the paper recyclables, saturating them and making the paper fibers unfit for the market. The old food container may be recyclable, but unless we make sure it's emptied out, contamination can still occur. A bit of liquid can go a long way in rendering your once perfectly recyclable paper products to a low enough quality that it might be sent to the landfill you were consciously trying to avoid.

Single-stream may increase participation because of its ease, but contamination rates also go up in this system, and as a result, the quality of recovered materials can decline. Purchasers of recycled materials for manufacturing expect to buy bales of reasonably clean recovered items, meaning ultimately free of any defects that would hamper their reuse. Contamination can cost companies like Waste Management $60 million every year and make up 35 percent of all materials that enter the stream.[7] This company, which ironically created the first single-stream system years ago, has been outspoken in acknowledging it's a tough issue to turn the tide on. While they're seeing improvements, it's going to be a long road.[8] It's clear the problem has grown in recent years, coinciding with the rise of single-stream, with contamination rates more than doubling from 2007 to 2013.[9]

You might wonder why anyone would bother switching to single-stream, given the higher risks of contamination. A common reason is the vehicles and costs necessary for collection. Hauling trucks are either open (mixed materials = single-stream) or built with partitions (for sorted streams). When residents have to sort materials, they are sectioned by material type, including paper, glass, metal, and plastics. Collecting sorted goods can be more time-consuming for haulers than dumping all recyclables in together.

Materials must be deposited into the right compartment from your bin, which takes more time and more labor. And if a neighborhood is recycling a lot of one material and less of others, one compartment might fill up more quickly and need to be dropped off at a facility before the truck can continue its route, which is less efficient. MRFs using single-stream likely prefer to contract with haulers collecting for single-stream to maximize the volume per truck. More stuff can be packed into one vehicle to reduce transportation costs and at-curb service requirements of haulers.[10] It all comes back to cost for companies, but any extra costs of having residents sort could very well be offset by the higher-quality materials they're recovering and able to sell.

Contamination can arise not only from dirty items but also when nonrecyclable things are put in the bin. Clothes hangers, VCR tapes, used diapers, old shoes, liquids and food waste, and bags of trash are just a few things contaminating recyclables. When people are confronted with a range of city-specific rules that limit what they can put in the bin, they may feel frustrated to find that some commonly used items they've been recycling for years are not accepted by their local MRFs. Well-intentioned "wish-cycling" is when someone attempts to recycle everything they can, whether they're certain if it's recyclable or not. Someone might look at an item like a plastic grocery bag and think, "This is plastic, so it should be recyclable" before tossing it in. The problem is that, while the item is technically recyclable, it is not accepted through curbside programs and instead needs to be dropped off at a local grocery store to be recycled. Individual flimsy plastic bags easily snake around machinery at the MRF and have even shut down entire facilities for a certain amount of time by jamming the machines. Small items can have a big negative effect, like plastic straws. These might be made from plastic, often polypropylene, but their size renders them useless to most recyclers. If we do try to recycle plastic straws, then they will be rerouted to the landfill because they aren't accepted at facilities, or if they aren't spotted and removed from the line, the small, lightweight size of the items means they can slip into other material lines, such as paper, during sorting. One plastic straw in a bale might not seem like much, but if everyone on your street does the same thing, this adds up, and because manufacturers only allow between 1 and 5 percent of the bale to be contaminated before purchasing, an entire bale of materials could be thrown out if it exceeds these standards.

Wish-cycling can be tempting for those of us who just hate tossing something into the trash, but in order to get the most benefit out of your recyclables, reducing contamination is key. Putting items not accepted at the local MRF actually increases the footprint of those items because they have to be trucked to the MRF, sorted out, and then eventually transported to the landfill. The costs of the entire system are also increased because along with those extra emissions are additional charges on the haulers, which gets passed onto the city to cover the cost.[11] Tom Szaky of TerraCycle, a company offering solutions for hard-to-recycle items, has said that up to half of the contents in an average recycling bin could be sorted and thrown out instead of recycled.[12] A common motto is "When in doubt, throw it out," but I prefer the alternative "When in doubt, go find out" to build better habits rather than give up on confusing items.

THE RECYCLING JOURNEY

After being lovingly placed on the curb for pick up, your recycling bin's contents are gathered onto a truck operated by a hauling company. Haulers collect recyclables and deliver them to either a transfer station (a facility where waste is deposited by collection trucks to be held and prescreened for hazardous items before it's put in larger vehicles to its destined disposal site[13]) or directly to a MRF. The truck is weighed when it arrives at the MRF to record the amount of materials being processed, and then emptied out onto a durable area known as the tipping floor. Envision a towering pile of materials, mounted on the tipping floor as they wait to be scooped up by the loader, a truck that guides items from the giant pile to a machine called a drum feeder. This spinning drum acts as a kind of popcorn machine, in which your recyclables bounce around to separate the items and make sure what's going into the facility isn't stacked high or stuck together. It leverages the load of materials onto an in-feeder conveyor belt, which moves the items into the sorting facility. When large improper items sneak their way onto the tipping floor, they can get caught in the drum feeder. For example, a troublesome garden hose can ensnare the machine, delaying the entire facility from operating while it's removed.

As you walk into the MRF, your eyes would be met with a web of conveyor belts guiding materials this way and that, with different machines situated throughout as pit stops to reroute certain recyclables. The items from the tipping floor glide into the facility to their first stop at presort. This quality-control measure is conducted by MRF employees, who pluck unfit items off the conveyor belt by hand. Workers have mere seconds to visually scan tons of materials, and in that time, they also may need to rip open plastic bags, dump them, and try to quickly sort before the next batch passes while still surveying the loose materials zooming by (this is one reason it's better to send our recyclables loose and not tied up in a plastic bag). They remove nonrecyclable items like dirty diapers, hypodermic needles, and twinkle lights. Occasionally, workers have even rescued wallets and other valuables from the machinery to return to their owners.

Once past presort, the items go through different machines designed to separate each type of material based on their physical and chemical traits and let the rest continue on the journey. One of the first is a series of rapidly spinning disc screens, which causes flattened, light old corrugated cardboard (OCC) to float above the screens while the other 3-D materials, like detergent containers and soda cans, drop through the discs onto a conveyor belt below. Then the materials head through the old newsprint (ONP) screen, a set of inclined spinning discs that filter out other fibrous items and allows containers to move along. Once the paper fibers have been sorted, the materials are dropped onto a glass breaker screen with rotating metal discs that break up the glass items and simply bounce around the other container types. The glass will later be sent through a cleaning system that removes debris from the broken glass (called cullet) using screens and blowers.

Another separation method is the trommel, which employs a tumbling action to keep materials from sticking to one another. It rotates and churns materials around, similar to how your dryer tumbles your clothes. It's necessary to keep materials separated so the other sorting technology can accurately function, and separation keeps density down on the conveyor belts. By using a specific rotation and angle, trommels can filter out small objects, like dirt and residue, through perforations in its walls. The rotation allows only the large recyclables to release out of the bottom of the trommel.

Workers throughout the processes pull any paper items mistakenly not captured by the screens and make sure the materials get to their correct places. After the fiber items and glass have been sent along their way, the plastic and metal containers are sorted. A large rotating magnet is employed to draw out steel items, which are ferrous metals (they contain iron).[14] Through the use of an overhead electromagnet, these metals are lifted away from the remaining materials and are dropped when they're positioned above the bunker for steel items. The rest of the nonferrous materials ramble onto a screening process, which divides materials into groups of like sizes.

Plastic items are separated through an optical sorting technology that can identify the desired type of plastic (like polyethylene terephthalate items; e.g., water bottles) and sort them into various bunkers to be baled. The optical sorter can determine the desired plastic and blow a small, strategic poof of air to knock the item into its proper bunker.

The remaining materials pass through a magnetic field system which taps into the electrons in aluminum objects and sparks an alternating magnetic field (an eddy current). When the two fields interact, the eddy field propels the aluminum into another area for collection. Your discarded soda cans are shot away from the rest of the materials because they are not attracted to this magnet.

Once all the materials have been sorted into their respective bunkers, they are moved to a machine that squashes them into compact bales held intact by steel wire. These bales are pretty hefty, weighing up to two thousand pounds, and are compacted into a 3 × 4 × 4 feet cube.[15] Bales are sent to a storage area to await sale to processing facilities, like paper mills and plastic processors. The exception is glass, which is deposited into a pile in a bunker and waits for a truck to transport it to a glass facility.

But there's one last bunch of items to dispose of: the residue, which is all the nonrecyclable items and debris removed during the sorting processes. The items unfit for recycling that were snagged at manual presort or removed later in the sorting process are shuffled onto a residue belt. With quality-control workers scanning this belt to rescue any recyclable materials, the unfit waste is then diverted to a landfill. A typical MRF can process hundreds of tons every day, and those materials are trucked from all across cities. Recycling objectors might point to the transport in proclaiming that the practice isn't as sustainable as we think. However, assessments show the emissions from transporting recyclables are generally minor and are less of an impact than those of virgin materials.[16]

These impressive sorting facilities process a plethora of items every single day, but they are only as effective as investments in the technology allow them to be. The original machines put in place and the maintenance and improvements of them (or lack thereof) determine how successfully our recyclables are sorted. Given the high level of competition among MRF machinery suppliers, it's possible the industry will continue to see advanced technology in the coming years. In 2016, 65 percent of U.S. recovery facilities were single-stream, compared to only 27 percent of all MRFs just a decade prior.[17]

Clearly, for all its drawbacks, municipalities are still intrigued by the promised participation rates and lower day-to-day costs of single-stream. Some towns report very positive results from making the investment in single-stream operations, but it's not a decision taken lightly. Adapting existing facilities to become single-stream can cost millions of dollars, and because there's likelihood of increased contamination with the switch, cities who have been achieving moderate recycling rates through other methods may decide it's not worth it to join the trend.[18] Even in dual- and multistream, incorrect placement of items or tossing nonrecyclable stuff can cause expensive problems. The town of London, Ontario, offers dual-stream recycling and has still spent up to $250,000 per year due to improper curbside sorting and contamination.[19] Contamination of material loads in single-stream can cost a facility $140 per ton. In 2014, processing costs for single-stream reportedly increased 20 percent in just two years.[20]

Collection costs are lower in single-stream, but processing costs and the expense of disposal for contaminated goods are higher than dual-stream.[21] Comparisons of various methods show that single-stream can collect around 20 percent more volume, but the costs for dealing with contamination can outweigh the benefits of more-efficient collection. These same comparisons show that single-stream MRFs lose roughly one-quarter of collected materials to contamination, compared to the 1 to 12 percent seen at facilities employing source separation or dual-stream. So, more volume may be entering single-stream MRFs than multi-stream facilities, but this doesn't equal more recyclables going out the door to manufacturers.[22]

Moving to single-stream to make recycling easier for residents does not eliminate the need for education on best practices. Like most things, we will get out of this system what we put into it, whether that be a company investing in and maintaining sophisticated sorting equipment or residents learning the acceptable items to place in the bin. If we want to have high environmental and economic benefits, then we must invest in the processes the system depends on to function.

There is another type of facility, historically called dirty MRFs, in which residents throw every bit of their waste into the same bin to be sorted (a.k.a., mixed-waste processing [MWP]). Banana peels, old newspapers, plastics, yard waste, used tissue—you name it—all goes in one bin, requiring absolutely zero sorting from residents. All municipal solid waste is sorted at a facility from this single-bin system and is sent onto the directed fate for each item, including recycling, composting, or incineration. The sorting requires equipment similar to a traditional recycling MRF, but this process needs more equipment to separate our leftover food scraps from junk mail. These all-in-one-bin plans have a significant logistical gap: the unrealistic expectation that tossing in all our garbage will churn out sellable recyclables. Contamination is a problem present in single-stream recycling systems, and adding more wet waste to the mixture offers more chances for contaminants to drive down the quality of recovered materials. There are also benefits of residents sorting recyclables from their trash. It allows us to remain in tune with what we're tossing out and how much. The one-bin method not only takes out the guesswork involved for residents but also removes any need to think about our waste at all, including the quantity of our trash, how we dispose of it, or even the workers sorting it for us. If we have no motivation to consider the types of things we're tossing and the volume of it, then why would we feel the need to reduce our consumption?

Such a project was set to take place in Houston, Texas, with a new facility to be built near an existing landfill, once again targeting specific communities to deal with any environmental and health impacts from the process. As evident in Dr. Robert Bullard's study of the placement of Houston waste-disposal sites from the 1930s to 1978, all city-owned landfills, three of four private landfills, and six of eight incinerators were placed in largely black neighborhoods. He notes that, as of 2014, all the city's waste was taken to landfills, transfer stations, and MRFs located in overwhelmingly black and Hispanic neighborhoods.[23] There is also reason to be wary of seeking employment in this type of facility: Because the process typically relies on a mix of machines and hand sorting, there is a high likelihood of workers coming into contact with rotten foods and hazardous wastes.[24] Although the mixed-waste model is said to make life better for busy households and provide jobs to communities, it doesn't seem to deliver on those ideal outcomes.

For cities like Houston, which has a low recycling rate of 6 percent,[25] this idea was one that city officials hoped would achieve more landfill diversion (lowering the city's cost to send trash to the landfill) and higher recycling results. Proponents of the one-bin-for-all plan suggested that it could yield a 75 percent diversion rate, which some interpreted as what the new recycling rate would be for the city. We are reminded of the problems associated with focusing solely on "zero-landfill" goals. One bin for all might be diverting high amounts of waste from landfills, but that doesn't automatically mean it's going to be found in your new recycled-content products. A similar system in Montgomery, Alabama, had promised 90 percent waste diversion, but this was never realized. The resulting recycling rate was so low that the company owed the city $2.5 million in costs to send waste to landfills during its first year.[26] The Montgomery facility had a short-lived operation from spring 2014 to fall 2015 due to low market prices for the materials being recovered. Another problem was that the city didn't generate the amount waste per month needed to make the venture profitable. The $37 million facility needed 150,000 tons a year to maintain costs of operation but got 78,000 and was even bringing in additional tons from other areas.[27]

As for Houston, if city officials thought everyone would be excited about the prospect of another waste facility to save them from sorting, then they were quickly proven incorrect. Tens of thousands of residents spoke out against the proposed one-bin plan and in favor of keeping curbside recycling by signing petitions, calling the mayor and city council, speaking at city hall, and using social media.[28] The discomfort of having one entity control a public service like curbside recycling along with the prospect of another waste facility built in underserved neighborhoods stirred residents to take action and make sure leaders heard how unwelcome the concept was in their community. The city's dismal recycling rate can in large part be attributed to the restricted access until 2015, when all neighborhoods finally were offered recycling services for the first time.[29] Houston's low recycling rate has long been skewed by the limited area it serves. The one-bin-for-all plan did not move forward, as the new mayor taking office denied the deal without full explanation, but it's entirely possible the plans buckled under public pressure against the system, including organizations and trade groups concerned about the quality of recovered items.[30]

Supporters of MWP note its effectiveness in some European cities for twenty years, after a European Union directive to divert biodegradable waste from landfills. They recycle what they can and then landfill or burn the rest at a waste-to-energy plant (it cannot be composted because the material is too contaminated).[31] But it's inability to function in the United States is clearly proven by dismal recycling rates from cities attempting it. For example, North Carolina mixed-waste facilities report only between 1 and 10 percent recycling rates, and it's been noted that contracts of these plants stipulate where waste in a community can go, meaning that they can decisively send all waste to the MWP facility.[32] This kind of situation allows the MWP company to control the

whim of waste disposal entirely and could potentially undermine recycling efforts throughout the city. When MWP operates alongside a recycling system and is not contractually above it, there have been reportedly more favorable results.[33] Recall the staggering amount of recyclable items still ending up in the landfill I toured despite having a fully
functioning recycling system. Some propose that a dirty MRF could be
in service to pluck out those recyclable goods from waste headed to be
buried at greater efficiency. But in this scenario, contamination risks are
still an issue for paper items. And the concerns of neighborhoods at
greatest risk for having yet another waste disposal site built and operating near their homes cannot be ignored.

While it is likely that companies will continue searching for advanced technology to make mixed-waste processing more successful, it
strikes me as an immense waste. With 94 percent of the country having
access to recycling and more than five million residents with compost
services (and growing),[34] why would it be productive to build massive,
costly facilities that could take the place of these programs, particularly
when the results are expected to be the same or lower[35] and materials
like paper fiber (which makes up more than one-quarter of most household recycling[36]) will unquestionably be degraded in quality? Estimates
show a mere 10 to 30 percent of the waste going into a mixed-waste
facility as recoverable to a sellable quality because of contamination.[37]

Proponents of mixed-waste facilities may continue to praise their
potential, but I wonder how many more cities will attempt this costly
change only to shutter it because expectations are not met. It seems
that a fraction of the cost to build a new system could be spent to better
our current systems through increased recycling education and other
incentive programs to reduce trash. And there will be more improvements as we urge cities to set zero-waste goals instead of fixating on
landfill diversion as the main metric of success. A large determinant of
the system's future comes back to us, the people making the choices to
recycle and to do it correctly. After all, 100 percent participation is
obvious when residents have no other alternative, but it does not trans-
late to a high recovery rate for those materials or ensure their reentry to
the market as new products. Where recycling and buying recycled
closes a loop, mixed-waste processing leaves many open holes for negative climate and societal effects to sneak through.

SEPARATE MATERIAL PROCESSES

Once they've been sorted, your old materials are taken to their respective processing facilities, where they will be cleaned and broken down to their new forms to make into products. I've listed the following material sectors with their recycling rates, meaning the rate of material recycled from total solid waste. This is the most common metric used for signaling if recycling is effective, but gauging success solely on recycling rate is not the most reliable indicator because everyone measures differently. Just weighing all the stuff in the disposal method doesn't convey if items are actually being recycled and displacing virgin materials in production. By focusing on the recycling rate, we are simply observing how much of the old items we get rid of go into the recycling stream versus the landfill. Using weight as a barometer for success also doesn't offer the full picture of an item's impact. Because it would take multiple plastic items to equal a heavier one like a large glass container, the impacts of those lighter-weight recyclables are diminished.

A more telling metric would be steering sectors and municipalities to report on contamination rates. We need to define success as a decrease in overall waste and effectively diverting items to recycling, but we must also celebrate leaders for low contamination rates. An impactful recycling program is more than the number of residents participating or the volume not being trashed or burned. Even if all residents in a city participated and a stunning 90 percent of waste was sent into recycling, in order to consider this scenario a triumph, these high-quality recyclables must displace virgin materials in manufacturing. As Helmut Maurer, waste management expert with the European Commission, has stated, "What counts is how much of that recycled material actually re-enters production."[38] Researchers at the University of Florida developed a metric called adjusted recycling rates to account for contamination in county recycling rates. For example, a county's reported recycling rate is 58 percent, but when its 28 percent contamination rate is considered, the recycling rate dips down to roughly 41 percent.[39] Until measuring successful recycling programs by contamination rates catches on, using recycling rates can offer a general idea of how much of a material group is going through the recycling stream.

PLASTICS: LESS THAN 10 PERCENT GLOBAL RECYCLING RATE [40]

Let's travel from the forest to the ocean for a moment. Our waters are full of unique creatures, reefs, waves, and sadly, a gruesome amount of plastic. Each year, another 19 billion pounds of trash makes its way into our oceans, and estimates show that this number will double by 2025 unless we all commit to action. [41] This plastic trash is largely made up of discarded fishing nets and single-use plastics from mismanaged waste disposal. Littered plastic items get blown away and find storm drains; then they float through our waterways and out to sea. Now imagine standing in waters with millions of these little moments where someone tossed trash out a window or didn't bother to recycle it, the plastic products of our hurried schedules bobbing around as far as the eye can see. This pollution takes a deadly toll on the wildlife in our waters, and Ocean Conservancy says plastics threaten at least seven hundred different species. [42] Plastics don't ever disappear; they just break down into smaller pieces, known as microplastics, that animals ingest on a regular basis at increasing rates. One in four fish have been found in U.S. markets with plastic in their bodies. [43] If you eat seafood, these plastics are highly likely to make their way back to you.

We use tons of plastic around the world every year, and this stubborn material is known for its resistance to disappearing without a trace. Many cleaners are packaged in plastic because the material is resistant to the chemicals found in the solvents we stow under our sinks. This tenacity comes at a cost because it's tough to get rid of this plastic stuff once its purpose has been filled. For example, Americans use millions of plastic straws every day, and it can take each of these nonrecyclable funnels centuries to break down. [44] Straws are just one piece of the array of plastic products clogging oceans.

It can be hard to see our individual choices as making a huge difference, but experts affirm that our seemingly cliché ecohabits of carrying reusable bottles and bags truly are a huge part of changing this landscape. [45] It's estimated one million plastic bags are used around the world every minute, and these items are typically in service for fifteen minutes before being tossed. Keeping a reusable bag can go far in reducing our additions to this ocean plastic pile. Half of all the plastic produced is used once and then tossed away, and too often, "away" is into our seas.[46]

If there's all this plastic floating around, then why aren't we recycling more of it? The reasons are a mixture of social habits and widespread demand for the material. Plastic is made using oil and in fact makes up 6 percent of global oil consumption.[47] When oil prices are low, manufacturers elect to use virgin plastic instead of recycled plastic because it makes more economic sense if they don't have to satisfy specific demands from companies for recycled content. Typically, companies are mostly concerned with the resin composition, color, and weight of the plastic to make sure their products are consistently recognizable to consumers.

Perhaps you've noticed the little numbers beneath your plastic products circled by the Mobius Loop, the familiar three arrows. Consumers see the symbol and eagerly toss their plastics into recycling, but these numbers are just clues to the kind of resin (the base of all plastics that can altered to suit different needs) used in the product. They were created to help recycling facilities know how to sort the different kinds. The numbers have confused people in the past and have led folks to accidentally place nonrecyclable plastics in the bin to recycle. This eventually led to changing the arrows around the resin numbers to a small triangle, but the resin labels are still often found in the recycling arrows.

These are commonly used plastic resins: polyethylene terephthalate (PET), which are your beverage bottles; high-density polyethylene (HDPE), where you'll see your larger beverage jug or detergent containers or plastic grocery bags; low-density polyethylene (LDP) for items like frozen food bags, squeezable bottles, and shrink wrap; polypropylene (PP) for plastic straws, medicine bottles, and yogurt containers; polystyrene (PS) for disposable cutlery, clamshell containers, and cups; and polyvinyl chloride (PVC) for more rigid plastic containers (think of those hard-to-open shells often used for electronics).[48] Fortunately, we don't have to know how to spell or pronounce these titles in order to recycle them correctly because most municipal programs use their corresponding numbers on a list of accepted items. After being sorted from other materials at the MRF, these resins are separated into streams by resin number and color.[49] Buyers want a simple process and often prefer clear plastics that can be dyed more easily to suit the customer's needs. The expectation is to put a variety of plastic types into the recycled stream and have marketable clear plastics come out of it, like a clean new canvas. Unfortunately, this makes collecting and sorting this material a bit tricky. Plastic PET bottles have historically had a low amount of recycled content. The bottles we put into our recycling bins are typically used to make synthetic fibers instead of new bottles. Converting recycled plastic into fiber for clothing and carpets is less intensive than converting it to food grade plastic packaging. But this is changing, as some producers are committing to boost the FDA-approved recycled content in their bottles, particularly as concern around plastic pollution grows.

Another cause of the low recycling rate is the sheer number of different plastic types out there and the challenge presented in recovering those properly. If there was greater design consistency in companies' use of plastics, then all the products could be recycled together, like aluminum, which does not have to be separated.[50] Another challenge ironically comes from a technique of practicing source reduction, when companies try to use lightweight plastic film for packaging or use thinner plastic for bottles. The goal may be to reduce overall use of plastic for the company (a good thing), but these thin films and laminated plastic pouches are generally not accepted in curbside programs (not so good). This is what occurs when a company is focused on just one part of a product's impact but neglects to make choices that ensure recyclability for disposal. So, there is a combination of design decisions that a company makes. In order to increase recycling rates, they must consider the end of life of their products, and we as consumers must urge companies to commit to using recycled content.

After your plastic recyclables have left the MRF and arrived at a processing plant, they are cleaned to remove any extra debris. Then they go through specialized laser sorting, in which clear and opaque plastics are separated, zipping down their respective conveyor belts. All plastics are then treated to a hot water bath, with just the right temperature to shed any labels and caps, before being sent through a shredding process. The tiny pieces are once again washed, dried, and given one last heating. Then they are packaged for sale to manufacturers. Plastic material destined to become new beverage bottles and food containers have added steps and are further sterilized to comply with federal regulations. They are melted down to even tinier pieces, the size of a grain of rice, before being sent to manufacturers.[51]

We've been using plastic packaging fervently for just a few decades, yet it's clearly delivered sizable impacts to the planet. The good news is that, though it's a problem we have created, it is also one we can help solve. While cleanups are great mitigating efforts, we need to focus on not letting plastics reach our waters in the first place. We can reduce plastic consumption and correctly dispose of them by recycling the plastics we can and throwing away the ones we can't (and ideally not buying single-use plastics at all). Nothing can show the powerful ripple effect of one movement quite like the water, and we are able to make small decisions that ripple across social habits and norms every day. If other people see you carrying a reusable bottle, then they are reminded and inspired to do the same.

ALUMINUM: 70 TO 95 PERCENT GLOBAL RECYCLING RATE,[52] 56 PERCENT IN THE UNITED STATES[53]

After various metals are sorted, aluminum, steel, and tin are sent to their respective treatment facilities. I focus here on the two main metals that you likely often use and are able to put in your local residential recycling stream: steel and aluminum. Brass and copper are recyclable but often need to be taken to a drop-off location instead of going through your curbside service. Some cities collect old cast-iron pans through curbside recycling, while others would direct residents to a drop-off center.

As noted, aluminum is an infinitely recyclable material, and it is able to be reused in a brand-new product or recast into its previous shape. Increasing our use of recycled aluminum can curb the harsh effects of bauxite mining operations. From pie pans and foil to cars and aircraft, this material is malleable and reliable. Aluminum has been called the most valuable item in the recycling stream due to its durability and infinite recyclability. Nearly 75 percent of all aluminum ever created is still in use in a new form today.[54] The sector leading the charge on recycled aluminum is the automobile industry, which boasts a 95 percent recycling rate.

Once sorted from other recyclables at the MRF, aluminum is cut into smaller pieces, baled, and sent to a treatment facility, where it is cleaned and then processed. It is melted into molten aluminum (it can be melted at a much lower temperature than bauxite, the virgin raw material, thus lowering energy needs), which removes the branding and inks from the material from its previous life. Then the molten aluminum is made into large blocks, called ingots, each containing what were once around 1.6 million beverage cans. An average plant can produce fifteen massive ingots a day.[55] The ingots are sent to manufacturing mills, where they are unfurled into a long, flat sheet of aluminum. In some cases, the molten aluminum is ground into a powder or pushed into a die or model. Then the aluminum is made into new cans for soups, foil, and pie pans to be sold back to you. Aluminum is recycled from larger items after usefulness has ended, like automobile and construction parts (90 percent of which are effectively recycled), but not through your residential curbside recycling service.

We go through a substantial amount of aluminum in the United States. Every three months, we toss out enough aluminum to rebuild every commercial American airplane. We do a decent job at recycling our metal refuse, but there's still room to improve. Beyond recycling rates, there is a need to improve the very facilities processing metal materials. These industrial operations are a preferred disposal method than landfills and incineration, but if unmonitored they can still result in harmful effects on communities. In 2012, Houston metal recyclers were called into question after nearby residents had complained of smoke and breathing difficulties for multiple years. This led to closer examination of Houston metal recyclers and five tested scrap yards were shown to emit dangerous levels of hexavalent chromium (or "Chrome VI"), which can ultimately lead to lung cancer when inhaled over time.[56] By identifying and targeting the problematic facilities, investigators from the Bureau of Pollution Control and Prevention scored each recycler, and companies began cutting emission-causing methods and reducing airborne particles. Until Houston's testing, the U.S. Environmental Protection Agency had not identified metal recyclers as a source of Chrome VI.[57] It's important to observe that while recycling is a better way to manage our materials, this does not mean its processes can go unchecked. This underscores the need for city officials to take residential concerns seriously and address root causes of emissions through regulation and enforcement, so companies are required to make necessary adjustments.

STEEL: 88 PERCENT GLOBAL RECYCLING RATE,[58] 92 PERCENT IN THE UNITED STATES[59]

The steel industry proudly declares it's the world's most recycled material, and with impressively high recycling rates, it has reason to brag. From aerosol cans to bottle caps and bicycles to food tins, this is the most widely used metal, and it can be recycled time and again without declining in performance. Its magnetic properties allow steel to be easily sorted in commingled recycling streams.

A steel item's journey after being sorted is like its nonferrous friend, aluminum. Once the steel arrives at a processing center, it needs to be separated from a layer of tin that often is used to keep steel items from corroding from oxygen. Tin is rust resistant and has a low toxicity, making it a great fit for where steel falls short. Recyclable steel items are dipped into a caustic chemical solution (it can corrode organic tissue), which dissolves the tin and leaves the steel to be rinsed off. The steel is then melted down, and high-purity oxygen is blown for further cleaning. After spending twenty to thirty minutes in a heated converter, the steel is rolled into coils, which is how it is sent to manufacturers.

Steel is often used in larger items, like cars, appliances, buildings, and bridges, meaning it can be employed for many decades at a time before being recycled as scrap (if ever). For this reason, the industry maintains the necessity of introducing some virgin-made steel into the supply chain to satisfy demand. Steel requires the mining of iron ore, and almost all of this mined material goes toward steel production. Raw iron ore is mixed with coal and limestone and blasted with extreme heat in furnaces, with oxygen added to reduce the carbon amount to form liquid steel. A major source of carbon emissions from the process is coking coal, which is heated at high temperatures for many hours to be used in furnaces for steel production.[60] The more carbon in the coke, the faster the process goes, but unfortunately, this also means more carbon emissions. Impurities like sand and clay are removed during the process, and the result is new raw steel ready to be manufactured. The production demands high amounts of energy and emits carbon dioxide throughout. In fact, producing one ton of steel releases nearly two tons of carbon dioxide, accounting for up to 5 percent of our global greenhouse gas emissions.[61] Chemists continue to work for a process that would drastically reduce carbon released, but as of 2015, it still contributes some of the highest emissions of any material production.[62] By contrast, recycled steel production requires 75 percent less energy and emits 58 percent fewer greenhouse gases than new steel.[63]

GLASS: 73 PERCENT RECYCLING RATE IN THE EUROPEAN UNION,[64] 34 PERCENT IN THE UNITED STATES[65]

Glass has the shortest turnaround time of any of your curbside goods, zipping through the recycling and manufacturing processes and back into stores in just under thirty days.[66] This material is endlessly and 100 percent recyclable, retaining its purity and quality throughout use in different products. Once glass is sorted at your local MRF, it is sent to a processing center, where it is further cleaned and sorted by color. Manufacturers have a limited amount of mixed-color cullet (ground glass) they can use to make new containers, so glass-processing facilities separate by color to meet customer standards. Then the cullet is sold to one of the forty-six glass manufacturers in the United States, where it is mixed with sand, sodium carbonate, and calcium carbonate before being melted in a furnace of more than 1,000°F.[67] The glass is then molded or mechanically blown into new shapes, making the jars and bottles for consumers to purchase.

Unfortunately, this material has shown some trouble in the markets and is sometimes left out of local recycling programs. Not all states have processing facilities for glass, so it often must be shipped across state lines. Some communities opt to not recycle glass and blame the costs of transporting to distant facilities. Cities like New Orleans and Nashville may be known for lively bars and music venues with lots of glass bottles to discard every night, but neither currently recycles glass due to the low market value and the concerns with collection costs. Houston also ditched glass when it reconfigured its recycling services after declining the one-bin-for-all proposal. Municipalities choosing to go without glass point to the cost of hauling a material with low market value as the reason, but other industry folks argue that the market for glass is not the problem. They consider the problem to be collection[68] and assert that, if glass could be collected in ways that reduce its role as a contaminant, then we would see greater success with the material.

The glass industry is no exception in concerns of contamination and it prefers to ensure its material isn't ruined. This makes drop-off recycling centers and commercial collection preferable for obtaining higher-quality recovered glass.[69] Customers of recycled glass need the correct glass color for their products, and colored glass can only be used to make more of the same color, so having a correctly sorted supply is very important.[70] Major industry members have advised dropping glass collection out of single-stream programs completely, as less than half of the states host glass manufacturers and just a few more than that have processors.[71] They say that, even if quality weren't a concern, transportation costs from the material's weight and distance are still enough to discourage a city from gathering our old bottles and jars. In 2013, 34 percent of all glass containers were recycled, most of which were beer and soda bottles (41.3 percent of this type were collected), and the smallest amount of glass products collected were food and glass jars (only 15 percent were collected for recycling).[72] The glass industry noted that the 34 percent recycling rate contributed the environmental savings equivalent of taking 210,000 cars off the road every year. Glass is a useful material, and many of us prefer glass packaging to plastic, so it's important to find solutions to recycling it. Bottle deposit systems have been a successful solution in many areas, and I expand on how to help grow these in a later chapter.

PAPER: 58.9 PERCENT GLOBAL RECYCLING RATE,[73] 67 PERCENT IN THE UNITED STATES[74]

Unlike metal and glass, which as noted can be recycled into perpetuity, paper fibers can be reused fewer than a dozen times, and the fiber shortens each time it's reused. By applying recycled fiber in a smart way, we can use it in many ways before it's no longer recyclable.

Paper is one of the more vulnerable materials in a single-stream recycling system because it can be damaged by the food and liquids lingering on other containers in a bin or truck. After the recoverable paper items have been separated from other materials at the MRF, they are sorted by grade and baled. The bales are then sent to paper mills, where the paper is placed into a pulper to be chopped into smaller pieces. Water is added to the paper and heated, so that the fibers can be broken down before the mixture is put through screens to remove any remaining nonpaper items like packaging tape and staples. All the pulp is further cleaned and goes through a deinking process to get rid of any glue or old ink from the previous paper use. The final refining stage is when the pulp is stripped of any lingering color and occasionally bleached with hydrogen peroxide and oxygen for white paper products. The pulp is sprayed on rapidly moving screens to drain the excess water so the remaining fibers can bond together, and then the sheets are put thought pressers to remove any excess moisture. The paper sheets are then dried and wound into rolls and sent off to manufacturers and printers to be made into the products we buy.

On average, each ton of recycled paper used conserves seven thousand gallons of water, seventeen trees, and more than three yards of landfill space.[75] There is ample fiber in the world to become new products; however, if a demand for it is lacking, then there's less incentive to strengthen collection methods that protect these paper fibers. To continue reducing environmental and social impacts of this industry, each product sector must maximize recycled content, and this is achieved through demands by companies (and us, of course).

While every material we send through our recycling system has its own unique set of criteria for processing, they all curb the impression our products leave on the planet. We can measure with certainty their energy savings, reduced greenhouse gas emissions, and of course the wide range of benefits from lessening virgin-material production. In any system, the mechanics of how it functions and the quality of the inputs and outputs are all necessary to consider. But one area that may feel a bit more unusual to quantitatively measure success is the psychology of those participating in the system. What might incentivize someone to recycle or how they engage with the process or even why you decided to pick up this book about recycling are all questions we can surmise only to the extent we understand it. A definitive reason an individual does or doesn't recycle or the way they purchase new products is slightly harder to pin down with precision than amounts of emissions when producing new materials. But if we are striving to better our habits and become more sustainable participants in our own ecosystems, then knowing how we approach decisions can be extremely valuable.

7

HOW PSYCHOLOGY AFFECTS RECYCLING AND WASTE

Introducing new habits into our lives can be tough. For example, perhaps we've all experienced striving to exercise more, but then a few hours later, indulged in some junk food or other empty calories. We often reason that successfully exhibiting some good behavior warrants the reward of some less-healthy decisions, despite knowing that doing so cancels the more positive habit. We see this same rationale in studies that show having recycling options actually leads people to waste more. Tossing a soda can into the right bin makes us feel good, like we've given back to the world and are doing our part. But experiments run by Boston University suggest this warm, fuzzy feeling could be problematic.[1]

During the experiments, participants were divided into two rooms, one with just a trash can and the other with only a recycling bin. They were asked to sample a few different beverages, with a stack of disposable cups to use in each room. In the recycling room, each participant used multiple cups to sample, while in the trash room, each person was more likely to reuse the same cup multiple times. The awareness that they could recycle the cups led to participants being more lenient in how much they were wasting. Researchers then replicated the experiment with wrapping paper and received similar results. In social science, this act of giving yourself freedom to be wasteful as reward for doing some good behavior (or even *thinking* about doing something considered healthy or virtuous) is called "moral licensing" (or self-licensing).[2]

When developing a new habit, it seems obvious that any warm, fuzzy feelings we can link to the behavior would help solidify the habit. If we feel proud of something, then we will continue doing it to relive that positive feeling. The problem comes when we decide to reward ourselves, and this can be as simple as leaving the water running while we brush our teeth. The satisfaction of recycling can give us a sense of permission to create more waste, which is a reward—the reward of convenience. We've made a deal with our future selves to recycle so that we can consume materials that make our lives easier. We then anticipate a reward for recycling rather than doing it out of habit. Sometimes the reward is defending our own environmentalism to others. How often have we heard or said some variation of, "I care about the planet. I recycle!" as justification for some behavior others judge as nongreen?

Recycling is good, but the altruistic sense of satisfaction and the exceptionalism that can come along with it may not be beneficial. The circular arrows are seen as neutralizing the existence of the product rather than a symbol of the best way to dispose of an item already carrying environmental impacts from its production. As Adam Minter states in *Junkyard Planet*, discarding something into a recycling bin has just outsourced the problem to someone else, either at the MRF down the street or overseas.[3] And while the process of recycling a material is far gentler on the planet than extracting a new material, what we've put into the bin (nor the efforts and energy spent making it) doesn't magically vanish. Using moral licensing when we recycle to assuage other wasteful behavior can be counterproductive for our ultimate goal of reducing our impact on the environment.

A study from Stanford University suggests we engage in moral licensing when facing ethical uncertainties in our social lives.[4] When our next action has the possibility of being immoral, we boost ourselves with past moral behavior to signal that we are not "bad" people. We lean on past experiences of positive actions to permit any acts we engage in that are considered wasteful, selfish, or even bigoted.

Experiments have shown that moral licensing can result in discriminatory or abusive practices. For example, in one experiment, a group of people were given opportunity to express nondiscriminatory hiring decisions for equally qualified candidates. The participants who had previously been told they were "more moral than other groups" by the researchers were more likely to state a job as better suited for white candidates than for black candidates.[5] This and other similar experiments suggest that once people have expressed a nondiscriminatory statement, they appear to feel licensed to espouse something discriminatory. It's like when someone begins a sentence with "I'm not racist, but..." They seem to feel that the preface gives them permission to reference a stereotype. They perhaps subconsciously view it as "canceling" offensive behavior.

Along with exhibiting discriminatory behavior, moral licensing can be damaging in the sense that it can undermine the very goals and ideals we want to achieve in our lives. It's likely many of us have had days where we are ahead on a task list and then take a deserved break. But when we allow that break to extend far beyond what's necessary to recharge, we once again find ourselves trailing behind on our next tasks. When people have been told that they've made progress on something, they're more likely to start slacking off because the message implies progress instead of a commitment. People receive the message that they've done enough and their job is complete.[6] This can allow us to disengage with the positive behavior, so better habits never form.

Companies contribute to our moral-licensing tendencies by inflating the positive effects of our purchases. A brand might affirm that the customer is "saving the planet" by purchasing their recyclable or organic goods. These messages might be well-intentioned (and are likely to urge a customer to buy more of the product), but they allow us to think we have done a feat worthy of indulgence rather a default behavior. By extolling a customer for their consumption of a more sustainable product and equating their decision to "saving the world," companies make the behavior seem all the more exceptional rather than the norm. So, how do we encourage more sustainable behaviors while also not inciting rampant moral licensing? Part of the solution could be giving praise in accordance with the impact of an action. Buying one cup of organic coffee is not necessarily "saving the world," but it does contribute to a system that is better for communities and the environment. Printing "Thank you for contributing to a more sustainable system to obtain this coffee! You're great!" is not as pithy as emblazoning superhero accolades on a cup, but it seems necessary for us to make these positive decisions more normal than extraordinary.

Another key could be eliciting community-praise messages rather than just customer praise. Maryam Kouchaki and Ata Jami, researchers from Northwestern University and the University of Central Florida, conducted an experiment to better assess how praise affects us. Volunteers were sent one of two messages from an organization they were affiliated with: one message praised the entire group of volunteers for their work, while the other thanked the recipient's individual work. Both e-mails ended with an opportunity to receive the gift of a luxury backpack or a utility travel bag. The individual-praise e-mails saw volunteers opting for the more indulgent luxury backpack, while those receiving the group-praise message were more likely to choose the utility bag. It turns out that, when we're praised for being more green, we begin to see ourselves with that trait, temporarily boosting our self-concept and the related behavior that reflects us as eco-friendly individuals.[7] The key word here is *temporarily*. As soon as choice on consumption arises later, we are more likely to do the more wasteful thing because we already did our good deed for the day. A noted exception was people who already considered themselves environmentally conscious; they were less likely to be influenced by any praise for sustainable habits, perhaps because they've adopted the habit as a norm. But these people haven't necessarily surpassed moral licensing because it's possible that they could exhibit it in other aspects of their lives, like delaying fitness goals or cheating in a casual board game.[8]

Moral licensing also works in the other direction. We feel compelled to do something healthy or "good" after we've done something indulgent. When we indulge too much or the amount of licensing we use is out of whack with the positive behavior we exhibited, it begins to undermine our goals. It takes a fair amount of research to determine if conserving in one area equals or outweighs wasteful behavior in another, though. It's hard for us to always know if our actions have a balanced impact, like if recycling regularly outweighs online shopping habits throughout the year. We'd have to look into the greenhouse gases (GHGs) emitted through each process and know more about the full life cycle of the products we order online, as well as the recovery rates for each item we put into the bin. In some cases, we can clearly see how moral licensing has worked against our intentions. An example is after making energy-efficient improvements to one's home yet seeing no change in bill amounts. If someone indulges in using more energy because of these new efficiencies, the savings could remain roughly the same as before when they used less energy but paid more for it.[9]

There is another contributor called the rebound effect, when people buy a lot of a recyclable product and possibly cancel out some of its environmental benefits.[10] It's entirely possible that our tendency to wish-cycle is in cahoots with the rebound effect, so we might be causing contamination with lots of items we think are recyclable. This can be seen beyond recycling; we might buy a more fuel-efficient car but then drive further or have greener bulbs but leave the lights on.

We might think these tendencies are just part of human nature and there's nothing to be done about it, but cross-cultural studies suggest otherwise. For example, researchers have found that North American participants in studies exhibited high moral licensing, but that Western European participants did so far less, and participants from Southeast Asia were found to engage in very little moral licensing at all. The study observed North American participants to have a strong desire to be considered a "good" person and strive for perfection, whereas Western European participants were observed to maintain a reasonable level of moral self-concept. These studies suggest that North American participants exhibited a higher fluctuation in behavior, possibly due to more rigid definitions of good and bad behavior. The pendulum constantly swings back and forth, as we attempt to exhibit strictly moral actions and feel shame when we fall short.[11]

If actions aren't viewed in such extremes, then the value of a "license to do something" goes down because there isn't as high of an urge to respond to certain behavior with the opposite act. Western Europeans in the study were observed to be less driven by a need to correct behaviors and thus were less inclined to indulge in bad actions after doing something charitable. For participants from Southeast Asia, there was even less evidence of moral licensing. Keeping consistency in behavior was observed to be more important, meaning a sustainable decision is likely to lead to more sustainable decisions. The study suggests that Southeast Asian participants would take recent behavior into account less; rather, their long-term behavior (both past and future) was more of a guiding principle, as opposed to North American participants, who bartered the morality of one decision with the next.[12]

Social judgments are often how we determine if something is good or bad in the first place, and any associated shame stems from how others perceive our actions or even how we anticipate our actions will be perceived. The distinction between guilt and shame is significant, as some guilt can propel us to do better, but shame can lock us further into negative behaviors. Guilt allows us to acknowledge when we fell short of our own standards (e.g., "I did a bad thing"), whereas shame punctures a deeper part of our self-identity (e.g., "I am a bad person").[13] Psychologists observe that, when someone is enveloped in shame, their capacity to experience guilt is actually lower because a coping mechanism for shame can be narcissistic behavior, meaning they have less concern for others.[14] In short, a feeling of guilt could be our moral compass at work, but a feeling of shame results in less space to consider the feelings of others. When we make mistakes, it's important not to heap on the shame. If we do, then we risk associating sustainability with chores that we should do to not feel ashamed, and we remove any joy from those habits. Green practices will seem daunting rather than a normal routine, and carrying shame about them will just make us distance ourselves from those habits.

If the system's goal is to reduce our impacts on the environment, then the psychology of how we approach our decisions of consumption and disposal is paramount to reaching that goal. Our small, daily purchasing habits are perceived as insignificant in the goals of turning the tide on climate change, but they have more of an impact than we think. In 2016, researchers set out to measure consumption impacts of major countries by looking into what's called the secondary effects, taking the export of goods into account. The United States and China are regularly pitted against one another as the country with the most greenhouse gas emissions, but this recent analysis observes that, when we take demand and consumption of goods into account, one far surpasses the other. China produces lots of products which are exported, and commonly to meet U.S. demand.

The study says consumers are responsible for 60 percent of the world's greenhouse gas emissions.[15] In looking at our effects per capita, the more wealthy and populated a country is, the higher each person's environmental impact. The United States leads in per-capita GHGs (18.6 metric tons), followed by Luxembourg (18.5), and then Australia (17.7). In a more distant slot is China, with just 1.8 metric tons of carbon dioxide; the reported global average is 3.4 metric tons. With this fuller view of our consumption effects, we can begin to address the habits and methods we use to make decisions that are more in line with sustainable values. The authors of this study affirm that the two best ways for us to have an impact are reducing our meat intake and cutting back on our purchases. They advise households to use a service instead of buying a new product whenever possible, such as renting or borrowing equipment for household maintenance. Coordinating lists of items neighbors own and are willing to loan to others through a tool library is a great way to help reduce consumption.

Moral licensing is clearly a complex phenomenon that has been well substantiated across many experiments, but there is still much to learn about how to change those impulses. What we can do is reframe how we make these decisions to curb the effects of our actions. The first step is to recognize when we're indulging in moral licensing and taking a pause. When faced with a decision, instead of bartering with past or potential future actions to permit negative behavior, we can ask ourselves if the decision is in line with our core values or goals. There is obviously a difference between truly immoral behavior (causing someone harm) and behavior that we prescribe as bad but is actually just in conflict with our goals (watching TV when we need to study). If we label a counterproductive action (e.g., not recycling when we value sustainability) as just bad, then our brains will begin looking for a way to swing the pendulum in another direction. The flipside is also true: If we view our good behavior as in line with our values or goals, then we are less likely to see it as an extraordinary feat deserving counterproductive behavior. For example, the buying an organic coffee in our minds will better match what we have done in reality: We've contributed to a better system, but we don't think of ourselves as individually saving the world because of it. This reframing is more likely to keep us at a neutral baseline of behavior so our actions are more consistent rather than swinging back and forth, frantically trying in vain to achieve a sense of balance.

We can instead strive to mindfully remain grounded, to notice when we're making a decision rather than doing it on autopilot. We can also be honest with ourselves and not allow shame to envelop us and promote inactivity when we fall short. And of course, we can identify a deeper reason for good actions rather than relying on social pressures to ensure longer-lasting change. If we accept sustainability as a core value within ourselves rather than something we should do to be considered a good person, then we are more likely to succeed in adjusting our habits.[16] We can then share the process with others and help each other learn more about how we make decisions so we all grow toward more mindful behavior.

HOW DO WE CHANGE OUR HABITS FOR THE BETTER?

A man by the name of John Francis observed an oil spill choking local wildlife as it seeped into the water in California in 1971. Two Standard Oil Company tankers had collided in San Francisco Bay, releasing 840,000 gallons of oil. This haunting image propelled Francis to walk one day instead of riding in a car. And then the next day he decided to walk, still meditating on the devastation the oil had caused. Then the following day and the following, he kept choosing to walk. Eventually, he had gone twenty-two years without using motorized vehicles. He had walked up the West Coast, across the forty-eight lower United States, and through much of South America.

Early on in his days of walking and discussing the merits of not using oil-powered transportation with people around him, he decided to spend his twenty-seventh birthday in silence to listen and learn as much as he could from those he encountered. Francis realized what he gained from not worrying about his verbal response and noticed his interactions were enriched (although sometimes complicated) by his decision to not speak. Just like choosing to walk, each day Francis made the decision to keep his silence, until seventeen years had gone by. During this time, Francis earned his bachelor's, master's, and doctorate degrees, which led him to be called to Washington, D.C., to work on federal oil-pollution regulations. He broke his silence in a speech on the 1990 Earth Day in Washington, thanking the audience for their attendance and expressing gratitude to his family and friends. His conviction and determination spoke volumes, even during the years he never uttered a word. This inspiring journey has resulted in truly phenomenal work to educate young people on their actions and how they can shape a more sustainable and just world. (I highly suggest you read his full story in *Planetwalker: 17-Years of Silence, 22-Years of Walking*.[17]) Dr.

Francis teaches and gives talks around the world and now serves as one of three commissioners of the Borough of West Cape May, New Jersey. Although he began talking again in 1990 and using vehicles again five years later, he continues to practice silence every morning to remind himself to listen and try to understand what people are really saying.[18]

What I find so compelling about Dr. Francis's journey is how he cultivated these habits by deciding to do so each day. One day at a time, the habits became woven into his lifestyle. I'm not suggesting to necessarily go the path of foregoing all motorized transport (although if that calls to you, by all means go for it!). I do suggest that we all follow in his footsteps by making a choice to change our learned wastefulness and overconsumption and to consume less, reuse items, and adopt better recycling habits. Drastically changing your life from the familiar is intimidating. Making small decisions throughout your day, each day step by step, until those new habits become familiar is entirely possible.

We often look for an incentive to change, requiring a reason for the effort of altering ingrained processes. Many organizations use moral incentives to urge us to adopt environmental habits, tugging at our desire to be good people. Moral incentives can achieve impressive results, but they're highly objective, based on the values of the individual. Their effectiveness even changes with the same individual's evolving mood day to day. They rely on the hope that, regardless of our hectic schedules, we'll still elect to do the desired behavior because it's what we *should* do. And while I think there can be beautiful effects from people choosing to be their best without financial gains, I also recognize that we are all dynamic beings whose lives and emotions can shift. One day I might prioritize making zero waste; then the next, I might have to prioritize accessibility or convenience.

Regardless of our fickle natures, moral incentives can work well in the right setting. Experimental economists learned that an offer to pay for blood donations would *decrease* the number of people willing to donate by nearly half.[19] But letting people donate with no offer of compensation had the opposite effect. Just as we make purchases or craft our images on social media in a certain light, we also tend to do more charitable acts in a certain light. We want to donate and not seem like we needed a selfish motivator polluting the decision. People even find it insulting when it's assumed that they need to be coerced into helpful actions. What drives us to do the right thing is that we want to align ourselves with what those acts represent, those morals that we want to see in ourselves. Financial incentives like a fine or a tax can be effective but can also stimulate the undesired behavior by allowing someone to buy their way out of the problem. This model does not necessarily limit an activity but allows those with the most money to partake in the undesired behavior.

We can improve norms and habits by employing a mixture of both moral and financial incentives. The ideal result is to achieve spillover behavior, so that the sustainable behaviors targeted by the incentives positively influence other choices a person makes. The bag tax has seen immediate results in reducing disposable plastic bags by enacting a mild financial incentive while delivering a bigger-picture message of protecting waterways. This is a policy that supports a desired outcome (less plastic bag waste) and taps into our self-interest (a bag tax for every disposal bag we use) and encourages community spirit (celebrating the reduction of disposable bag waste in a nearby river). After Ireland began a plastic bag tax, there was a 95 percent reduction in plastic bag litter in just a few weeks, and the positive impacts are still observed years after the tax began. As residents noted, it had become socially acceptable to carry reusable totes and was no longer acceptable to use disposable plastic.[20]

To tackle waste and consumption, we need to use a set of tools rather than relying on just one. A bag tax might be effective in reducing disposable bags, but it doesn't necessarily spill over to our use of disposable coffee cups or straws. Policy makers pushing for different incentive programs for sustainability could strengthen these ideas by considering the cognitive effects of incentives. If the monetary incentive is valued above the environmental and community benefits, then the participant's attention can shift from the desired outcome and distract them with the monetary reward.[21]

We might wonder, "Who cares why people do something beneficial as long as they're doing it?" But problems can arise in the behavior's impermanence; if the incentive is removed, it's possible the positive behavior might decrease. Financial incentives tap into our self-motivated decisions, but by focusing on the self-transcendent effects—the larger societal and environmental ones—more positive spillover behavior can occur.[22] Favorable outcomes can be achieved by using a combination of incentives and a larger narrative explaining why the act is important for the community.[23] And if we celebrate environmentally beneficial actions without over-inflating their effects, we can incorporate the habits into our core values, normalizing them and affixing them in our routines.

One habit we can examine and strive to change is our desire to consume things we don't need or even truly want. Gleefully embarking on some retail therapy may seem like we're seeking a buy-one-get-one deal on shoes, but what we're chasing is the chemical reaction in our brains of satisfaction we receive from buying new items. The pleasure we experience from buying something new is an effect of the excitement and anticipation, not necessarily about the new thing itself.[24] And in pursuit of renewing those feelings of excitement, we might spiral with purchasing, as one new thing can lead us to "need" more new things. We want to ensure our nice new purchase has other things that suit it, so buying a new wrench can easily escalate into upgrading all your tools and maybe even snagging a new workbench. This phenomenon, called the Diderot effect, leads us to consume things that our previous selves never required to feel content and fulfilled. Denis Diderot, an eighteenth-century French philosopher, acquired a new robe, quickly leading to a spree of buying all new things so his possessions would all meet the quality of his new robe. Diderot then found himself in debt and lamented the snowball effect of his consumption in his work "Regrets for My Old Dressing Gown," where he states, "I was the absolute master of my old robe. I have become the slave of the new one."[25]

We create a deficit in our own minds and fill it with overconsumption. We are aided through this process by the presentation of small, last-minute, grab items as you near a store register or online when shown items similar to one you just added to a cart. These subtle (and not-so-subtle) gestures give us unbridled permission to continue creating a perceived deficit in our lives and endless chances to fill it with new things. Once presented with the idea that we are lacking, we become consumed by that thought, although it might not have occurred to us the day before when we felt content with what we already had. With planned obsolescence and the Diderot effect united in orchestrating our overconsumption, it may seem like we have little control over how much and how often we buy new things. But there are real steps we can take to make sure our consumption habits are kinder to both the environment and our bank accounts.

A first step to consuming less is removing the ease and temptation of buying new stuff. If you find yourself easily swept away with emails and posts from certain brands, resist the urge to join their mailing lists. Marketing emails sliding into your view every day with sales or new products could spark a bit of unnecessary shopping. Keep control of deciding when you shop without offering brands a chance to influence that choice for you. This way you can visit sites or stores when you need something specific rather than have a company guide you to their wares with their interruptions.[26] When buying an item that's new to you, try to pick what compliments your existing things. For example, buy clothes that match pieces you already own so they can be worn in a variety of ways. To curb impulse purchases, try to put a cushion of time between considering items and actually buying them. When online shopping, try putting items you like in a cart, and then close the tab before buying. You can go back a day or two later and comb through the saved cart to determine if you still want or need what you've selected. Just as we're advised not to grocery shop on an empty stomach, it's also wise not to do any kind of shopping when hungry or fatigued. When our internal resources are depleted, we're more likely to make reckless purchases and can end up feeling the buyer's remorse of getting an item home and regretting it. Try having a set of questions you ask yourself before a purchase, like "Is this something I had planned to buy?" "Is it compatible with other things I own?" "Does it have a specific place to be stored in my home?" "Is the item covered in my budget?"[27] Above all, we can be aware of how we make decisions that keep our consumption mindful.

While old habits die hard, they can still change and be replaced with ones more in line with our goals and values. Our lifestyles and actions evolve as our interests do and as we absorb new information throughout our lives. We can think of changing habits more as growth and an adventure rather than something that is cumbersome and difficult. This is where our creativity and ingenuity can craft new ways of reducing and reusing in our lives. My journey to use less has been gradual, and every time I run out of a product, I research how I can replace it with a lower-waste or DIY solution. It's enjoyable to try new solutions and feel a sense of accomplishment when replacing a disposable item with something reusable.

It might be tempting to set a huge goal ("I won't buy any plastic for the next year"), but we need to be realistic with ourselves. Starting with one specific goal ("I'll carry my reusable bottle and not buy any plastic bottles this month") can be a more successful way to incorporate less-wasteful habits into our lives. If we change one habit at a time, then we can create our own spillover effect by adding another goal to help us become more sustainable.[28] We also can make our environment more conducive to those new goals. Try removing some of the cues that trigger habits you'd like to change (like hopping off the marketing e-mails from companies where you tend to overspend), and create opportunities to practice habits you'd like to take on (such as having lots of wash rags more accessible than paper towels). These small disruptions of an old pattern can be an effective way to help us use less.[29]

I was once in a department store buying a pair of shoes that were on a small piece of plastic without a shoe box. When I bought the shoes, I said, "Thank you, but I don't need a bag." The cashier froze, as she pulled her hand back from the plastic bag and replied, "Are you sure? They'll think you've stolen it," and followed with trying two more times to push the bag, but I firmly declined, thanked her and left. I'd successfully passed on a bag but left the encounter feeling like a high-maintenance customer. It's no wonder people avoid challenging these commonplace social norms—it feels awkward to be the subject of even perceived confusion. Why should we subject ourselves to this record skip of a moment, when we could take the plastic bag and prevent any delay? We might argue that we could "make up for it" by doing something like donating to a group cleaning plastic bags out of rivers. But we have to change social norms to get to the root of the problem. We can support river clean-ups and also do our best to change habits that put trash in the rivers in the first place. Everyone who challenges a social norm feels uncomfortable and even ostracized for that act but has the confidence to continue doing what they know is right anyway.

Changing habits is a difficult thing, and it can feel quite awkward. But, by taking your reusable bottle and sharing information about recycling benefits, you offer other people the encouragement to follow suit and think about ways they can reduce consumption or instill better recycling practices in their own lives. And lastly, be kind to yourself when you fall short of your ideals, and do not let those mistakes discourage you to the point of giving up. We are indeed creatures of habit, and those ingrained processes we've developed can't be simply unwound and rerouted overnight. Humans are complex, and our behaviors are not always rational, but we also show phenomenal capacity to learn and change. Progress can happen when we take a brief pause before engaging in a seemingly automatic habit and ask if it serves our core values and goals. The depth of that pause can be so vast, despite the moment itself being brief, because it's letting ourselves consider another way. Recognizing your habits just before they happen is a victory—just not a victory deserving some indulgent, wasteful moral licensing afterward.

In an attempt to not disappoint ourselves or others, we may lower the bar to the mildest positive behavior and cheer when we gingerly traipse over it. But our goals to create a better society are not served by thinking so poorly of ourselves that we believe reaching a higher bar is impossible. Beating disappointment to the punch by never feeling the hope or drive to do better is not a success or even a failure; it's apathy. Finding a balance of stretching ourselves to new heights and supporting instead of shaming ourselves during times when we fall short can shift careless consumers to mindful individuals. We can become more self-sufficient and as needed, purchase something useful or to make our lives more enjoyable. Humans aren't perfect, but we have the ability to grow, harness our creativity, and stubbornly rise to meet new goals we can set together.

WHY DON'T MORE PEOPLE RECYCLE?

Because you're reading this book, it's likely that you're somewhat passionate about recycling, and perhaps you've felt the frustration of seeing someone throw a bottle in the trash when a recycling bin sits just inches away. Recycling has become increasingly accessible over the past decades, but a 2011 survey exposed that only half of adults recycle daily, with 13 percent confessing that they never recycle at all.[30] A quarter of those surveyed say they don't recycle because they lack curbside service and live too far from a drop-off center.[31] Social norms also play a significant factor in the success of recycling programs. A 2016 Pew Research Center study found that 28 percent of Americans said their community's social norms strongly encourage recycling; 22 percent said they received little to no encouragement to recycle; the rest stated that their areas express a moderate amount of encouragement.[32] People respond to social cues, and if a community encourages recycling, then the residents are more likely to participate.

Convenience is not the only factor, as research from Remi Trudel at Boston University suggests. We are also more likely to recycle items that are fully intact, with branding we recognize, than crumpled or torn pieces with no logo. These curious results show what Trudel calls distortion bias, when we think an item is more valuable and should be recycled the more pristine it is, and identity bias, the idea that trashing an item with a logo we feel connected with results in lower self-esteem. Simply put, if our names are written on a cup, then we're more likely to want to recycle it because "it feels bad to throw a piece of ourselves in the trash."[33]

Some individuals don't recycle because they don't consider themselves environmentalists or even want to be associated with the label. In 1990, 76 percent of Americans considered themselves environmentalists, but by 2016, that number had dropped to 42 percent.[34] That twenty-six-year gap saw the term become heavily politicized, and what both Democrats and Republicans once aligned themselves with now divides them on anything, such as practices like recycling. Even individuals identifying with progressive political parties are somewhat hesitant to loop themselves into the green label. It's possible many people feel that they don't qualify as environmentalists if they aren't chained to a tree or living off the grid. Sometimes environmentalism is perceived as an exclusive or sanctimonious movement, particularly if those wearing the label proudly shame others for knowing less about sustainability and blame them for escalating climate change.

Some people might not recycle because they vehemently deny climate change exists, so they avoid practices connected to environmentalism. Others may believe climate change is real, but find it so overwhelming that they don't see how daily acts like recycling could combat it. In discussions with people harboring these viewpoints, we can share the proven positive effects of recycling for both the environment and the economy, rather than focus solely on the consequences of not recycling. When we enter a conversation from fundamentally different reference points, focusing on where there is overlap can be challenging but ultimately a space where change can sprout. If the person you are sharing information with cares more about economic prosperity than climate change, explain how managing materials through recycling bolsters domestic manufacturing and creates jobs. Addressing climate change denial is important, but if you're casually talking with a neighbor while taking out your recycling, starting from a place that resonates with them may achieve further results than opening with why they should care about the climate. Undoing the damages of misinformation spread by anti-science politicians and fossil fuel interests refuting climate change is no simple feat. Open a conversation with recycling and you could lay the foundation for a road that leads to larger discussions to begin tackling inaccuracies about climate. For people you encounter that feel powerless in the face of climate change, you can help them see that breathing sustainable habits into our daily lives creates small shifts. When we each strive for those changes, a powerful movement towards greater sustainability occurs. In many cases, small choices in our daily lives contributed to the problems we are grappling with, and making better choices can contribute to solutions. We can evolve our habits to be more sustainable while we also support wide systemic changes like climate policy. Those who do consider ourselves environmentalists can work to be more understanding and helpful to people who may not be as informed on the related issues, and we can avoid shaming others to prevent distancing them from sustainable habits. We can raise awareness by discussing the results of overconsumption and suggest concrete steps to improve habits.

Last, people might not participate in recycling if they feel skeptical or confused about how it works. A poll conducted by the Institute of Scrap Recycling Industries (ISRI) found that U.S. adults do not accept typical statements about recycling to be true, even if they were. Those surveyed had to identify eight statements as believable or not. More than half of the participants said none of the statements were true, when actually four were true and four were false. Meaning fortunately, most people thought the false statements were false, including statements claiming recycling has no economic benefits or that recycled products are lower quality—no one was buying those myths. But the disappointing results were that participants assumed two important (and true) statements were false: that recycling reduces greenhouse gas emissions (51 percent thought this was a lie) and that there are enough materials recycling in the United States to satisfy production needs of domestic manufacturers (73 percent thought this was false).[35]

The survey showed that people understand the benefits of recycling, but some were wary of how far those benefits extend. Many might be curious how lucrative a system could be when it's built on taking stuff we no longer want. Some critics argue that landfilling is the better option because they say it's cheaper and more straight-forward. However, recycling proponents note the economic upsides of the revenue and job growth the system generates. Understanding the investment and upkeep costs, but also the economic value generated, is crucial to evaluating the system as a whole. We now know what the point of recycling is, how it works, and even how our mental processes influence it, so let's go onto resolve the bottomline questions: is it worthwhile and who pays for it?

8

ECONOMICS OF RECYCLING

The forest's waste system operates without money, but there are plenty of investments and payments occurring to sustain decomposition. Fungi, bacteria, and some insects set to work when an organism's life ends, effectively releasing the carbon the organism had sequestered through its existence. These decomposers receive payment for their labor in the food created by the process, and the time investment varies with the size of the organism being broken down. We can't ask fungi their thoughts, but can speculate that the decomposition work is plenty costly in time and energy (an evergreen tree in a cool climate can take more than 100 years of this work).[1] The process decomposers facilitate permits the entire forest to thrive and continue its growth. These little organisms may seem unglamorous, but their work is indispensable.

We wander through the woods aloof to the decomposers humming along, working to clean the forest floor and distribute vital nutrients throughout the system. We may take for granted the investment they make to keep the ecosystem operating smoothly. We may similarly consider the seamless whisking away of our recyclables as a magical occurrence. We don't receive a recycling bill in the mail or a receipt of service taped to our bins; it just seems to happen. But, like most services, recycling costs money to maintain and those investments have to come from somewhere. There are some who see the system as too costly and not worth further investing to untangle its snags. This perspective sees these costs as negating recycling's benefits, and believe that it would be better to just send all refuse to the landfill. This view does not encompass the depths of benefits we receive from recycling and how those will expand if we strengthen the system. Additionally, there are externalized costs to not recycling that we must consider. For starters, let's do a cost comparison of the different waste disposal options to frame the discussion on expenses and values of recycling.

The companies who collect, transfer, sort, and manufacture recycled goods need capital to pay workers and invest in necessary equipment to keep the process moving. Other costs to sustain the system include the transportation of the materials from thousands of curbsides or drop-off locations. This involves maintenance on the trucks, fuel, and the payment for workers to haul recyclables. Then we have the sorting and handling costs, including the energy to power facilities, pay workers doing quality control and hand-sorting throughout the process, and the purchase and upkeep of equipment. Building a single-stream materials-recover facility (MRF) can cost up to $15 million.[2] On average, it costs between $50 to $150 per ton to recycle our old materials.[3]

By comparison, collecting and disposing of our garbage can cost from $70 to $200 per ton.[4] The average tipping fee (meaning how much someone pays the landfill just to take their trash) for one ton of municipal solid waste is $49. These fees have seen steady increases over the past few years, attributed to landfill space (part of why pricing varies by region), population density, regulations, and waste management companies trying to avoid "market share wars" (when companies in a sector keep lowering prices to remain competitive). Areas with more population density tend to see higher landfill fees; for example, in the United States, the Northeast averages $77 per ton, while states in the West pay $34 per ton.[5] Depending on the site, building a new landfill can cost between up to $800,000 per acre (just the construction, not the land acquisition or permits needed to break ground).[6] Landfill sizes can be anywhere between a few dozen acres up to the largest landfill in the country, Apex Regional Landfill (located outside of Las Vegas), at 2,200 acres.[7] When municipalities contract with businesses who operate their recycling programs, there is an expectation to pay less tipping fees as a result of an expanded recycling service.

Here's where it becomes more complicated: There are companies who make money off recycling programs and landfills simultaneously. In the United States, more than half of our waste is hauled by two major companies, Republic Services and Waste Management. Both control billions of dollars in recyclables but make a huge return on waste going to landfills or incinerators.[8] In some ways, it makes sense for companies to handle all the waste because they have expertise in collecting and disposing and generally have in-depth understandings of city infrastructure for these types of services. But when they make money whether residents recycle or not and sometimes make significantly more when more trash goes to the landfill, there's a glaring conflict of interest at play.

The upfront costs of a waste-to-energy (WTE) plant can be between $500 and $900 million.[9] Disposal costs for WTE plants are up to 50 percent higher than disposing at landfills.[10] It's even estimated that incinerators are the most expensive source of electricity, with a projected cost of $8,232 per kilowatt for a new facility.[11] This costly process is made even more so when you consider their health impacts on communities, as past studies have shown that mercury emissions from WTE plants were six times higher than that of coal plants.[12] Also keep in mind the loss of usefulness items might have offered in recycling streams when we bury or burn them instead. Recycling our waste saves three to five times the energy incineration can generate, thanks to its reduction of extraction and manufacturing of new materials.[13]

Although they are difficult to fully assess, we must consider the costs we will pay if we do *not* recycle. The long-lasting costs are more challenging to conceptualize than the costs of buying a city a set quantity of bins. Rather than simply comparing costs of dropping trash in a landfill or recycling it, we need to look at the start of manufacturing processes. When we consider all of the environmental degradation from virgin material production, then the scale pulls down, despite the explicit price tag attached to the other side. These externalities are the effects of industrial or commercial activity that isn't reflected in the cost of the good or service and it's usually where government becomes involved with the market.[14] An example of a negative externality is pollution from a factory that creates health issues for communities downstream. The health care and clean-up costs from the pollution are not reflected in the upstream company's direct costs. Social and environmental costs are levied on external parties, while the producer of these indirect costs is only burdened with their costs of production. When discussing the costs of recycling, we need to stay cognizant of the impacts new material production can cause and the cost we incur by not using recycled materials.

Price fluctuation for virgin materials can affect the value of its recycled counterparts. For example, the cost of producing new plastic goes up and down with oil prices because the material comes from petrochemicals of fossil oil and gas production. So, when oil price is low, it is cheaper to buy new plastic than to buy recycled. Manufacturers just need a reliable source of good material to make products, and new plastic comes with a chemical composition that can be precisely adjusted, so the companies know exactly what they're getting, and manufacturers are happy. But as markets are ever changing, these low oil prices are not permanent. If at some point the real cost of oil becomes a part of the price for manufacturers, then new plastic production could take a nosedive.

Government subsidies affect the cost of production and energy generation. In the past, tax codes, laws, and regulations have favored virgin material over recycled. The EPA has affirmed that this is no longer an issue and subsidies do not hinder the recycling system.[15] But the same financial support offered to waste-to-energy plants has not necessarily been extended to MRFs. For example, WTE companies receive a tax credit for each kilowatt hour generated. On the other hand, using recycled materials saves energy, like aluminum, which uses 95 percent less energy than virgin production.[16] But there is no system in place offering credit for the energy saved by using recycled materials. While there are grants for helping a facility update some of its equipment, subsidies could be doing more for recycling by offering credits to internalize some of the benefits we receive. Such subsidies could support companies in times of upheaval within the industry. When the landscape changes, such as drastic market drops, companies may need assistance from the government to weather these changes. And as Frank Ackerman observes in *Why Do We Recycle*, another possibility to better take externalities into account could be a tax on virgin material production.[17]

Regardless of what monetary value the market has deemed for materials, recycling consistently requires less resources and produces fewer greenhouse gases (GHGs) than production of new materials. When we consider the negative externalities from new material production and other disposal methods that recycling eliminates,[18] we can see there are significant savings the process provides. Clean air and water are public goods and when they're available to all, they aren't defined by property rights, so society has a tendency to undervalue them. For example, climate change is resulting in costs from devastation through more powerful storms and depletion of resources and biodiversity. In 2017, damage from natural disasters cost the United States an estimated $306 billion.[19] Human activity has escalated climate change, and the negative externalities of our actions are levied on the entire world. Because the atmosphere is essentially a global public good, internalizing these costs and identifying policies that target GHG emitters on a global level has been notably difficult,[20] which is why policies like the Paris Agreement have been so significant. We need to evaluate the reduced emissions from recycling across multiple sectors to determine the full costs. When we measure the costs of new material production in the loss of natural resources, health effects on communities, and the devastating extreme storms due to climate change, our not recycling becomes all the more costly.

There are ways we as individuals can make the system more economically viable; beginning with recycling in accordance with our local rules. In 2014, the District of Columbia rolled out bigger recycling bins for residents. An unfortunate result was the high volume of nonrecyclable items going into the bins, increasing processing costs and decreasing profits of recyclables by more than 50 percent.[21] Our wishcycling has a sizable cost and is something critics point to when they say recycling is not financially efficient. If we better educate ourselves on recycling practices (which I dive into in chapter 9), we can improve the quality of items going into facilities and achieve a win-win for the environment and our economy.

EXTENDED PRODUCER RESPONSIBILITY

You may be wondering who foots the bill for recycling. From the 1990s into the early 2000s, recyclers would offer their services for cheap because they were so eager to obtain materials that could be sold for record high prices. Much of this desire for recyclables was due to China's economic growth and their demand for our materials. China was eager to import raw recyclables, and recycling companies in the United States were equally eager to oblige, making recycling profitable. But when the 2008 financial crisis hit, recyclables took a nosedive in value, and companies had no incentive to do cheap collection for items that were not as lucrative.[22] The service shifted to rely more heavily on taxpayers to keep it afloat. Now, recycling is part of the solid waste tax residents pay every year. Depending on where you live, you could be paying anywhere between five dollars and twenty-five dollars per month for curbside recycling services.[23] But imagine if the downstream costs of disposal were also internalized in a product's inception.

Recall those antilittering ads paid for by companies making the products being littered and how this was an effort to shift responsibility from the producers onto consumers. There has been a movement, called extended producer responsibility (EPR), to apply some of that accountability back onto the companies selling products that end up in our waste stream. One EPR method is having the producer pay a fee to municipalities equivalent to how much of their product is going on the market, which helps cover the collection and recycling services. Major corporations producing thousands of plastic soda bottles every day will have to pay accordingly, and companies might increase the cost of a product to contribute to the EPR fee, so the disposal cost becomes a part of the item's price tag. However, the fee can be adapted to how easy it is to responsibly dispose of the product, which is something producers can incorporate into the way they design and package items.[24]

The idea was born in the late 1980s by Thomas Lindhqvist, an environmental policy expert from Sweden, and his goal was to reduce the burdensome effects of production on the environment.[25] Lindhqvist set to achieve this by putting the cost of the entire life cycle of the product, from cradle to grave (or cradle to cradle), back on the company manufacturing the product. The theory is that the entity currently in charge of disposal for these items, municipalities, are not as equipped to change the packaging and product materials to be easier to dispose. But companies who create the design and select the components of their products are able to transform their goods into items that can be deconstructed and dealt with more sustainably. When a product is flawed and multiple customers complain, a company does not expect the user to determine how to make it work; instead, they go back to the design stage. In EPR, companies would ideally design products and packaging to make it more cost effective to dispose; another method they can use is a deposit/refund. For example, dairy companies have given new life to the old glass milk bottle. The deposit tacked onto the fee for the milk encourages the customer to return the glass bottle after use. Packaging for food, beverages, body care products, technology, and other items makes up almost one-third of municipal solid waste in the United States,[26] so it's in our best interest to maximize our use of recycled content and account for responsible disposal.

Europe has had a wider use of the concept, with thirty European Union countries implementing EPR legislation.[27] Belgium boasts more than five thousand companies that follow extended producer responsibility, representing 92 percent of the packaging materials in its market. The result of this is an impressive 95 percent recovery rate for packaging materials in the country.[28] American lawmakers have attempted EPR legislation in the past but have not had success passing such a bill at the national level. But there are over eighty EPR laws in thirty-four states for products like used electronics, mattresses, and other hard-to-recycle items.[29]

But, there are challenges presented with EPR. While the concept is generally agreed to be positive, the implementation can have negative repercussions. If EPR turns entire control of the waste stream to producers, this could result with investments in incineration being used as a "solution", and most urgently, could take away decision-making power from communities in how to manage their own materials and waste. For example, large corporations Pepsi, Coca-Cola, and Nestle have led an effort to apply EPR to all printing, paper, and packaging (PPP).[30] The companies would be in charge of determining the fate of these materials, and would remove the abilities of citizens to vote on their own waste management and recycling programs. Citizens provide a critical role of expanding recycling programs in their communities by using our voices to advocate for wider access to services. Good EPR would include strong recycling targets and a stated zero-incineration policy. It would result in shifting some responsibility of disposal back onto producers, urging them to rethink designs of their products to be better suited for recycling streams. But when EPR is used to also shift all decision-making power from other stakeholders and place it into the hands of corporations, this can lead to inequitable results. The multi-year long debate of EPR-PPP in Connecticut ended in 2018 with a resounding vote against the plan. A task force appointment by the state's General

Assembly produced a report advocating for voluntary initiatives, more consumer education, more programs incentivizing trash reduction, and other similar strategies to tackle waste instead of EPR-PPP.[31] The report advised strengthening and fixing recycling programs and the state's existing bottle deposit bill, citing this route would be more efficient, less expensive, and "less susceptible to abuse." The Institute for Local Self-Reliance (ILSR) is an non-profit organization that has worked for forty years to help cities and countries maximize economic development value from their waste streams. It is at the forefront of healthy criticisms of EPR and has suggested that formal EPR policies may not be necessary. ILSR cites the elimination of microbeads as an example. The United States has banned the use of plastic microbeads in personal-care products to protect waterways. The expressed concern of organizations and individuals and irrefutable research on the amount of microbeads entering aquatic habitats first brought state-level bans, and 2017 saw the ban rise to the national level, without the use of EPR. One thing is certain: Demanding producers to find efficient, sustainable ways to construct products and having reliable recycling in place to handle them is essential.

SENDING RECYCLABLES OVERSEAS

Variables influencing recycling prices extend beyond fluctuations of virgin material prices and the evolving material compositions of our goods. Another huge variable is international trade and the prices countries are willing to pay for raw materials rejected by U.S. manufacturers.

One of the wealthiest self-made female billionaires in the world started her work gathering scrap paper in California to be shipped back to China in containers that had delivered goods to the United States.[32] These containers would have been empty vessels gliding back to Asia, but Zhang Yin (also known as Cheung Yan) saw an opportunity to use this transport for paper many had thought to be trash.[33] Her company, Nine Dragons Paper, boasts that recovered paper makes up 95 percent of the total fiber it uses[34] and has been hailed as the world's largest recycled-paper manufacturer.[35] For quite some time, waste from the United States has been exported to find its usefulness abroad and resulted in significant profits. When materials arrive at our MRFs unsuitable for domestic sale, they have routinely been sold overseas to countries with lower standards for material purity, sometimes to be burned for energy. The vast majority have gone to China, which has been importing 12 million tons of the world's discarded plastic each year.[36] But the United States became mistakenly complacent with depending on exports. When China's GDP slowed, it began recovering more recyclables domestically. U.S. companies faced big changes. In 2013, China put forth an inspection policy called Green Fence to temporarily strengthen the quality of imports.[37] What were once routine inspections on random arrivals became stringent searches of every shipment container. Shipments were rejected at ports if they didn't meet new standards for lower contamination and were sent back to the United States without payment. American recyclers lost revenue and shipment expenses and had to pay fees assigned at the ports to store the material waiting to be inspected. Hundreds of companies had their licenses suspended, and some lost their licenses to sell to China entirely.[38] And the value of some recyclables plummeted with the decreasing demand for low-quality materials.

The Green Fence was a wakeup call that rang throughout the industry forcing heightened standards because, simply put, no one would buy junk anymore. It created an immediate incentive to strengthen our domestic recycling system. American companies had to adapt quickly by improving technology, which meant higher overall processing costs. This is good for procuring better recycled materials, but it presented a challenge to operators' budgets. In 2011, over 52 million tons of paper and paperboard was recycled in the United States, and nearly 16 million tons of that was exported.[39] Scrap was the top export to China, with $11.3 billion in revenue for the United States.[40] But in just the first three months of enforcing Operation Green Fence (OGF) in 2013, about 55 scrap transactions and 7,600 metric tons of recyclables were rejected. Within the six months of enforcing OGF, the rejected amount reached to 800,000 tons of recyclables.

Clearly, the policy had made noticeable changes in the ten months it was operational, but it had been designed to be temporary. In 2017, another policy loomed over the industry: the National Sword. More permanent and severe than the Green Fence, China furthered its efforts to end smuggling through its ports by using X-ray exams and vigorous searches of all bales coming into its country to target contaminated items. There was notable upset throughout the industry, as people anxiously awaited to learn the depth of the new policy. Toward the end of 2017, China announced its new 0.5 percent contamination standard and rolled out a ban of 24 types of imported materials. There was a palpable defensiveness from the industry and some companies desperately began searching for new foreign markets to maintain business as usual.[41] This has certainly brought to light more problems associated with single-stream recycling and has reopened conversation on the merits of multistream. But some companies have felt forced to drop materials because the mounting piles of unmarketable items are filling their plants to the brim. Avid recycling residents in Portland, Oregon, have been dismayed to find local facilities turning away plastics. Rogue Waste Systems in Oregon reports that its warehouses are filled with stacks of recycling bales that no one wants to buy, and they have begun to spew out into the parking lot. Sadly, the company says there's no option other than depositing to the landfill.[42]

A significant change to a complicated system understandably takes time for companies to adjust. It would always be more ideal to change systems at the most convenient time for all its stakeholders, but inherent in change is a certain level of discomfort and friction. Nothing feels convenient about shaking up the status quo, but we needed a driving force to urge us to look at the system and find ways to strengthen it. Otherwise, the industry would continue along, each stakeholder placing blame on another for its hiccups, and we would see very little movement to address problems. The National Sword policy has induced turbulence for some U.S. recyclers, as twenty-nine states reported noticeable or heavy changes within months after the more stringent contamination standard was announced.[43] But this is an opportunity to remiagine our system. We can respond with more consumer education on best practices to reduce contamination and innovate in processing technologies. Trade groups can (and have begun to) respond by urging producer companies to commit to upping their use of recycled content and to identify new, creative end markets for these materials.[44] One of the most important lessons from the policies is our need for domestic demand for these materials. Demand could provide the needed motivation for MRFs, haulers, and municipalities to work together towards recovering higher quality materials through the system.

Government could step in to help create better market conditions for domestic recyclables. The industry and government must operate together for recycling programs (or any waste management, for that matter) to succeed. Industry lacks the authority that government provides, but it offers capabilities for operating the system that the government cannot. The government can help balance the supply and demand in the recycling system by creating incentives for recycling and partnering with well-skilled organizations to explain the complexity of recycling to a wide audience. A central role the government has not played in the recycling system is one of coordinator between the many other stakeholders. In the 1980s and 1990s, the EPA spearheaded initiatives to provide financial help in job creation in the recycling industry and increase demand for materials. But the creation of new efforts stalled as different political administrations sought new avenues for these funds and the export markets shot upward. Recycling experts Betsy Dorn and Susan Bush observe that the strategies needed to tackle problems must be different from the past because the materials we recycle and the technology to sort them have changed.[45] But the consistent, essential need is to have partnerships between the private industry stakeholders and public entities.

An example of a very prosperous relationship between recyclers and the local government can be found in the Bay Area. San Francisco has long held a reputation of environmentally conscious habits, and the company Recology offers a range of waste services as a key part of the city's success with its zero-waste goals. Recology has uniquely been entirely employee owned since 1986. It creates innovations and sets goals from within, so the company is not beholden to outside shareholders.[46] It has another unique piece that seems to ensure Recology's consistent flourishing success in a somewhat tumultuous time for other industry players. An entity with long-standing history in the area, it has other affiliated companies that came before Recology. Predecessors of the company, two haulers, were written into the city charter through a vote as exclusive official waste collectors for the city. As long as voters were pleased with the haulers' services, the arrangement would continue, with the ability to overturn the decision should things go badly. In the 1990s, the city had its sights set on becoming zero waste, and Recology took the plunge along with it. San Francisco aided Recology to adapt its practices to work toward landfill diversion and zero waste. In cooperating with one another, the two entities have maintained a fascinating and unusual working relationship.[47] This is an intriguing case study of what can flourish when two stakeholders in a system coordinate and strive for individual and collective goals.

WHO ARE ALL THE STAKEHOLDERS?

As the federal government's role in the recycling system stagnated in the 1990s, other stakeholders from local governments, like San Francisco, kept things moving through innovation and expansion of programs.[48] City and state leaders stepped up to fill the hole left as federal leaders backed away from the system. Local governments had to navigate markets using the materials they were able to collect and sell. But one result is the multitude of recycling programs and rules throughout the country, which causes confusion at the bin.

A system operating the way in which it's designed is not always a positive thing for everyone. When a system is designed to put certain results above others, like profit above all else, it can allow for exploitation, oppression, and degradation of people and the planet. When these systems are functioning, they can create devastating consequences for those who do not benefit from the results. A determining factor of positive or negative outputs of a system is the stakeholders who are involved in creating and maintaining it. Maximizing one output and sacrificing others does not yield a productive system. When recycling operates at its best, it can provide an array of benefits for the environment, communities, and the economy. When each stakeholder can speak up for the part of a system it represents, people affected by the system's functions are more able to influence its mechanics. Achieving sustainability means that we must have systems in place within our societal ecosystem that sustain both the environment and all people within it.

Residents, municipalities, waste management haulers, transfer stations, sorting facilities, manufacturers, and companies are among the many participants in the recycling system. You can see their roles throughout the recycling system in figure 8.1. Recycling is a system with a wide range of industries that must communicate effectively for it to succeed. But consumers and residents are heavily involved in making the system work, too. Our unique role both creates the demand and provides supply when we choose to purchase recycled-content products and make sure we recycle all we can. The haulers are companies specializing in the collection and transport of our materials to and from various locations, whether from our neighborhoods to a transfer station or to a MRF. As we've discussed, the MRF employs workers who aid in hand-sorting items and operating machinery to quickly group like materials together into bales. Then these bales are sold to U.S. processing plants or foreign markets, which facilitate taking the recyclables into their raw form, cleaning them, and selling them to the next stakeholder group, the manufacturers, to be made into new products. These provide a supply to meet the demand of companies whose brands we likely recognize. Another step in the system are the storefronts that purchase these goods from companies to sell on their shelves. And then, of course, it's back to us, the consumers. Both public and private sectors overlap in this system, and how much each is involved varies by municipality. A city might choose to contract recycling services or to take on some of the work itself, depending on staffing capacity and resources available.

THE JOURNEY STARTS AT HOME

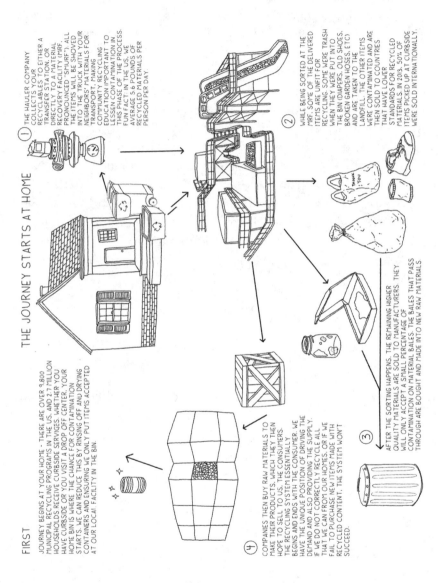

FIRST

JOURNEY BEGINS AT YOUR HOME – THERE ARE OVER 9,800 MUNICIPAL RECYCLING PROGRAMS IN THE US, AND 2.7 MILLION HOUSEHOLDS RECEIVE CURBSIDE SERVICES. WHETHER YOU HAVE CURBSIDE OR YOU VISIT A DROP OFF CENTER, YOUR HOME BIN IS WHERE THE CHANCE FOR CONTAMINATION STARTS. WE CAN REDUCE THIS BY RINSING OFF AND DRYING CONTAINERS AND ENSURING WE ONLY PUT ITEMS ACCEPTED AT OUR LOCAL FACILITY IN THE BIN.

1. THE HAULER COMPANY COLLECTS YOUR RECYCLABLES TO EITHER A TRANSFER STATION, OR DIRECTLY TO A MATERIAL RECOVERY FACILITY (MRF, PRONOUNCED "SMURF"). ALL THE ITEMS WILL BE SHOVED INTO THE TRUCK WITH YOUR NEIGHBORS' MATERIALS FOR TRANSPORT, MAKING COMMUNITY RECYCLING EDUCATION IMPORTANT TO LESSEN CONTAMINATION IN THIS PHASE OF THE PROCESS. FUN FACT: IN THE US, WE AVERAGE 5.6 POUNDS OF RECYCLED MATERIALS PER PERSON PER DAY.

2. WHILE BEING SORTED AT THE MRF, SOME OF THE DELIVERED ITEMS ARE UNFIT FOR RECYCLING. SOME WERE TRASH WHEN THEY WERE PUT INTO THE BIN (DIAPERS, OLD SHOES, BROKEN GARDEN HOSES, ETC) AND ARE TAKEN TO THE LANDFILL. THE OTHER ITEMS WERE CONTAMINATED AND ARE THEN SOLD TO COUNTRIES THAT HAVE LOWER STANDARDS FOR RECYCLED MATERIALS. IN 2013, 50% OF ITEMS PICKED UP AT CURBSIDE WERE SOLD INTERNATIONALLY.

3. AFTER THE SORTING HAPPENS, THE REMAINING HIGHER QUALITY MATERIALS ARE SOLD TO MANUFACTURERS. THEY WILL ONLY ACCEPT A SMALL PERCENTAGE OF CONTAMINATION ON MATERIAL BALES. THE BALES THAT PASS THROUGH ARE BOUGHT AND MADE INTO NEW RAW MATERIALS.

4. COMPANIES THEN BUY RAW MATERIALS TO MAKE THEIR PRODUCTS, WHICH THEY THEN HOPE TO SELL TO US, THE CONSUMERS. THE RECYCLING SYSTEM ESSENTIALLY BEGINS AND ENDS WITH THE CONSUMER. WE HAVE THE UNIQUE POSITION OF DRIVING THE DEMAND AND ALSO PROVIDING THE SUPPLY. IF WE DO NOT CORRECTLY RECYCLE ALL THAT WE CAN FROM OUR HOMES, OR IF WE FAIL TO PURCHASE NEW ITEMS MADE WITH RECYCLED CONTENT, THE SYSTEM WON'T SUCCEED.

Figure 8.1.   Map of Recycling Journey. Iris Gottlieb

More than 55,000 businesses employ 1 million people as drivers, sorters, technicians and maintenance workers, sales representatives, and more.[49] These jobs result in an annual payroll of $37 billion and generate more than $200 billion in annual revenues, as well as saving more than $3 billion in avoided landfill disposal costs.[50] Recycling creates jobs throughout each sector; for example, recycling one thousand tons of glass creates just over eight new jobs, according to the Container Recycling Institute.[51] By investing in the collection infrastructure, California has seen returns in investments and job growth from manufacturers. The state employs more than 84,000 people in thousands of recycling and reuse locations, resulting in $14.2 billion in annual revenues.[52] California reports that every job it's seen created in collection, an additional eight jobs become available in manufacturing our old items into new products. Economic analysis shows that there are more benefits to be unlocked in the industry at a national level, and the system can generate three times as much revenue per ton and almost six times as many jobs as the landfill industry.[53] Also, people who work in the industry have a demonstrated dedication to communities, as seen in their assistance to victims during natural disasters. As hurricanes and storms are becoming more intense and frequent, emergency resources for towns can become strained, and recycling haulers have donated their time and trucks to transporting residents to safer ground. Workers in the industry have helped not only in evacuations but also in the clean-up process of gathering debris and wreckage these storms leave in their wake.[54]

But like many industries, an increased use of automation presents a bit of uncertainty on the horizon for some recycling jobs. Bulk Handling Systems manufactures sorting equipment for many of the MRFs throughout the United States. Its research facility is humming with experiments in using robotic arms, cameras, and artificial intelligence to rapidly sort items on conveyor belts. The company's CEO, Steve Miller, says the technology can pick and sort eighty items per minute, whereas a person might achieve thirty picks in the same time.[55] This sophisticated technology comes at a price, though, and might not be a realistic purchase for most companies. In the future, companies might find the investment to automation worthwhile, as estimates suggest it could cut sorting costs in half in the long run.[56] And with increased pressure for more purity in baled materials, MRFs may feel they have no other option.

There could be positive effects from increased automation because the jobs being replaced pose safety hazards to workers. Trash and recycling collectors have the fifth-most dangerous job in the country, with 34 deaths per 100,000 workers.[57] Recycling workers may also experience long-term health effects from breathing in dust that is potentially filled with toxins and the contamination if they suffer a cut at work, sometimes despite protective gear they wear.

We contribute to these risks when we put improper, hazardous items in our bins. Workers have been faced with dead animals on conveyor belts, along with medical waste, needles, and even human feces.[58] Workers may or may not have safeguards in place, depending on the private company's decisions, and might even be given minimal training for a dangerous job.[59] A recycling company could be claiming to have sustainable values for its business, but then neglect these values by treating its workers as disposable. As residents, we can e-mail or call our municipality's recycling office and ask if there are safeguards or unions in place for the workers who handle our recyclables. By applying that pressure and demanding transparency, we can call attention to what the company might be neglecting and put our local government in the position (as the customer) to demand better practices. And we can do better right away by only putting accepted items in the bin and considering the real people on the other side of our bins who have to contend with what we choose to toss their way.

IF YOU'RE NOT BUYING RECYCLED, YOU'RE NOT RECYCLING

As Carl Zimring writes in *Cash for Your Trash*, "public recycling is environmentalism based upon traditional consumer behaviors."[60] Recycling is a business with the materials as commodities whose value is in many ways determined by us. For recycling to thrive, we, the customers, must demand recycled products to close the loop of our actions. Tossing our discarded goods in the bin is only part of our role, but if there's no interest from consumers, then companies have less incentive to use recycled materials. When brands are urged by customer decisions to include recycled content in products, an expectation is set for competing companies to follow suit, and we eventually see changes flowing throughout industries. Walmart has set goals to increase the postconsumer recycled plastic in products on its shelves by three billion pounds by 2020. Despite the additional costs of recycled plastic in the market, the company has said that its decision was influenced by the massive pressure they are under about the material polluting the environment, specifically our oceans.[61]

We steer these decisions through voting with our dollars and choosing to buy products made with recycled materials. You may have noticed that some recycled products are more costly than nonrecycled, making them inaccessible for everyone to purchase. Those who are able to buy these products and wish to see recycled materials become the norm can make decisions that will contribute to this goal. Increasing the demand will encourage improvement of collection and sorting. Making buying recycled the default rather than the exception will allow the costs for such materials to be more accessible to those at lower economic levels. And we can all commit to asking companies we patronize how much recycled content is used in their products. We can inquire at a store, on their social media platforms, or via e-mail. Simply communicating that we want recycled options sparks an incentive for a company.

Recycling and composting programs are affordable ways to manage our waste. By strengthening these cyclical systems throughout the country, we can access the measurable benefits they provide for the economy and also reduce our effects on the climate. In 2014, the amount of municipal solid waste that was recycled and composted provided carbon dioxide emissions equivalent to removing 38 million cars from the road annually.[62] Recycling generates hundreds of billions in revenue each year, provides employment opportunities, and reduces the demand for landfills and incinerators. For all these reasons, we must strengthen the system for it to thrive, and we can begin by learning ways to take action in our homes and our communities.

9

TAKING ACTION FROM YOUR CURBSIDE TO CAPITOL HILL

Forest dwellers perform their respective roles to satisfy their individual needs while fueling the larger ecosystem. Each role contributes to the sustainability of resources on which all organisms rely for survival. In our recycling system, the role you play is essential, and as Adam Minter points out in Junkyard Planet, it is more of a "harvester" role. [1] The actual recycling process occurs at industrial facilities. Minter notes that, compared to harvesting, recycling is actually quite routine and simple, calling on practiced procedures to break materials down into their raw useful forms. The harvester has the more challenging task of providing enough quality items to keep the system functioning. We are charged with acquiring materials that are both recycled and recyclable. This leads back to the role of the individual as one who provides a supply of materials as well as steers demand for them.

People want recycling to be as easy as possible and we want to recycle everything. Sometimes local rules can feel restrictive and we might be tempted to put items in recycling anyway, because it feels better than throwing things into the trash. However, we need to decide if we want the best results for our time investment or not. Most systems are only as worthwhile as their inputs, and recycling is no exception. In short, we get out what we put into recycling. Many problems in our recycling system come from people's misinterpretations of the process, and fortunately, this can be fixed. If we are part of the problem, then we are able to make great strides in solving the problem, and once we couple personal accountability with systemic improvements, real change can take place. You can strengthen recycling in small daily decisions, such as knowing what your local MRF accepts and sharing information with others about the problem of contamination and wish-cycling.

This chapter is devoted to harnessing all the ideas and information I've presented and equip you to address the challenges the system faces through a variety of action steps. If you are ready for a flourishing materials management system that reduces pressure on the environment and supports domestic manufacturers, then this chapter is for you!

HOW TO BETTER YOUR BINS

Recycling rules are tricky to pin down because they can vary by location based on what companies are able to collect, sort, and sell. With confusing labels and evolving rules, people may feel doubtful about what to recycle and a few may even stop recycling altogether. When you ask if something is recyclable, a typical (and unsatisfying) response you might receive is, "It depends." This is frustrating when you want a simple yes or no, but it reflects the thousands of recycling programs in this country, each with their own rules of what items are accepted. What your local program accepts will depend on what its sorting technology can manage and if there's a marketable value (and an end buyer) for the materials, which lets the system remain healthy and profitable. Value is also propelled by customer demand, which closes the loop and makes an item go from "cradle to cradle" instead of "cradle to grave." In the following section, I'll offer some tips for common items, but the first step is to always check out the local rules to make sure you aren't wish-cycling incorrect items.

Someday, I'm sure recycling will be a process humming along perfectly, with high recovery for materials, and perhaps the United States will see more than a 90 percent recycling rate with scarce contamination in sight. If this is your reality, then I'm sure you're reading this book for historical purposes and are probably shocked that there was a time our country idled at 34 percent for so long. For those reading this between 2018 and when we've achieved an ideal recycling system, here are some small steps to reduce contamination and provide quality materials to keep the system thriving:

- **Don't bag them.** Avoid tying up your recyclables in plastic garbage bags. Having to rip open sturdy garbage bags and dump your recyclables onto the sorting line can cause a traffic jam and can be difficult for workers who have to open them by hand. If you're able, keep your recyclables out in a reusable box or bin and dump them into your larger container for pick-up.
- **Clean them up and empty them out.** While it's not necessary to scrupulously scrub your recycled goods until they are shining (and in the case of paper, I'd advise against scrubbing them at all), you also don't want to toss items that are covered in wet food and beverage residue. Give plastic food containers a quick rinse and if you can, run a dish towel over them or just shake the excess water off before tossing them in the bin. For glass and plastic bottles and aluminum beverage cans, be sure to empty out any lingering liquid.
- **Make them safe.** The safety of workers is important, and while there are protections in place, broken and jagged materials can still cause injuries. For your safety and that of others, don't put a loose, jagged-edged lid into the bin. As for broken glass, it can pose a hazard to workers and can also contaminate material bales like paper. Leave broken glass out of your recycling.
- **Don't squish them (too much)** Many of us collapse empty plastic containers before tossing them into the bin to save space. But this flattened plastic can be misidentified at your local MRF. Sorting technology is smart, but sometimes it can't tell the difference between a flat plastic milk jug and a folded piece of cardboard, so squished plastics can be erroneously sorted into paper bales. Plastic containers that are left in their original state are more likely to be sorted correctly.[2] If you prefer to compact items a bit to save space, try not to flatten them entirely. As for cardboard boxes, the opposite is true. In order to help haulers and ensure boxes are sorted correctly, make sure to collapse them.
- **Separate their caps (sometimes)** This has confused people for quite some time. Should we leave the plastic caps on or take them off? Plastic bottle caps are often made from plastic number 5, but

the bottles are often a different type of resin and because different plastics require different melting processes, it's been thought best to separate them. But then there's the problem of these small items rolling around recycling facilities. Plastic recycling associations have said to leave the caps on now that the recycling process has improved.[3] After being sorted and sent to a processing facility, the cap and bottle are separated during a water float/sink process, so it's been suggested to attach bottle caps back to plastic bottles but not to screw them on too tight. Check if your local facility accepts plastic bottle caps, or you can deposit them at Gimme 5 drop-off locations like Whole Foods, where other plastic number 5 items can be taken.

Metal bottle caps are either steel or aluminum. Their small size means that trying to recycle them individually can cause problems at the facility (once again—check your local facility to confirm how they accept metal caps). You can keep two cans in your kitchen or recycling and trash area of your house to collect metal bottle caps: one for steel and one for aluminum (although most caps will likely be aluminum). You can tell the difference with a simple refrigerator magnet test: If it sticks, then it's steel. If it doesn't, then it's aluminum. Keep the aluminum caps in an aluminum can and steel caps in a steel one. Once your can is just over half filled, crimp it closed so the caps won't fall out before putting the crimped can into the recycling.

ITEMS NOT MEANT FOR YOUR BIN

Now that you know more about the sorting process, you can visualize where your items are going. For example, recognizing the challenge of sorting small items, you now know why things like wine corks and plastic condiment containers are not recyclable through our systems, despite the fact that they could technically be recycled. You can determine if something should be kept out of recycling by asking yourself questions, like: *Is it smaller than 2 inches x 2 inches? Can it tangle around equipment? Is it hazardous? Is it unsanitary? Is it a textile or an electronic device?* If you answer yes to any of these, keep it out of the recycling bin. Let's dive into a few ubiquitous items that usually aren't accepted through your municipal recycling program and which ones can be recycled through other methods.

- **Candy wrappers:** Candy wrappers are complex items made from different materials, including plastic, paper, and aluminum, and it's challenging to separate them. Because MRFs receive huge volumes of stuff every day, the amount that candy wrappers yield just wouldn't add up to the volume of materials that have more market demand, plus they're small, lightweight and tricky to sort. But solutions do exist for these kinds of items. Terracycle is a company that recycles things not accepted in city recycling, from empty toothpaste tubes to old musical instrument strings. Some retailers pay for Terracycle to accept their brand's packaging, so consumers can freely mail them or drop off at a local store listed on Terracycle's online map to be recycled.[4]
- **Paper cups:** Paper coffee cups have traditionally not been recyclable because of the chemical lining on the inside of the cups. It's difficult to separate the lining from the recyclable paper fibers in an efficient and effective way. But, there are efforts to push major producers of the billions of paper cups tossed out every year to make them recyclable. Some cities have begun accepting them, so check to find out if yours is on that list. The paper sleeves often used are recyclable, so make sure to put those into the recycling bin. Obviously, the best choice is to use a reusable mug, and many coffee shops will give you a discount on your drink for bringing your own mug.
- **Paper receipts:** These little paper slips have surprisingly large environmental impacts and an estimated 93% of them are coated in bisphenol A (BPA) or bisphenol S (BPS), which are substances connected to endocrine-disrupting health problems.[5] The coatings are quickly absorbed through the skin of people handling them. Trying to recycle these receipts can lead to these coatings contaminating new recycled paper products, like bathroom tissue and food packaging.[6] This is another evolving topic, as employees and customers continue urging retailers to use better receipt options, but unless you know a retailer is using phenol-free paper, toss the receipt into the trash. Another solution is to skip the

paper receipt and ask for no receipt at all or use digital receipts instead.

- **Pizza boxes:** These items have sparked disagreements during party clean-ups across the country. The general rule is to leave used pizza boxes out of your curbside recycling. Although some cities have begun accepting the non-greasy parts of the box, since grease contaminates recyclable fiber. Check your local rules; if they accept pizza boxes, then rip off the pieces with visible grease stains and toss those out before recycling the cleaner parts.

- **Plastic straws and utensils:** Americans use 500 million plastic straws every day, but straws are not recyclable through your municipal recycling program. Their small size makes them difficult for machines to sort and there is a lack of alternative methods to recycling straws. It's best to say no thanks on the plastic straw when you're ordering your drink to keep your server from automatically putting one in there. If you love straws, then there are many reusable options made of glass or steel, as well as paper and compostable options. As for plastic utensils, their complex shape and range of resin types make them poor candidates for recycling. These small, rigid items can jam sorting machinery and have a low market value. Most recycling programs do not accept them. As with other disposable plastics, replacing them with reusable options are the best choice.

- **Foamed Polystyrene:** Also known as Styrofoam or plastic number 6, for you resin buffs. People tend to cringe when being handed this material because of its wasteful reputation. It's forever floating or blowing aimlessly through our environment or buried in a landfill. Polystyrene only makes up 2 percent of the total municipal solid waste by weight, but it's also 30 percent of the total volume in landfills because this lightweight material is so regularly used in packaging.[7] Some cities have banned it from being used as takeout boxes for restaurants. There's not much of a market for recycled foamed polystyrene, and it's not accepted through curbside recycling. Check your local government's recycling website to determine if it accepts the material through a specific drop-off center. There are companies trying to develop a market and value for the material, but it's best to keep it out of your recycling bins at home.[8]

- **Certain types of glass:** Glass packaging of your food and beverages can be recycled through your curbside program, but there are other types of glass that cannot. Because glass products are treated differently depending on their intended use (e.g., to hold hot liquids), the temperatures at which they melt varies. Windows, mirrors, and crystal or Pyrex glass cannot be placed in curbside recycling. And as a reminder, broken glass shouldn't be placed in your curbside bin because it can injure workers collecting and sorting it.[9]
- **Shredded paper:** It is recyclable, but just dumping loose shredded paper into your bin can wreak havoc for collectors and the MRF. Facilities accepting shredded paper ask that you bag it before tossing it into the bin to keep the shreds contained. Shredding might be needed for security or legal reasons, but in recycling paper, longer fibers are more valuable because they have more life in them. Shredding paper shortens those fibers and potentially the number of future products they can be recycled into. If the document is not sensitive, then recycle it without shredding.
- **Plastic bags:** This is one of the biggest problem items for MRFs. When you put one flimsy bag into your curbside recycling, it can get jammed in machinery and slow down the whole facility. They're also easily sorted into incorrect materials, like paper, because they are so lightweight. Most grocery stores take plastic bags back, and some also accept plastic film from food packaging. And of course, the best choice is to carry a reusable bag.
- **Complex cartons:** Tetra Pak is a massive producer of beverage and food packaging, and it's known for those containers that look like thick paper packaging coated in plastic, like the packaging for juice, soup broth, ice cream, or other dairy products.[10] This item is tricky to recycle because it's made using very thin layers of paper, aluminum, and plastic.[11] If paper mills do not have the equipment to separate carton layers to get the fiber they can use, then there's no point in buying these containers from MRFs, making it too costly and inefficient for MRFs to accept them.[12] Separating these into different streams is not possible through many municipal recycling facilities, but 60 percent of community programs do accept these cartons, and checking your local rules will

tell if you live in one of those areas.[13] The Carton Council has a goal to make recycling cartons more widely accessible and works to connect MRFs with brokers who can find end buyers for cartons.[14] These buyers could be facilities with capacity to separate out the carton materials or companies using the entire carton for wall boards or other construction materials. Strive to pick products with less-complex packaging (like glass jars and metal cans) to ensure recyclability.

- **Rigid plastics:** Old lawn furniture and laundry baskets made of plastic are too bulky to be recycled through the curbside process. Someone in your area might like to use your old large plastic items, so try putting them on the free section of your local Craigslist or make a quick post on your community forum. If there are no takers, then call your local recycling facility to inquire about drop-off possibilities for these items (make sure you can tell them the number of the plastic, found on the item in the three arrows symbol).[15]

- **Batteries:** A wide range of battery types are recyclable, including, alkaline, lithium, and lead acid batteries. From common household appliances to automobiles, these batteries can be recycled for new products but should not be disposed of in your curbside service because they require specific methods of extracting the recyclable minerals and metals. Improper placement of batteries in recycling can even lead to dangerous instances of fires at MRFs. If batteries are landfilled, then the heavy metals can react with rain water and contribute to leachate discharge,[16] which is another reason to recycle them. You can find a drop-off location for batteries near you through an online search (hardware stores are typical drop-off points) or request a mail-in box suitable for the amount you have through a company like Battery Solutions. The best decision is to use rechargeable batteries as long as you can and then properly recycle them.

ELECTRONICS RECYCLING

Our insatiable appetite for new electronics has a decidedly massive impact, in both the production of these items and the complex disposal of them. We typically think of e-waste as smartphones and laptops, but the category also refers to items like air conditioners, heat pumps, lamps, other home appliances, calculators, and electronic toys.[17] According to a 2017 United Nations report, we discard 44.7 million metric tons of electronic waste worldwide every year, roughly 6.1 kilograms or 13.4 pounds per inhabitant.[18] This is expected to increase in the coming years, but only 20 percent of that waste is gathered to recycle, per documentation from the forty-one countries with official numbers on e-waste.

In the U.S., twenty-five states have mandated electronics recycling, servicing 65 percent of the country's population, and almost all policies require the manufacturer to fund the recycling effort for its products.[19] Sadly, due to lack of documentation, the fate of 76 percent of electronic waste is unknown. Not all countries have national legislation on disposing and accounting for e-waste, and even among countries with legislation, the types of waste covered varies and makes it difficult to accurately assess the devices we're discarding and how. The United Nations estimates that the potential value of materials in e-waste in 2016 was €55 billion.[20] For every 1,000 tons of used electronics, 200 repair jobs can be created; a robust recycling system for devices could bring 45,000 new jobs.[21] Recycling these items is challenging due to the variation of materials used (and the fluctuations of market values for each material), as well as the sheer volume we toss out every year.[22] Devices can have such materials as lead, mercury, cadmium, PVC, and plastics with flame retardants, and separating these materials can be dangerous if appropriate safeguards are not in place for workers. Although increasing awareness of dangerous materials in electronics has resulted in some companies phasing out hazardous materials, there are still devices circulating that have those components, and at some point, they will be discarded. Like batteries, devices that are disposed of irresponsibly can contaminate land and water around waste facilities. And because devices are designed to obtain data from users, a key part of refurbishment requires reputable recyclers that have specialized resources and workers for removing sensitive information.

You can drop off electronic waste at many locations, including some nonprofit organizations, retailers, recycling facilities and through take-back programs in which you send the device back to the company through the mail or their storefront (some even offer cash back—check the company website).[23] Programs can be found through stores like Best Buy and Call2Recycle. The items are then assessed to see if they can be refurbished and resold or if the parts can be removed and reused. If it's too old or beyond repair, then it goes into recovery, in which hazardous pieces are removed and the remaining materials are treated. The device can then be broken down in size through a process like shredding, and the metals and plastics can be separated and sold. All useful parts with market value go onto manufacturing, while the remaining materials are landfilled or incinerated.

We have a tendency to keep old devices stored in a drawer or box somewhere in our homes, and years tick by while we forget to discard them properly. The problem is that electronics entering the recycling process years after their release date decline in value. They are less likely candidates for refurbishment and are sent to be broken down, its parts garnering lower prices due to the time lag. Electronics recyclers have an uphill battle in trying to keep up with the range of device types and continuous upgrades of models each year. It's tough for them to estimate items they'll receive now and what they'll need to adapt for in the future. Smaller and lighter-weight electronics are more convenient for consumers, but it means less materials poised for recovery. The return on investment sometimes is not high enough for companies to make a profit in breaking apart and selling our old devices.[24] You can help by recycling your e-waste as soon as possible in order to keep the value of the item high. Also, buy refurbished electronics instead of brand-new items, and urge companies you patronize to invest in strengthening the electronics-recycling system. Companies need to hear that you value recycling and also see it in your purchases for used items.

LABELS, SEALS, AND SIGNALS

Products typically have two things on their packaging that we can peek at before buying: ingredients and instructions. This is an avenue for producers to communicate directly with customers about their products, and it's also where we look to find out if something is recyclable or made with recycled materials. The Mobius Loop, the official name for those three arrows, is commonly associated with recycling. Gary Anderson, an architecture student from California, designed the symbol in 1970 to win a contest sponsored by the Container Corporation of America.[25] Anderson won a cash prize and college scholarship, but he also created one of the most pervasive and recognizable logos still in use today. His vision was to symbolize "continuity within a finite entity" in the image.[26] Anderson was inspired by the Mobius strip used in mathematics (think of taking a strip of paper, half-twisting it, and taping together the ends to form a loop—it's still one strip of paper with two sides, but the connection makes it appear to be only one side).[27] The design is available for broad use, but if a company uses it and can't back up recycled or recyclable claims, then they can get into big trouble. They might be fined, sometimes hundreds of thousands of dollars, by the Federal Trade Commission (FTC) for green-washing practices.[28]

As people have grown more concerned with environmental impacts over the years, brands have tried to remain competitive by using more green lingo in their marketing. Unfortunately, some companies try to ride the coattails of those actually implementing better practices by just adding claims of sustainability to their websites, ads, and packaging. For example, companies latched onto using the word *natural* to remain competitive with USDA organic foods. Consumers have become savvier and aren't being fooled by a "natural" label as often, but companies are finding new ways to green wash with their marketing.[29] The FTC updated its *Green Guides* in 2012 to specify what behavior is prohibited because of its deceptiveness and to demand more clarity from companies claiming to be green.[30]

The FTC notes distinctions between the components of a product that are recyclable. For example, a plastic soda bottle might be made from recycled plastic, but that doesn't mean recycled plastic was used in the lid. While the commission doesn't consider this deceptive, it's something consumers should be cognizant of when determining recycled content or recyclability for an entire product. Another marketing trick is when companies inflate environmental benefits to sound significant when they're really negligible. A company might claim its product has 50 percent more recycled content, so at a quick glance, it appears to be 50 percent recycled content. But the key word here is more. If the product previously only had 5 percent recycled, then the claim just means the product now has 7.5 percent. The FTC prohibits this kind of deceptive marketing, but it's possible that companies will still try to use such tactics or find similar methods to fake environmentally friendly products.[31] Some companies might affirm what they're selling is "environmentally preferable" to another company's products, but this could be unfounded if they don't specify how (e.g., concrete information about their production or actual recycled content with comparison to other brands). Also, a company may claim to be using greener packaging than it was prior, but in reality, they might just be using lighter-weight material that isn't recyclable or made with recycled content. While it might be practicing source reduction by using less material than before, if it doesn't have the potential to be recycled then the packaging is not necessarily a better choice.

Because the FTC exists to protect consumers, we as individuals can contact the agency through their website (https://ftc.gov/complaint) to flag a company engaging in deceptive green marketing. In many cases, specificity is the key, and if a company is vague about the recycled content or environmental benefits and has no substantial evidence to back those claims, then it could be engaging in deceptive behavior.

Recyclability in a product is very important to consider, such as buying something in a recyclable glass container rather than in a nonrecyclable flimsy plastic bag. However, in order to close the process loop and ensure that we are achieving the full environmental benefits from the system, we need to buy recycled-content products. To be a responsible consumer means to have complete information that allows us to make the best decisions for our values and budgets. Unfortunately, we often make decisions with incomplete knowledge of the product, not knowing if it's the more sustainable option on the shelf.

To demand recycled items, we need to know which items are made with secondary materials. It can be tricky to locate the information we need when branding and design vary from company to company, but we can identify some key details from the Mobius Loop label on products, like if it's made with postconsumer or preconsumer recycled content. Post-consumer material means it was discarded and collected from some kind of end user, whether that's household, commercial, or industrial use (it's the stuff we put into our bins). This differs from preconsumer material, which is diverted from the waste stream during manufacturing. This could apply to trimmed-off scrap, shavings, or sawdust that is discarded during production and doesn't get purchased by consumers. This can include unsold items, which might be in their final form, but they're considered pre-consumer because they weren't used by a consumer.[32]

Buying a product with either is much better than buying something with no recycled content at all. But, if you're given the choice between the two, postconsumer material has more environmental benefit. Recycled materials that are postconsumer have been through a useful life cycle, and they have a higher potential of being discarded into the waste stream. Preconsumer materials are less likely to be thrown out because manufacturers often find ways to use them in their production or sell them to another company to be used. Choosing post-consumer material signals demand and creates more incentive to strengthen the collection methods for recovering those materials.

When debating a purchase, check to see if the recycling symbol on the product references a percentage, often printed within the three arrows. Products may specify what percentage is preconsumer and postconsumer (some are mixes of both). You might see a statement like "Please recycle" next to the symbol, which indicates the recyclability of it but not the content. Conversely, if a product is made with recycled material, it's not necessarily recyclable (think of single-use products like napkins). To add more complexity, just because the three arrows are printed on an item doesn't mean your local recycler accepts it. You can find a list of what's accepted in your program by searching for the recycling rules on your towns' website. A 2016 survey showed that 59 percent of the public thinks that "most types of items" are recyclable in their town, perhaps without knowing the local rules.[33] This wish-cycling and confusion risks damaging the positive outputs of the entire system.

If confusing labeling has been contributing to the problem, then better labeling can help solve it. Cue standardized recycling labels, which explain succinctly and consistently what items can be recycled in matching-labeled bins. The nonprofit organization Recycle Across America (RAA) provides municipalities and entities (like national parks and sports stadiums) with society-wide standardized labels for bins. Nearly nine million standardized labels are in use across the country, and RAA reports the success of increased recycling levels and significantly lower contamination in bins with the labels. For example, once the Orlando Public K–12 Schools began use of standardized labels, it saw substantial improvements in the very first year. The school district's recycling levels increased 90% from previous years, saving a net

$370,000 in trash hauling fees. Another example is the U.S. Bank Stadium, host of the 2018 Super Bowl, whose use of the standardized labels played a key factor in the game being deemed the first zero-waste Super Bowl in history and achieving a 91% diversion rate.

These labels were evaluated by industries and end users to ensure their accuracy and effectiveness. They include photos, easily read fonts, and color-coding based on disposal methods. The standardized labels provide information in a universal format so we can easily recycle wherever we are. Recycle Across America labels are great solutions for sorting at the bin, and another helpful label applies instructions for recycling right onto products. The How2Recycle label uses insight from the FTC, along with recycling data, material trade groups, and industry experts to craft labels advising us how to responsibly discard an item. [34] The labels explain how to prepare it for recycling and if it can be recycled through your curbside program or needs to be taken to a drop-off location.[35] Categories like "Widely Recycled" or "Check Locally" offer more insight to the recyclability of the material in most cities and can easily remove the guesswork for consumers. Over 75 companies have adopted the How2Recycle labeling because they know it's something customers value.[36] We can communicate to brands that we want them to incorporate these changes to their product designs, and social media offers a fast way for us to voice these concerns.

THIS OR THAT

Would you like paper or plastic? A drink in an aluminum can or a glass bottle? Even though we realize that everything we consume has a footprint and takes resources, we can still try to make a less-impactful choice when buying a product. Gauging those impacts can be tough to do in a store. If you are worried about plastic pollution in oceans, then you might avoid using any plastic at all. If you're focused on reducing effects of virgin paper production, then you may attempt to go paperless as often as possible. And if you're trying to make choices that curb harmful impacts on all ecosystems and communities, selecting a product can be a dizzying experience. Using less is better for the environment, but we don't always remember our reusable bottles, and in those times, we shouldn't dehydrate ourselves. We need to choose the most preferable option from what's available rather than neglecting our needs.

There are three qualities to look for when picking an item: recycled content, recyclability, and longevity. By checking for a percentage, you can signal a demand for products made with recycled materials. You can ensure recyclability by choosing items that you're certain are accepted in your local program. If you are given the choice between a compostable item or a recyclable one and you don't have access to a composting service, then it's better to opt for the latter. Composting is an excellent way to handle organic items like food scraps but, things like cups and utensils that are labeled as compostable don't quickly break down in a landfill. If your only option is to throw the item in the trash, then it will sit in a landfill without the proper aeration to decompose. For these situations, selecting a product that you know is recyclable in your local system is the best option.

Some recyclables are more valuable than others based on economic markets. For example, instead of buying a beverage in a plastic bottle, opt for one in an aluminum can, because there's typically a strong market for recycled aluminum, and it's infinitely recyclable with high environmental savings. This is another instance where being up to date on any local rule changes can be helpful. If you see that a material has been added to or removed from your community's recycling list, you can change your purchasing choices accordingly. And the third quality to check for is long-term durability. Try to invest in quality products that can be repaired rather than replaced. This will help you curb encounters with planned obsolescence. You can pick products that are compatible with any existing accessories you may already have (like electronics that will connect with a power cord you have or an item of clothing that can be paired with many others you own). Instead of falling down a hole of "this or that" conundrums, you can look for items that are recycled, recyclable, and made to last. These determinations can help guide you to find a product that has a lighter impact on the environment.

HOW TO INSPIRE YOUR COMMUNITY

An ecosystem is made stronger by the diverse qualities and skill sets of its inhabitants. When communities can unite in ways that encourage each members' unique abilities, powerful systems can be achieved to benefit all. Individuals adjusting their practices and sharing their experiences with others are essential facets of driving systemic change. We pluck social cues from each other, and neighbors observe our public habits to determine how things are done in a community.

Enacting change throughout your neighborhood and town begins with individuals deciding to change their own habits and going on to share those experiences with others. We pluck social cues from each other, and neighbors observe our public habits to determine how things are done in a community. Those cues are sometimes cosmetic, such as keeping lawns kept in a particular fashion, or they can be courtesy, like cleaning up after your pet. And of course, the cues can be geared toward a larger system of stewardship, for instance (yep, you guessed it!), recycling. In one study, researchers compared two messages about recycling in one neighborhood. Some signs stated the moral obligation to recycle, and others stated how many neighbors were already recycling. Curbside recycling increased 19 percent when the social-norm signs were up.[37] Real-world face-to-face interactions can result in behavioral impact and habit changes. When we strike up conversations with neighbors or friends or strangers at a volunteer or community event, we can help people to better understand recycling and share ideas on how to reduce waste. We can help people feel less confused or alone in trying to confront climate change and brainstorm ideas for how to live better and adopt habits that have less environmental impact. We can entwine these goals within our existing groups in order to help those participants learn and strive for improvements. You may be focused solely on the previous section of improving your home habits, which will provide ample help in allowing recycling to thrive. If you have the capacity to extend your work on waste beyond your homes, the following are series of ideas for how to share these concepts with your larger community. This is not meant to be a checklist of tasks, but instead is a collection of ideas. Following any of these paths could be a way to boosting the three R's in your area, so review and see which resonates the most with you!

HOW TO SPREAD THE WORD

One of the most effective ways for people to learn better recycling practices is through word of mouth. Recycling knowledge is available everywhere online. Sites like Earth911 allow you to simply enter an item and zip code, and they present options for recycling. Despite these online resources, family and friends still regularly text me their questions. These messages convey curiosity about the process and their desire to recycle right, and I love helping tackle these questions. It seems people prefer to ask someone they know about recycling habits rather than Google their way to a definitive answer about what to do. Word of mouth is essential in spreading recycling know-how and ideally, every neighborhood would have a point person who knows the local rules. You could be the savvy recycler in your community who can take people's blue-bin questions at block parties, yard sales, potlucks, and so on.

We need more widespread education and community support to help people reduce, reuse and recycle. The Master Recycler Program is an example of how Oregon and Washington States are offering residents a way to participate in building that community support. The program offers passionate individuals a new understanding of recycling and how to educate others. More than two thousand Master Recyclers have completed the course since 1991.[38] Graduates have then committed to teach others and have gone onto creates projects to help their community such as starting Repair Cafes, collection events, and organizing green teams to improve recycling in their workplaces. Community-based interest has spread the program throughout the Pacific Northwest, and the organization receives calls from around the country from others hoping to replicate the idea. The program aims to shift the paradigms of its participants, who often join the program because they are concerned about keeping items out of landfills. Master Recycler teaches materials management instead of discards management and urges people to consider the impacts of an item's production and use, not just its disposal. The Oregon Department of Environmental Quality adopted a holistic approach of assessing impacts throughout the life cycle of materials, and materials management uses that wide lens to inform actions to reduce overall impacts.[39] This includes the design, extraction, and production of materials, as well as their impacts during use and end-of-life management (such as recycling or disposal). Master

Recyclers are taught how recycling is affected by markets and demand and how we must displace virgin materials with secondary ones, beyond just avoiding the landfill. The program also focuses on behavior change and also explores how to remove the barriers that keep communities from taking action.[40] You can reach out to current chapters to learn how to get involved where you live or start a new program. They are all independent of one another, but the existing ones are always happy to share their model.

For reducing waste, you can use the method of peeking into your waste basket to determine what you're throwing out and spread that information to your community. For example, if you live in a neighborhood, there's likely a lot of organic waste that could be composted. If you don't have that service provided, you can coordinate with neighbors to participate in a composting service with a local company (usually a monthly fee, with the scraps picked up weekly) or donate to a nearby farm. Another way to curb waste is to start a tool-sharing program where neighbor borrow each other's tools and large appliances for occasional use. The first step is to check myTurn (formerly, Local Tools), an online map of these programs, to determine if one already exists near you.[41] If not, then you can reach out to neighbors to see if others would be interested in starting one. myTurn is a software platform for sharing and managing place-based sharing programs in communities, whether that be neighborhoods, schools, or businesses. You can develop a sharing system among a group of neighbors and work to designate a space where items are stored, like a shed or garage or office. Some programs use a small rental fee (one dollar for seven days) to help maintain the library and ensure that tools are returned. myTurn reports that most locations are lending hundreds or even thousands of items per week, delivering powerful tangible results in promoting reuse in communities. There are different formats to share items among neighbors, and depending on the size of your neighborhood, even a simple email group could be sufficient.

Towns have also operated tool sharing near or in their local public library, and residents can check out a tool with a simple swipe of their library cards.[42] Starting a tool library can be daunting, and you may bump into a number of questions that could even deter you from launching one. Fortunately, as of 2018, more than 150 tool libraries are on myTurn, which means many others have grappled with and solved the concerns you may have with starting a tool share. Share Starter is an online resource full of guidance to help communities begin their own lending libraries and can advise you every step of the way, from budgeting and funding to securing volunteers. There might even be a similar program (or the potential for one) operated by your local government, such as the parks and recreation department. Do some internet searching and ask around before trying to reinvent the wheel. It's possible that an existing program could use some volunteer work, too, so make sure to offer your time if you can!

And of course, there's the Repair Café, which has been an impressive model of reuse and increasing self-sufficiency for people throughout the world. If you don't have the resources to set up a devoted space with tools for repair, then you can explore hosting a skill-sharing and repair club. Think of it like a book club, but with a focused theme of the three R's. During the meetings that no one has any repairing skills to share, your group could brainstorm new ways to reduce and reuse waste, plan neighborhood recycling competitions, have a potluck, and just enjoy each other's company. Reconnecting to our waste practices doesn't need to be a painful, burdensome reckoning. It can be an opportunity to deepen connections with neighbors and friends and a chance to explore new solutions together.

On the other hand, in trying to improve our neighbor's habits we might feel annoyed when we see someone neglect their recycling bin, or argue about which items are recyclable. While we might feel compelled to vent those frustrations directly to those not taking part, we could undermine our ultimate goal of furthering recycling habits. When we approach a conversation about any green habit from a place of condescension or exasperation, we lose not only the potential to learn why our neighbor doesn't participate but also the chance to connect a positive, community-building experience with recycling itself. I should know because I've allowed my desperation to get the better of me at times and have been guilty of lecturing those whose actions I found wasteful or unproductive. My abrasiveness shifted the conversation to my anger, tone, and disappointment rather than the solutions I hoped to see the person consider adopting. Having a negative reaction to wasteful behavior is normal and even understandable, but if we truly seek change and not just an avenue to air grievances, then the way we communicate should be oriented for solutions rather than shame. In the same way we have reasons to recycle, people may also have reasons they do not. There could be time constraints due to working multiple jobs and raising kids or just feeling confused about the whole process and deciding not to bother. Maybe they've heard misinformation about how recycling isn't worthwhile and doesn't make a difference. In any of these cases, you can help remove these barriers for them. Perhaps you can offer to teach neighborhood kids how to recycle and let that be a contribution to their household chores. You can listen to the recycling information they've received that has contributed to their disengagement and share your knowledge for a more balanced view of the system.

USING YOUR LOCAL CHANNELS

There are creative ways to captivate and excite people about recycling, and you can determine which could be effective in your neighborhood or let those ideas serve as a jumping-off point to develop your own. The first step is to look up your local government's recycling website or call their office to determine if they have existing education guidelines or tools. After you're familiar with the local dos and don'ts, you can begin exploring the available channels for communicating best recycling practices to your wider community. This is also a chance to use your unique skillset. For example, if you're an artist then you can create a poster with images of items for community centers, making the divide very clear between the recyclable stuff and what's not meant for the bin. Or you could submit a column on the rules (either as a reminder or an update to the recyclables list) to your local neighborhood forum or newsletter. A good tip is to include an encouragement for readers to comment on the post or reach out to you directly with any confusion or misinformation they may have received from other sources to clear those up.

What clogs our recycling system are a lack of communication between stakeholders and confusion about how the process works. As residents, we are important stakeholders and can reach out to other groups in the recycling system to learn what they need from us and voice what we want from them. You can see who in your town would be interested in making a group trip to the local recycling facility to see firsthand how items are sorted and call the facility to schedule tours. To tackle contamination, reach out to your local recycling facility and ask if they can give you their top five tips for communities to do better. Rather than just researching problem items for other cities or even simply relying on this book, go straight to the source to learn the specific challenges for your area. Once you've learned the issues, try addressing them in your home recycling and share the information with your neighbors through community forums. You can send a letter to the editor or an opinion editorial to your local newspaper on the benefits of recycling and how your town can better participate.

Like the great Nebraska scrap drive during World War II, competitions can be effective to inspire participation. In 2001, an initiative called RecycleMania sought out sports rivalries between colleges and built on the existing competitive spirit to pose a new recycling challenge to rival schools. They held a competition to determine which school could recycle the most per student over a ten-week period, and the idea spread into a national tournament, mostly through word of mouth. Since it began, more than one thousand colleges and universities in North America have competed with their recycling rates, waste minimization, or composting efforts.[43] The winners receive national recognition, but the driver seems to be the spirit of competition through something we feel we have control over: our own waste. Schools teaching all grade levels can offer indispensable support for recycling by helping students to understand how our consumption of goods affects the world and how we can do better. If you are not a teacher, then connect with a school you're affiliated with and suggest a trip to your local recycling facility. You could even coordinate a recycling education event at your local library and make it family friendly with sorting games to show which material goes in which bin.

EXPANDING YOUR RECYCLING PROGRAM

During my freshman year of college, the campus had not yet implemented a recycling program. The environmental club was doing demonstrations, like explaining how many plastic bottles were needed to make a new T-shirt and dumping trash to sort out the massive amount of recyclables and useful materials we were sending to the landfill.

Eventually, students could recycle throughout the entire campus, but during the program's development, I gained a reputation as an environmental kid, and students in my dorm began bringing me their recycling because I offered to drop it off at my family's nearby house every week. My dorm closet became a temporary host to empty bottles, rinsed-out plastic food containers, and tin cans. Thankfully, my generous roommate merely teased me about my bizarre hobby. It's always fun to be the go-to person in a dorm for something, and I was glad my reputation was linked to something sustainable rather than something less endearing, like the longest shower-taker. Eventually, though, having residents drop their empty containers at a room barely the size of a Winnebago became inconvenient and pretty ridiculous (although, if you'd ask my patient roommate, I'm pretty sure she'd admit it was both of those things sooner than "eventually"). Thankfully, the campus began offering recycling services, and the problem was solved.

If your town doesn't offer any recycling services or only offers to select neighborhoods, I don't suggest stockpiling your neighbor's bottles and cans in your home closets. Instead, reach out to your city officials to ask why no recycling services exist, and learn what barriers they faced with failed recycling programs in the past. Knowing the history or concerns from their perspective allows you to research similar problems in other cities and their solutions. To show the interest in recycling, get a good old-fashioned petition into your community and gather signatures online; door to door; and at community centers, galleries, libraries, and places of worship. Present to your local council meeting the request of starting or expanding a recycling program, and show the number of eager citizens behind the initiative. A public statement during a town hall or forum will not only reach the many people in the room but also will become part of official meeting minutes to be referred to in the future if necessary. Demand is essential to many parts of the system, from achieving recycling services in your neighborhood to urging local businesses to use recyclable and recycled-content materials. Posing the suggestion and proving its momentum is sometimes necessary to produce a change. It might feel like an uphill battle at times, or it might feel inconvenient, but remember the many other people throughout the history of recycling who pushed through obstacles to enact a convenient and sustainable service for the community. Recall why it's important to have a circular loop of resource use and recovery for reuse, and let those reasons motivate you. And remember you don't need to do all of this alone. Don't be shy in asking for help from people who express an enthusiasm to address waste in your community. As we've seen, it may take one person to get the ball rolling, but there is strength in numbers, and uniting with others not only accelerates the strength of that ball, but it allows you to share the task of pushing it forward.

If your town has a program already, does it regularly report recycling and contamination rates to the public? Has it set new goals for those rates by a specific date? We recycle in our homes but also in our broader communities. Some places have strong recycling programs, and people can easily access a recycling bin to toss their bottles in while out and about. Perhaps there are curbside residential services but a lack of public recycling bins. Call your local facility or government to request recycling bins for parks, sidewalks, or wherever a public trash can currently sits. These are requests you can make of your city officials, and they can even be incorporated in a larger competition to increase participation to meet those goals. For example, residents of Laurel, Maryland, engage in a recycling competition, with monthly updates on each neighborhood. Each month, the winning neighborhood is announced on the government website and awarded accolades based on the largest reduction in refuse from the previous month, the smallest gap between refuse and recycling, and increases in recycling from previous totals.[44] The competition not only encourages an increase in recycling but also decreases overall waste.

Many critics scoff at the reverence people have for recycling. Op-eds and blog posts are written to pull the rose-colored glasses off avid recyclers and replace them with more cynical lenses, able to see recycling for the waste of time and energy they declare it to be. Sometimes, their points expose an uncomfortable truth: that the recycling system is complex and challenging. However, the best course of action is not to abandon a habit with tangible environmental and economic benefits that people feel good about participating in. It's unproductive and wasteful to tear down enthusiasm for recycling. We need to maintain our excitement. We can be proud to take part in something and also call into question the nonworking parts of it, holding up a magnifying glass to understand the flaws and why they occur. Instead of using the problems as a reason to discard the entire system, we can repair them. Through technological advances, better practices in our curbside bins, and appropriate and strong communication between stakeholders, we can raise recycling to meet our standards.

POLICIES TO SUPPORT

Baltimore, Maryland is one of many cities with a historical pattern of burdening certain neighborhoods with industrial facilities, like oil refineries, chemical plants, and sewage treatment. There are dangerous and long-lasting effects of prioritizing these industries over communities. A 2013 study concluded that Baltimore was the deadliest city for emissions-related mortality rates, and 130 out of every 100,000 residents were likely to die each year from long-term exposure to air pollution. This environmental crisis led Destiny Watford to co-found a student group, Free Your Voice, devoted to social justice and community rights. They raised awareness on the approved plans for what would be the largest trash incinerator in the United States to be developed by Energy Answers. The proposed location was in Curtis Bay in southern Baltimore, less than a mile from two public schools. Equipped with environmental studies confirming that the incinerator would emit more mercury than a dirty coal-powered plant, the students of Free Your Voice mobilized a countereffort. They learned more about the depth of the environmental injustices Curtis Bay had been dealt over the years from longtime residents. In 2014, upon learning that Baltimore City Public Schools had agreed to purchase energy from the incinerator, the students of Free Your Voice were able to urge the school board's divestment. After nearly a year of petitioning on behalf of Watford and other students and families, the school board voted in favor of ending its contract with the developer. All customers then canceled contracts with the proposed incinerator, and it lost its market. Free Your Voice then mounted pressure on government agencies to pull the project's permits entirely, and in March 2016, the Maryland Department of Environment announced the permit to be invalid. Community members now have their sights set on ensuring the site will be used for a renewable energy source, like a community solar panel farm and recycling center.[45]

We can take political action to support and bolster sustainable systems and defy unhealthy ones. Policies can create a goal for a system to adapt and strive toward, and regulations can be paramount in molding a system to have a more positive impact on people and the environment. However, as mentioned, individuals who are responsible for crafting and shepherding the policies change, and those changes in roles are accompanied by a change in goals and philosophy. Thoughtful, strong policy can help set the marker for the society we want to see; however, political agendas can fundamentally change as other individuals with different goals are voted into office. When economic systems exist and function the way ours currently does, the relentless pressure and power we can wield by choosing where and how to use our money (or not use it) can speak volumes. In the case of bauxite mining in Malaysia, the temporary ban on the mining was a necessary step, but as the demand continued for the material, certain companies with enough means disregarded and continued mining operations. We can keep moving toward our societal vision through the decisions we make in our everyday lives.

A democracy can only work when we engage in it and voice our values, not only at the ballot box, but also at the grocery store and bank. It is imperative that we use this two-pronged approach in which we not only push for policies and systemic change to advance our society but also remember that our purchases and actions convey our values, regardless of who currently sits in office. Policies and goals like zero waste can set benchmarks and there is a myriad of solutions. Policy can help achieve the environmental and economic benefits of recycling from your town, county, state, and even the country.

A MANDATE TO RECYCLE

On a visit to Dublin, Ireland, I noticed labeled colored bags sitting outside homes, presumably waiting to be collected. When I asked my cab driver what the bags were for, he explained that, in an attempt to shed its "Dirty Dublin" nickname, the city enacted a recycling program using labeled bags and hefty fines for residents who failed to correctly bag their waste and littered. This gentleman enthusiastically shared how the city became stricter about trash for human health reasons. You can be fined €150 for neglecting to clean up your dog's bathroom business, and if you don't pay promptly, then you risk the maximum fine of €4,000. In under a decade, the country's recycling rate shot up from 11 percent to 36 percent. Ireland was the first country in the world to introduce a plastic bag fee, in which consumers had to pay fifteen cents for a plastic bag. Immediately successful, the fee caused a 90 percent decrease in the plastic bags in circulation, and over time each resident went from 350 bags per year down to only 14 bags.[46] In later years, the bags per capita slightly increased, and the bag tax did so accordingly, to twenty-two cents, which solved the problem. Ireland, ranked third in the European Union for its recycling efforts, has bolstered its recycling rate thanks to a landfill tax, which was thirty euros per ton as of 2010.

Recycling mandates exist in varying degrees all around the world. Some target specific materials, whereas others include fines for improper sorting of all recyclables. Taiwan has seen great success with a unique model that combines a lot of the strategies I've mentioned. Using social norms, it makes recycling a public event, strives to keep streets healthier and cleaner, and relies on rigorous sorting in thirteen material categories. The solution revolves around a musical truck that collects refuse directly from residents multiple times every week. Cheery music from the road might fill our minds with nostalgic ice cream trucks, but in Taiwan, the upbeat tune is the soundtrack for a public event for tossing out trash. The country struggled with trash in public spaces and rivers for decades, during which landfill capacity was dwindling and environmental awareness was rising. There were also challenges with resource limitations on the small island, which led to its reliance on imported raw materials. But in 1997, the Waste Disposal Act of 1979 was amended to require more regulations of certain waste materials. As a result, the four-in-one program was established to reduce municipal waste, boost recycling, and make the industry safer. The program has clearly defined roles for all participants, which are separated into four major groups. Residents, or waste generators, are required to separate their trash from recyclables at community waste-collection sites. Then private collectors, the second group, gather items from communities and retailers. Local governments provide public collection for communities and then sell recovered materials to recyclers, using some of the acquired revenue to finance the collection sites. And the fourth group is the funding source, called the Recycling Fund, in which manufacturers and importers finance municipal collection and private recy cling companies compliant with environmental and safety standards.

The fee-and-subsidy program is operated by a Recycling Fund Management Board, which calculates fees for manufacturers and importers based on the cost to collect and recycle an item. The Recycling Fund's status is reported to a committee of representatives from governments, trade associations, environmental and consumer protection NGOs, and academia. This committee discusses possible modifications to fee or subsidy rates and how to achieve them. What is also unique about the program is that it includes categories for electrical and electronic appliances and has spurred an increase in formal recyclers of those items. By increasing convenience for residents, Taiwan has achieved collection rates of 50 percent or more for electronic devices, which is twice as high as in the United States. A mandatory take-back program also is in effect for home appliances; for example, retailers must provide collection of televisions and washing machines for residents who discard old ones and buy new appliances.[47] In population-dense areas, the familiar music echoes out five nights a week, as large, yellow garbage trucks trundle through community collection sites, followed immediately by open-bed recycling trucks for sorting materials into paper, plastic, glass, and so on. There are even bins for food waste, separated as cooked and raw; the cooked waste is fed to animals, and the raw is composted. Residents can use a mobile app to track the trucks and be alerted when their neighborhood is next to offer ample time for them to escort their waste outside. People caught violating the rules are warned, and repeat offenders can face fines up to two hundred dollars. Add in the social norm of being with all your neighbors, participating in a process in which everyone can observe each other's engagement, and you've got some strong incentives at work. Workers even ride along on the back of the recycling trucks to help people sort.

This may sound like a lot of trouble, but it's designed to ensure that there are quality returns on investment to manage materials sustainably. As noted, we get out of recycling systems what we put into them. And Taiwan is getting quite a lot, including a 55 percent diversion rate and billions of dollars from recovering quality materials for manufacturers.[48] Because they are more intricately involved in the process, Taiwan's residents remain acutely aware of their material consumption. A country once nicknamed "Garbage Island" has successfully shed its reputation to become home to one of the most impressive and sustainable material and waste management systems in the world.[49] In fact, it has the second-highest recycling rate for municipal solid waste (leaving incinerator ash, commercial and industrial waste, and biowaste out of the equation), after Germany.[50] This system makes it harder to mindlessly throw away items. Everyone is more connected to the waste, and it's not just someone else's problem but also a responsibility shared by the entire community, from residents to government to the very companies producing items. Hardly any trash cans can be seen in public spaces, with a few small exceptions at transit centers.[51] People typically take any trash they accumulate during the day to their homes and then out to the garbage truck when the familiar music wafts through the air.

There are accessibility questions to address for communities replicating this system, such as ensuring residents with heavy work schedules or those who have difficulty carrying out materials will all be able to participate effectively. These concerns can be addressed through varying trash pick up times and workers in the truck assisting specific homes with carrying out waste. It might seem far-fetched to ever see a similar method in the United States, particularly considering that each American resident tosses out more than 4 pounds of waste every day, compared to an average of 0.8 pounds in Taiwan. But Taiwan wasn't always so sparse with its waste generation, and the mandates have used incentives to reduce trash. A key reason the city of Taipei has a 67 percent waste-diversion rate is its Pay as You Throw (PAYT) program, in which residents buy specific blue bags for garbage in a range of sizes from corner stores.[52] The more trash a household tosses out, the more blue bags they have to purchase, but recycling is free, and residents can use any sort of bag for these materials.

This system has also been successfully implemented in thousands of communities in the United States. PAYT employs a strategy of making landfilling more unappealing to the consumer. The program makes disposing of trash more expensive, and the more you throw away, the more you have to pay. There are different approaches, such as residents paying by weight of their trash, but the most cost-effective is a proportional pricing program with the use of specialized bags. Residents purchase printed bags designated for trash, and haulers only remove these specific bags, leaving trash in any other nonlabeled bag on your curb to greet you when you come home; then the resident must figure out a means of disposal outside this program. It is a common concern that people un-willing to participate would result to littering throughout the commu-nity. However, the Environmental Protection Agency reports that, of the thousands of towns practicing PAYT none have had issues with increased littering, and with reliable recycling and composting services, residents can easily reduce their overall waste.

This incentive program is often cheaper than what most households are paying for traditional trash services. Households that have trash pick-up don't always take into account what it costs them every year through property taxes or trash fees. If a municipality has a trash tax to help cover the tipping fees for dumping garbage at the landfill, then all the citizens are paying the same amount for this service regardless of how much they throw away. Imagine having to pay a flat fee for elec-tricity, no matter if you conserve energy and live in a small household or live in a huge mansion using significantly more resources. You'd have zero control over the fee, regardless of smart appliances and efficient light bulbs. A key reason for the increased demand of efficiency appli-ances is that they save money from reduced utilities. If we had no incentive to care about the amount of electricity being used, then peo-ple would likely be far more careless with usage. If your house needs five large trash bags every week at $1.50 each (this price includes all costs associated with the service), then you'd be paying less than half the traditional trash tax many municipalities charge.[53] And for house-holds facing economic strain, there is a precedence of voucher pro-grams to help.

There are twenty-two states across the U.S. that have at least one recycling requirement, including Georgia, Indiana, New Mexico, and California. But these laws aren't all statewide mandates on all recyclable materials and instead represent specific materials, including banning the disposal of lead acid batteries and waste oil.[54] Some target more commonly used materials, such as North Carolina's 2009 law banning all plastic containers (except for motor oil or plastic pesticide bottles) from disposal. The Carolinas Plastics Recycling Council has raised awareness to boost plastic recycling through its Your Bottle Means Jobs campaign. It estimates that, if each household in both North and South Carolina recycled two more bottles every week, then there would be three hundred new jobs created to sort and process the items and manufacture new goods.[55] Many states target specific items, but only a few have made a mandate for recycling a wide range of materials.

An example is the classic bottle bill: container deposit legislation that requires a minimum refundable deposit on beverage containers to ensure recycling. A distributor sells its product to a company and charges a deposit for each can or bottle purchased for resale. The consumer then pays a deposit of a few cents to purchase the beverage and receives the change back when taking the container to the company's storefront, a redemption center, or a type of reverse vending machine.[56] In this elegant system, the up-front fees capture the true value of an item's resources, leaving the choice to the consumer if the costs are worth recuperating. Ten states enforce their own bottle bills, and the collection rates of recycling beverage containers are much higher than in states without the legislation, 66 to 96 percent beverage container recovery versus an average of only 24 percent in non-bottle-bill states.[57] For those who toss their items in the trash, people will scavenge bottles and cans to earn some cash. The cost-effective system has been proven to work, but what about states who want to go for an across-the-board recycling mandate of many materials?

Vermont's universal recycling law was unanimously passed in 2012. Its goal was to address the state's stagnated recycling rate, which had hovered between 30 and 36 percent for decades (not unlike our national rate). The law has been implemented in phases over the past few years. For residential recycling, the government put an emphasis on education, but the law did not include a specific consequence of fines for those residents not in compliance.[58] Haulers are required to notify customers of the trash and recycling separation rules and have used "oops" stickers on bins not following those rules. The law has ushered in upward movement for recycling and composting after years of remaining static.

In 2015, one year after the law was implemented, more Vermont citizens had access to recycling than ever before. That year, baseline recyclables, including paper, cardboard, aluminum, steel cans, glass, and plastic number 1 and number 2 containers, were all banned from going to the landfill. From 2014 to 2015, trash disposal decreased 5 percent, and recycling and composting increased 2 percent. Food donations grew by 40 percent, as reported by local food banks.[59] These numbers may sound trivial, but they reflect movement in the recycling system for the first time in nearly two decades. The improvements also are expected to continue because the mandate is going into effect in phases over the course of a few years until 2020, when the law culminates with a full ban of food scraps from landfills. All Vermont municipalities enforce PAYT programs, allowing their residents to exercise more control over their solid-waste costs to pay less for trash and use the free recycling and composting services. As a result, towns have seen recycling jump 50 percent from previous numbers and conversely have had trash volumes cut in half. [60]

Recycling mandates that consider all baseline recyclables and organic materials have many benefits. They necessitate widespread education efforts on recycling, how to adopt the new practices, and the benefits of reducing our waste. Mandates can stimulate a local economy by boosting jobs to ensure recycling and compost services are offered to all residents. One drawback of recycling mandates is the potential to have low compliance because some households and businesses will avoid changing habits and throw recyclables into the trash regardless. Perhaps the hauler will have to pick up the tab of any consequential fines. This is where PAYT programs are extremely valuable companions to recycling mandates, as it makes placing materials into recycling streams all the more appealing. You can work to start incentive programs like PAYT and recycling mandates in your community through raising awareness about the benefits among neighbors and appealing to your local city council to pursue them. Urge policymakers on state and federal levels by attending town hall events or lobbying at their offices and ask that they advocate for good waste management policies. Vote for and support candidates who are committed to sustainability. When we push for policies like these and when we follow standards set by our local facilities, we can curb contamination and boost the quality and marketable value of our community's recyclables. This means that the system remains profitable for the city, haulers, and sorters to continue providing services to all our neighborhoods. Bringing more stability to the full system and ensuring all its stakeholders are fulfilling their roles can result in a flourishing process that sustains itself from start to finish (or in this case, start to start again).

A CALL FOR JOYFUL ACTS OF SUSTAINABILITY

It is my hope that you have developed a clearer understanding of the mysterious world behind our recycling bins and the important and unique role we as individuals fill. When we carry out a role in a system, we are not merely following steps and pulling our assigned levers in isolation from our personal thoughts and idiosyncrasies. You bring all your life experiences and values every time you buy a new item, choose how to use it, and decide when to dispose of it and how. We allow our personal values to guide and navigate major life decisions, like careers, civic engagement, and travels. These same values influence our daily choices and are arguably just as important. Our lives are built from routine habits, and this foundation of little choices is what makes those milestone moments possible. We must infuse our ethics into everything we do for these steps to have wide-reaching results. This might sound like an intimidating goal, but similar to how a forest is created from one seed at a time, we can achieve this through small adaptations to our behaviors.

Why do you as an individual choose to recycle? The system of recycling is one many of us opt into day after day, and if you are choosing to engage in an action countless times throughout the year, then it likely is something you find worthwhile. You have a valuable and unique role in this system, and you can extend that role beyond putting the right items in your recycling bin. Perhaps you are able or interested in just learning your local rules and following them. This is an essential role to fill with minimal time investment, yet you will provide high-quality materials for manufacturers and reductions in greenhouse gas emissions. Or perhaps you have the time and enthusiasm to go a step further and help educate your friends and neighbors and become the local recycling expert in your community. Maybe you're more intrigued by incentives and policy and want to push those initiatives in your municipality. There are tons of ways to get involved on a myriad of levels, and you decide how to take action based on your passion and skill set. The notion of the consumer role being insignificant is one of the most pervasive and defeating myths of the recycling system. We have countless opportunities to use our power as individuals creatively and strategically to create a society that is more considerate of our environment and natural resources. We are influential and powerful. You can enact change at this very moment and choose to keep doing so the next day and the following one. Recycling one cardboard box will not save the world, but it contributes to a system far greater than just that one box. It is one act in a continuous line of habits that shapes the society we want to live in, a society that is more mindful of the demands and services we coerce from the planet.

I do my best to practice sustainability, call attention to how humans affect the planet and each other, and share choices we make that can alter those practices. We are consuming too much and have historically been quite reckless with how we use and discard resources. In order for us to operate in this global ecosystem more sustainably (for the well-being of both the planet and ourselves), we need to adapt those behaviors and consider the entire system. Human beings have expansive ingenuity and ability to solve problems, particularly those we have ignited. The practices of reducing waste, creative reuse, and effective recycling are pieces of a solution that we can start at any time. I hope you have found some inspiration from the stories of all the people who expanded and improved recycling simply by deciding to do it. I wish for us to not only keep the enthusiasm for recycling but also to allow a sense of joy for all methods of sustainability rather than a foreboding shame or burden. Every day, our choices are small opportunities to contribute to the society we want. I hope you approach problems and lend your unique view of the world to solve them and let your sustainable choices be something you celebrate with others.

Lastly, I have spent pages and pages discussing the necessity of consuming less, saving more, and recycling effectively. And yet, I wrote this book—which used resources to produce. Although it is printed on a recycled-content paper, it still has an environmental impact. Recognizing this, I hope that if you enjoyed or benefited from this book in any way and you'd like to share it with others, please consider donating to your local library or sharing your copy with a friend. The forest will appreciate it.

TIPS FOR RECYCLING

- Always rinse food from recyclable packaging and be sure no liquid is lingering in the containers. Rinse and shake or towel dry containers before putting them in the bin.
- Don't tie up recyclables in a garbage bag. This is time-consuming for MRF workers who are already dealing with high volumes of stuff because they must rip open your bag, dump the items, while simultaneously sorting other materials on a moving conveyor belt.
- No jagged edges or broken glass. For workers' safety and to reduce contamination, do not put broken glass into your recycling. Be mindful of tin cans with jagged edged lids and try to push the lid down into the can.
- Check for the three arrows symbol on a product, but know that this doesn't always mean it's recyclable or accepted in your city. Plastics, for example, use a small number within the three arrows to tell what kind of resin is used in the product. This can be misleading because not all resin types are accepted in recycling programs. So, always check your local rules for what is or is not okay.
- Squishing containers saves space in your bin, but if you flatten a container too much, it might get sorted into fiber when it should be sorted into plastics. Don't flatten them entirely from their original shape to ensure they're sorted correctly by machinery at the MRF.
- Tops and lids: this depends on where you live (like all recycling rules) and what material the lid is made of. For plastic bottles with plastic lids, you can leave the lid on but not too tight, so that it can be separated from the bottle during processing. I give it one twist before

tossing into the bin. It you have a glass jar and a metal lid, separate them before putting into the bin. But visit your local facility's website to know whether they take lids and caps at all because they are small items and can cause issues with sorting machinery. For caps like the tops of glass beer bottles, you can keep those in a metal container and then crump it closed before tossing into the bin. This keeps the tops contained from wreaking any havoc.

- A few items to NOT recycle (some of these may seem obvious, but they are found at MRFs): Dirty diapers, old shoes, broken garden hoses, hypodermic needles, plastic grocery bags, foamed polystyrene (Styrofoam), ceramic glass (also no mirror glass, wine/drink glasses, light bulbs, or Pyrex), animals (one MRF has on record found a 6-foot shark[1]), and plastic straws.

1. Stewart-Severy, Elizabeth. "Sharks and Hand Grenades: Recycling Companies Sort out the Trash." Aspen Public Radio. March 5, 2018. http://aspenpublicradio.org/post/sharks-and-hand-grenades-recycling-companies-sort-out-trash.

BUYING RECYCLED

As we've noted, to close the loop and truly recycle, we need to buy recycled content products when we make a purchase. Look for the familiar three arrows, but try to spot a percentage in or near it. This will show how much of the product has recycled content in it, whether it's 10% or 100%. The label might reference if it has preconsumer or post-consumer waste (some are mixes of both!). If you don't see a percentage or explanation of the materials and only see the recycling symbol by itself, this might mean the item is recyclable, not that it was made with recycled content. You might see a statement like "Please recycle" next to the symbol, which also indicates the recyclability of it but not the content. Conversely, if a product is made with recycled material, it's not necessarily recyclable (think of single-use products like napkins).

ADDITIONAL RESOURCES

Art of Recycle (https://artofrecycle.org/our_neighbors.html). Art of Recycle has put together an amazing list of scrap stores across the world. You can find a place for creative reuse and items for projects that have been rescued from disposal! There's a long list of locations, but if you don't see your city, then you can reach out to them and learn how to help start one.

Earth 911 (https://earth911.com). This site has endless blog posts answering recycling questions and a very handy search function, where you can enter a material and your zip code to learn how to recycle an item. To keep recycling info at your fingertips and impress all your friends in casual conversation, you can download their app, iRecycle, for the same great search function.

Green America (https://greenamerica.org). Learn how to reduce, reuse, and recycle and about tons of other sustainable habits for your daily life. Green America helps individuals learn how to green their lives and connects us to solutions that protect people and the planet. You can learn more ways to infuse your values into your daily decisions through their resources and take action through campaigns.

How2Recycle (www.how2recycle.info) and Recycle across America (http://recycleacrossamerica.org). These two resources supply labels to boost our recycling system. You can advocate that companies use the How2Recycle labels on their products to help consumers sort better, and you can urge your mayor's office to implement standardized recycling labels for the bins with Recycle across America.

Institute for Local Self-Reliance (http://ilsr.org). ILSR provides innovative strategies, working models and timely information to support environmentally sound and equitable community development. It works on issues such as growing community based composting and transforming waste into a resource through methods that are healthy for people and the environment.

I Want to Be Recycled (https://iwanttoberecycled.org). This Keep America Beautiful initiative offers a wide range of recycling education resources and great ways to engage kids (or just yourself) through activities and games.

myTurn (http://localtools.org). The place to discover how to launch and maintain a sharing program for your community. From small tools to large ones, you can start reducing waste and saving money by creating a lending library of useful items. You can even share this resource with your local government and urge them to help in starting and running the program.

Repair Cafés (https://repaircafe.org/en). Learn more about these community hubs for reuse and repair. You can find out how to start a location in your area through the extensive starter kit on their site.

Waste Dive (https://wastedive.com). Your source for daily waste and recycling news. They cover industry news and provide original analysis, with the goal to offer you a bird's-eye-view of the waste industry in 60 seconds. They keep anyone who is passionate about the system up to speed on changes in the related industries.

Waste Zero (http://wastezero.com/start-the-conversation). This organization partners with over 800 towns, cities, counties, and other entities to help them reduce waste and boost recycling. Waste Zero is striving for cutting trash in half across the United States, and you can help by starting a Pay As You Throw trash program in your community. Use their Start the Conversation toolkit above.

WORKS CITED

Achen, Paris. "Mandatory Recycling? There's Little Enforcement." *Burlington Free Press*, July 18, 2015. http://www.burlingtonfreepress.com/story/news/local/2015/07/17/mandatory-recycling-little-enforcement/30327889/.

Ackerman, Frank. *Why Do We Recycle? Markets, Values, and Public Policy*. Washington, DC: Island Press, 2013.

Advanced Disposal. "Recycle Right." http://www.advanceddisposal.com/for-mother-earth/recycling-tips-trivia/recycle-right.aspx.

Agency for Toxic Substances and Disease Registry. "Landfill Gas Primer—An Overview for Environmental Health Professionals." November 1, 2001. https://www.atsdr.cdc.gov/HAC/landfill/html/ch2.html.

Allan, Patrick. "How to Program Your Mind to Stop Buying Crap You Don't Need." *Lifehacker*. March 9, 2015. https://lifehacker.com/how-to-program-your-mind-to-stop-buying-crap-you-don-t-1690268064.

Aluminum Association. "Recycling." September 24, 2014. http://www.aluminum.org/industries/production/recycling.

———. "Study Finds Aluminum Cans the Sustainable Package of Choice." May 20, 2015. http://www.aluminum.org/news/study-finds-aluminum-cans-sustainable-package-choice.

American Disposal Services. "The Rundown on Plastic #6 (Styrofoam)." https://www.americandisposal.com/blog/the-rundown-on-plastic-6-styrofoam.

American Forest and Paper Association. "U.S. Paper Recovery Rate Reaches Record 67.2 Percent in 2016." May 9, 2017. http://afandpa.org/media/news/2017/05/09/u.s.-paper-recovery-rate-reaches-record-67.2-percent-in-2016.

American Iron and Steel Institute. "Steel Is the World's Most Recycled Material." *SteelWorks*. 2017. http://www.steel.org/sustainability/steel-recycling.aspx.

American Psychological Association. "Making Lifestyle Changes That Last." http://www.apa.org/helpcenter/lifestyle-changes.aspx.

Angelides, Philip, Sophie Glass, and Frank Locantore. "Green in All Grades." Green America White Paper. July 23, 2012. https://www.greenamerica.org/sites/default/files/inline-files/GreeninAllGrade_72312_FINAL_z.pdf.

Associated Press. "BP's Reckless Conduct Caused Deepwater Horizon Oil Spill, Judge Rules." *Guardian*, September 4, 2014. https://www.theguardian.com/environment/2014/sep/04/bp-reckless-conduct-oil-spill-judge-rules.

Association of Plastic Recyclers. "APR Announces Recycling Demand Champion Campaign." October 18, 2017. https://plasticsrecycling.org/news-and-media/735-october-18-2017-apr-recycling-demand-champion-release.

Bagchi, Amalendu. *Design of Landfills and Integrated Solid Waste Management*. New York: Wiley, 2004.

Baldé, C. P., V. Forti, V. Gray, R. Kuehr, and P. Stegmann. *The Global E-Waste Monitor 2017: Quantities, Flows, and Resources*, Bonn, Germany: United Nations University, International Telecommunication Union, and International Solid Waste Association, 2017.

Barboza, David. "China's 'Queen of Trash' Finds Riches in Waste Paper—Business—International Herald Tribune." *New York Times*, January 15, 2007. http://www.nytimes.com/2007/01/15/business/worldbusiness/15iht-trash.4211783.html.

Barringer, Edwin C. *The Story of Scrap*. Washington, DC: Institute of Scrap Iron and Steel, 1954.

Battery Solutions. "Battery Recycling Benefits." https://www.batterysolutions.com/recycling-information/recycling-benefits/.

Bellassen, Valentin, and Sebastiaan Luyssaert. "Carbon Sequestration: Managing Forests in Uncertain Times." *Nature News*, February 12, 2014. www.nature.com/news/carbon-sequestration-managing-forests-in-uncertain-times-1.14687.

Boboltz, Sara. "We Buy an Obscene Amount of Clothes. Here's What It's Doing to Second-hand Stores." *Huffington Post*, November 20, 2014, www.huffingtonpost.com/2014/11/20/fast-fashion-thrift-stores_n_5798612.html.

Bolderdijk, Jan Willem, and Linda Steg. "Promoting Sustainable Consumption: The Risks of Using Financial Incentives." http://www.verdus.nl/upload/documents/Bolderdijk%20%26%20Steg%20-%20REVISED.pdf.

Bottle Bill Resource Guide. "What Is a Bottle Bill?" http://www.bottlebill.org/about/whatis.htm#how.

Bowles, Samuel. "When Economic Incentives Backfire." *Harvard Business Review*, July 31, 2014. https://hbr.org/2009/03/when-economic-incentives-backfire.

Breslin, Mike. "Advanced Waste MRFs Tackle Diverse Challenges." *American Recycler News*, January 2016. http://americanrecycler.com/8568759/index.php/news/waste-news/1460-advanced-mixed-waste-mrfs-tackle-diverse-challenges.

Brinded, Lianna. "The 9 Richest Self-Made Female Billionaires in the World." *Business Insider*. March 10, 2017. http://www.businessinsider.com/hurun-global-self-made-women-billionaires-list-2017-3/#9-peggy-cherng-and-husband-andrew-cherng-net-worth-44-billion-cherng-and-her-husband-found-their-fortune-through-panda-express-in-the-us-which-is-now-one-of-the-worlds-largest-family-owned-restaurant-chains-1.

Brummet, Paul, et al. *Paper Task Force Recommendations for Purchasing and Using Environmentally Preferable Paper*. New York: Environmental Defense Fund, 1995. https://www3.epa.gov/warm/pdfs/EnvironmentalDefenseFund.pdf.

Bryant, Kelly. "8 Surprising Facts and Misconceptions about Recycling." *Mental Floss*. April 22, 2015. https://mentalfloss.com/article/63240/8-surprising-facts-and-misconceptions-about-recycling.

Bullard, Robert. "Houston Recycling Plan Will Hit Minorities Hardest." *TribTalk*. September 8, 2014. https://www.tribtalk.org/2014/09/08/houston-recycling-plan-will-hit-minorities-hardest/.

Bullard, Robert Doyle. *Dumping in Dixie: Race, Class, and Environmental Quality*. 3rd ed. Boulder, CO: Westview Press, 2000.

Bureau of International Recycling. "Ferrous Metals." http://www.bir.org/industry/ferrous-metals/.

Burgo, Joseph. "The Difference between Guilt and Shame." *Psychology Today*, May 30, 2013. https://www.psychologytoday.com/blog/shame/201305/the-difference-between-guilt-and-shame.

Burton, Neel. "The Psychology of Embarrassment, Shame, and Guilt." *Psychology Today*, August 26, 2014. https://www.psychologytoday.com/blog/hide-and-seek/201408/the-psychology-embarrassment-shame-and-guilt.

Bush, Jessica. "Taiwan Has Found a Brilliant Way to Get People to Recycle More." *Buzzworthy*, August 30, 2017. https://www.buzzworthy.com/taiwan-garbage-disposal/.

Carr, Robert. "Contamination Continues to Hurt Recycling Efforts." *Waste360*, January 26, 2016. http://www.waste360.com/source-separation/contamination-continues-hurt-recycling-efforts.

Carson, Rachel. *Silent Spring*. London: Penguin Books, in Association with Hamish Hamilton, 2015.

Carton Council. "About Carton Recycling." http://www.cartonopportunities.org/carton-recycling.

———. "Communities: Steps to Take." http://www.cartonopportunities.org/add-carton/communities-steps-take.

Casella, John. Interview with author. September 19, 2017.

Casella Waste Systems. "Landfills." 2017. www.casella.com/services/landfills.

Chandler, David L. "One Order of Steel; Hold the Greenhouse Gases." *MIT News*, May 8, 2013. http://news.mit.edu/2013/steel-without-greenhouse-gas-emissions-0508.

Chow, Emily. "Malaysia's Bauxite Exports Rise Despite Mining Ban." *Reuters*, July 5, 2017. https://www.reuters.com/article/us-malaysia-bauxite/malaysias-bauxite-exports-rise-despite-mining-ban-idUSKBN19Q32I.

Cialdini, Robert B. "Crafting Normative Messages to Protect the Environment." *American Psychological Society: Current Directions in Psychological Science*. 2003. http://www.pmair.net/doc/cialcraf.pdf.

City of Houston. "One Bin for All: Recycling Reimagined in Houston." https://www.houstontx.gov/onebinforall/.

City of Laurel, Maryland. "Recycling Competition." January 18, 2018. https://www.cityoflaurel.org/dpw/collections/recycling-program/recycling-competition.

Clean Water Action Council of Northeast Wisconsin. "Environmental Impacts of the Paper Industry." 2017. http://www.cleanwateractioncouncil.org/issues/resource-issues/paper-industry/.

Clear, James. "The Diderot Effect: Why We Want Things We Don't Need—and What to Do about It." *Huffington Post*, November 1, 2016. https://www.huffingtonpost.com/james-clear/the-diderot-effect-why-we_b_12756576.html.

ClimateWatch. "CAIT Emissions Data (Except PIK or UNFCCC Data Sets)." 2017. https://www.climatewatchdata.org/ghg-emissions.

Cline, Elizabeth. "Where Does Discarded Clothing Go?" *Atlantic*, July 18, 2014. www.theatlantic.com/business/archive/2014/07/where-does-discarded-clothing-go/374613/.

Column Five. "Infographic: Why Don't Americans Recycle?" *GOOD Magazine*, April 6, 2012. https://www.good.is/infographics/infographic-why-don-t-americans-recycle.

Complete Recycling. "Paper Recycling and Refining Process." https://www.completerecycling.com/resources/paper-recycling/process.

Complexity Labs. "System Boundary." October 17, 2016, http://complexitylabs.io/system-boundary/.

Confino, Jo. "We Buy a Staggering Amount of Clothing, and Most of It Ends Up in Landfills." *Huffington Post*, September 14, 2016. https://www.huffingtonpost.com/entry/transforming-the-fashion-industry_us_57ceee96e4b0a48094a58d39.

Conservatree. "Conservatree Staff." http://www.conservatree.org/about/Who.shtml.

Consumer Reports. "How to Recycle Old Electronics." April 22, 2017. https://www.consumerreports.org/recycling/how-to-recycle-electronics/.

Container Recycling Institute. "Bottle Bills Complement Curbside Recycling Programs." *Bottlebill.org*. 2016. http://www.bottlebill.org/about/benefits/curbside.htm.

Cookie, Joe, dir. *Recycle Here! Detroit*. 2014. https://vimeo.com/125065242.

Cosgrove, Ben. "'Throwaway Living': When Tossing Out Everything Was All the Rage." *Time*, May 15, 2014. http://time.com/3879873/throwaway-living-when-tossing-it-all-was-all-the-rage/.

CostOwl.com. "How Much Does a Recycling Pickup Service Cost?" http://www.costowl.com/home-improvement/home-services-recycling-pickup-cost.html.

Council for Textile Recycling. "The Facts about Textile Waste." 2017. www.weardonaterecycle.org/about/issue.html.

Davis, Lee. "DesignView—Garbage Design: Modesto Invented Curbside Recycling." *Modestoview*, May 3, 2017. https://www.modestoview.com/designview-curbside-recycling/.

Denison, Richard A., and John F. Ruston. "Recycling Is Not Garbage." *MIT Technology Review*. December 30, 2013. https://www.technologyreview.com/s/400100/recycling-is-not-garbage/.

DeSilver, Drew. "Perceptions and Realities of Recycling Vary Widely from Place to Place." *Pew Research Center*, October 7, 2016. http://www.pewresearch.org/fact-tank/2016/10/07/perceptions-and-realities-of-recycling-vary-widely-from-place-to-place/.

Diderot, Denis. "Regrets for My Old Dressing Gown; or, A Warning to Those Who Have More Taste than Fortune" (1769). In *Oeuvres Complètes*, vol. 4 (Paris: Garnier Fréres, 1875). https://www.marxists.org/reference/archive/diderot/1769/regrets.htm.

Dijkgraaf, Elbert, and Raymond Gradus. "An EU Recycling Target: What Does the Dutch Evidence Tell Us?" *Environmental and Resource Economics* 68, no. 3 (2016): 501–26. doi:10.1007/s10640-016-0027-1.

Dorn, Betsy, and Susan Bush. "In Our Opinion: How to Develop Resilient Markets at Home." *Resource Recycling News*. November 17, 2017. https://resource-recycling.com/recycling/2017/11/14/opinion-develop-resilient-markets-home/.

Douglas, Steve. "History and Design of the Recycle Logo." *Logo Factory*. September 11, 2015. http://www.thelogofactory.com/history-design-recycle-logo/.

Dubanowitz, Alexander J. "Design of a Materials Recovery Facility (MRF) for Processing the Recyclable Materials of New York City's Municipal Solid Waste." PhD diss., Columbia University, 2000. http://www.seas.columbia.edu/earth/dubanmrf.pdf.

Duggan, Joe. "Remembering the 1942 Nebraska Scrap Metal Drive." *Lincoln Journal Star*, March 18, 2007. http://journalstar.com/news/local/remembering-the-nebraska-scrap-metal-drive/article_44b311bb-ca27-556b-b4d4-716a0fd9b801.html.

Dunaway, Finis. *Seeing Green: The Use and Abuse of American Environmental Images*. Chicago: University of Chicago Press, 2015. http://press.uchicago.edu/books/excerpt/2015/Dunaway_Seeing_Green.html.

Earley, Katharine. "Could China's 'Green Fence' Prompt a Global Recycling Innovation?" *Guardian*, August 27, 2013. https://www.theguardian.com/sustainable-business/china-green-fence-global-recycling-innovation.

Earth911. "How to Recycle Glass." https://earth911.com/recycling-guide/how-to-recycle-glass/.

———. "Mixed Feelings on Mixed Waste, Still." November 8, 2016. https://earth911.com/business-policy/mixed-waste-mixed-feelings/.

EarthTalk. "Is Recycling Worth It?" *Scientific American*, November 5, 2015. https://www.scientificamerican.com/article/is-recycling-worth-it/.

Eco-Cycle. "Be Straw Free Campaign: Frequently Asked Questions." 2016. http://ecocycle.org/bestrawfree/faqs.

Editorial Staff. "US Steel Recycling Rate Hits 92%." *Recycling International*, November 29, 2012. https://www.recyclinginternational.com/recycling-news/6718/ferrous-metals/united-states/us-steel-recycling-rate-hits-92.

E Magazine. *Earthtalk: Expert Answers to Everyday Questions about the Environment: Selections from* E—The Environmental Magazine's *Nationally Syndicated Column*. New York: Plume, 2009.

Environmental Paper Network. "Paper Calculator." 2017. http://c.environmentalpaper.org/home.

Environmental Research and Education Foundation Newsletter 19, no. 2 (2015). https://erefdn.org/wp-content/uploads/2016/04/Winter-2015-EREF-Newsletter.pdf.

Etchart, Linda. "The Role of Indigenous Peoples in Combating Climate Change." *Palgrave Communications* 3, no. 17085 (2017). doi:10.1057/palcomms.2017.85.

European Container Glass Federation. "Glass Recycling Hits 73% in the EU." Press Release. September 2015. http://feve.org/wp-content/uploads/2016/04/Press-Release-EU.pdf.

Extended Producer Responsibility Alliance. "Belgium." http://www.expra.eu/countries/belgium/2.

————. "Extended Producer Responsibility at a Glance." http://www.expra.eu/uploads/downloads/EXPRA%20EPR%20Paper_March_2016.pdf.

Federal Trade Commission. "Green Guides for the Use of Environmental Marketing Claims." October 12, 2012. https://www.ftc.gov/sites/default/files/attachments/press-releases/ftc-issues-revised-green-guides/greenguides.pdf+.

Flynn, Meagan. "The Long Rise and Fast Fall of the Ambitious One-Bin Recycling Program." *Houston Press*, July 13, 2017. http://www.houstonpress.com/news/what-happened-to-ecohub-and-houstons-one-bin-for-all-recycling-plan-9601564.

Food and Agriculture Organization of the United Nations. *Global Forest Products Facts and Figures, 2016.* Rome: Food and Agriculture Organization of the United Nations, 2017. http://www.fao.org/3/17304EN/i7034en.pdf.

Francis, John. "Experience: I Didn't Speak for 17 Years." *Guardian*, November 25, 2016. https://www.theguardian.com/lifeandstyle/2016/nov/25/i-didnt-speak-for-17-years-experience-planetwalker.

Frandsen, Jon. "The Money in Recycling Has Vanished; What Do States, Cities Do Now?" *Pew Charitable Trusts.* March 29, 2016. http://www.pewtrusts.org/en/research-and-analysis/blogs/stateline/2016/03/29/the-money-in-recycling-has-vanished-what-do-states-cities-do-now.

Frechette, Alain, Katie Reytar, Sonia Saini, and Wayne Walker. "Toward a Global Baseline of Carbon Storage in Collective Lands." November 2016. http://rightsandresources.org/wp-content/uploads/2016/10/Toward-a-Global-Baseline-of-Carbon-Storage-in-Collective-Lands-November-2016-RRI-WHRC-WRI-report.pdf.

Fresh Kills Park Alliance. "The Park Plan." http://freshkillspark.org/the-park/the-park-plan.

Gandy, Matthew. *Recycling and the Politics of Urban Waste.* Abingdon: Routledge, 2017.

Gendell, Adam. "2015–16 Centralized Study on Availability of Recycling." *Sustainable Packaging Coalition.* 2016.https://sustainablepackaging.org/resources/spcs-centralized-availability-recycling-study/.

Gerlat, Allan. "Casella Waste Partners on Solar Project at Vermont Landfill." *Waste360.* May 6, 2014. http://www.waste360.com/landfill-gas-energy-lfgte/casella-waste-partners-solar-project-vermont-landfill.

Gershman, Brickner, and Bratton. "The Evolution of Mixed Waste Processing Facilities: 1970–Today." 2015. https://plastics.americanchemistry.com/Education-Resources/Publications/The-Evolution-of-Mixed-Waste-Processing-Facilities.pdf.

Geyer, Roland, Jenna R. Jambeck, and Kara Lavender Law. "Production, Use, and Fate of All Plastics Ever Made." *Science Advances* 3, no. 7 (July 19, 2017). doi:10.1126/sciadv.1700782.

Gibbs, Constance. "UN Sees Global Rise in E-Waste, but Very Little Is Recycled." *New York Daily News*, December 13, 2017. http://www.nydailynews.com/life-style/u-n-sees-global-rise-e-waste-properly-rec-article-1.3696437.

Glass Packaging Institute. "Recycling." 2017. http://www.gpi.org/recycling/glass-recycling-facts.

Global Aluminium Recycling Committee. "Global Aluminium Recycling: A Cornerstone of Sustainable Development." 2009. http://www.world-aluminium.org/media/filer_public/2013/01/15/fl0000181.pdf.

Goldenberg, Suzanne. "BP Oil Spill Blamed on Management and Communication Failures." *Guardian*, December 2, 2010. https://www.theguardian.com/business/2010/dec/02/bp-oil-spill-failures.

Goldman Environmental Prize. "Destiny Watford: 2016 Goldman Prize Recipient North America." http://www.goldmanprize.org/recipient/destiny-watford/.

Goldsberry, Clare. "New Poll Reveals That Many Americans Are Confused about Recycling." *PlasticsToday.* January 5, 2017. https://www.plasticstoday.com/recycling/new-poll-reveals-many-americans-are-confused-about-recycling/44320612647240.

Gonen, Ron. "Yes, Recycling Is Still Good Business—If This Happens." *GreenBiz*, July 30, 2015. https://www.greenbiz.com/article/yes-recycling-still-good-business-if-happens.

Government Advisory Associates. *Materials Recovery and Processing Yearbook and Directory.* November 2016. https://governmentaladvisory.com/ordering/.

Grabianowski, Ed. "How Recycling Works." *HowStuffWorks Science*. https://science. howstuffworks.com/environmental/green-science/recycling2.htm.

Grandmont Rosedale Development Corporation. "Rosedale Recycles Turned 24 This April." 2017. http://grandmontrosedale.com/rosedale-recycles-turned-24-april/.

Granger, Trey. "Truth about Glass Recycling." *Earth911*, June 22, 2009. https://earth911. com/earth-watch/truth-about-glass-recycling/.

———. "The Verdict Is In: Keep the Bottle Caps On." *Earth911*, July 1, 2010. https:// earth911.com/food/the-verdict-is-in-keep-the-bottle-caps-on/.

Green America. "Sweatshop-Free Clothing." 2017. www.greenamerica.org/green-living/ sweatshop-free-clothing.

———. "What Is Fair Trade/Fair Labor." 2017. www.greenamerica.org/end-child-labor-cocoa/dean-foods/what-fair-tradefair-labor.

Greene, Eleanor. "What Does It Mean to Vote with Your Dollar?" *Green America*, June 20, 2017. https://www.greenamerica.org/blog/what-does-it-mean-vote-your-dollar.

Green Spectrum Consulting and Resource Recycling. "Making Sense of the Mix: Analysis and Implications of the Changing Curbside Recycling Stream." February 2015. https:// plastics.americanchemistry.com/Education-Resources/Publications/Making-Sense-of-the-Mix.pdf.

Greentumble Editorial Team. "How Is Plastic Recycled: Step by Step." *Greentumble*. October 22, 2015. https://greentumble.com/how-is-plastic-recycled-step-by-step/.

Gregory, Paul R., and Robert C. Stuart. *The Global Economy and Its Economic Systems*. Mason OH: South-Western Cengage Learning, 2014.

Grigoryants, Olga. "Turning Garbage into Profit." *Pacific Standard*, September 2, 2015. https://psmag.com/environment/turning-garbage-into-profit.

Hammad, Becky. "Trash Planet: The Netherlands." *Earth911*, July 6, 2009. https://earth911. com/earth-watch/trash-planet-the-netherlands/.

Harlan, Jessica. "The List: 7 Truths about Glass Recycling." *Recyclebank*. March 17, 2017. https://livegreen.recyclebank.com/the-list-7-truths-about-glass-recycling.

Harvey Mudd College. "The Möbius Strip." https://www.math.hmc.edu/~gu/curves_and_surfaces/surfaces/moebius.html.

Head, Jonathan. "Bauxite in Malaysia: The Environmental Cost of Mining." *BBC News*. January 19, 2016. http://www.bbc.com/news/world-asia-35340528.

Healy, Shawn. "When Good Deeds Lead to Bad—Moral Self-Licensing." *Lawyers Concerned for Lawyers*. June 28, 2017. http://www.lclma.org/2016/06/28/when-good-deeds-lead-to-bad-deeds-moral-self-licensing/.

Heisman, Rebecca. "When a Tree Falls in a Forest." *Northern Woodlands*, January 20, 2016. https://northernwoodlands.org/knots_and_bolts/tree-falls-in-a-forest.

Heist, Kristin. "How Packaging Protects the Environment." *Harvard Business Review*, July 23, 2014. https://hbr.org/2012/06/how-packaging-protects-the-env.

Helbling, Thomas. "Externalities." *International Monetary Fund*, December 2010. http:// www.imf.org/external/pubs/ft/fandd/basics/index.htm.

Hertsgaard, Mark. "John Francis, a 'Planetwalker' Who Lived Car-Free and Silent for 17 Years, Chats with Grist." *Grist*, May 10, 2005. https://grist.org/article/hertsgaard-francis/.

HowMuchIsIt.org. "How Much Does Garbage Pickup Cost?" http://www.howmuchisit.org/ garbage-service-cost/.

iFixit.org. "It's Time for a Repair Jobs Revolution." https://ifixit.org/revolution.

Industry Council for Research on Packaging and the Environment. "Facts about Packaging." www.incpen.org/displayarticle.asp?a=2&c=2.

International Council of Forest and Paper Associations. "2017 ICFPA: Sustainability Progress Report." 2017. http://www.icfpa.org/uploads/Modules/Publications/2017-icfpa-sustainability-report.pdf.

Isbell, Forest, et al. "Biodiversity Increases the Resistance of Ecosystem Productivity to Climate Extremes." *Nature* 526, no. 7574 (2015): 574–77. doi:10.1038/nature15374.

Ivanova, Diana, Konstantin Stadler, Kjartan Steen-Olsen, Richard Wood, Gibran Vita, Arnold Tukker, and Edgar G. Hertwich. "Environmental Impact Assessment of Household

Consumption." *Journal of Industrial Ecology* 20, no. 3 (December 18, 2015). http://onlinelibrary.wiley.com/doi/abs/10.1111/jiec.12371.

J. Poyry and Skumatz Economic Research Associates. "Paper Recycling: Quality Is Key to Long-Term Success." March 2004.

Jambeck, Jenna R., Roland Geyer, Chris Wilcox, Theodore R. Siegler, Miriam Perryman, Anthony Andrady, Ramani Narayan, and Kara Lavender Law. "Plastic Waste Inputs from Land into the Ocean." *Science*, February 13, 2015. http://science.sciencemag.org/content/347/6223/768.full?ijkey=BXtBaPzbQgagE&keytype=ref&siteid=sci.

Johnson, Chrystal. "Recycling Label Seeks to Clear Consumer Confusion." *Earth911*, April 20, 2016. https://earth911.com/business-policy/recycling-label-how2recycle/.

Johnson, David. "The Top 10 Most Dangerous Jobs in America." *Time*, December 22, 2017. http://time.com/5074471/most-dangerous-jobs/.

Jones, Jeffrey M. "Americans' Identification as 'Environmentalists' Down to 42%." *Gallup*. April 22, 2016. http://news.gallup.com/poll/190916/americans-identification-environmentalists-down.aspx.

Jones, Penny, and Jerry Powell. "Gary Anderson Has Been Found!" *Resource Recycling*. May 1999. https://logoblink.com/wp-content/uploads/2008/03/recycling_symbol_garyanderson.pdf+.

Jørgensen, Finn Arne. "A Pocket History of Bottle Recycling." *Atlantic*, February 27, 2013. https://www.theatlantic.com/technology/archive/2013/02/a-pocket-history-of-bottle-recycling/273575/.

Kaufman, Alexander C. "The Trash Incinerator Industry Is Trying to Tank a Massive Renewable-Energy Effort." *Huffington Post*, June 27, 2017. https://www.huffingtonpost.com/entry/trash-incinerator-renewable-energy_us_594d7fede4b05c37bb767c15.

Kaur, Harpreet. "Low Wages, Unsafe Conditions and Harassment: Fashion Must Do More to Protect Female Workers." *Guardian*, March 8, 2016. www.theguardian.com/sustainable-business/2016/mar/08/fashion-industry-protect-women-unsafe-low-wages-harassment.

Kaye, Leon. "Recycling Jobs Now Even More Dirty and Dangerous." *Triple Pundit: People, Planet, Profit*, September 6, 2012. https://www.triplepundit.com/2012/09/recycling-jobs-dirty-dangerous/.

Keep America Beautiful. "Keep America Beautiful National Recycling Survey." November 2016. https://www.kab.org/sites/default/files/ARD_National_Recycling_Survey_Highlights_11.15.16.pdf.

Koehn, Nancy F. "From Calm Leadership, Lasting Change." *New York Times*, October 27, 2012. http://www.nytimes.com/2012/10/28/business/rachel-carsons-lessons-50-years-after-silent-spring.html.

Koplow, Douglas. "Federal Energy Subsidies and Recycling: A Case Study." *Resource Recycling*, November 1994. https://earthtrack.net/sites/default/files/Alum%20Subs%2C%20Res%20Recyc%20Article.pdf.

Koplow, Douglas, Kevin Dietly, and Terry Dinan. "Federal Disincentives: A Study of Federal Tax Subsidies and Other Programs Affecting Virgin Industries and Recycling." August 1994. https://nepis.epa.gov/.

Kouchaki, Maryam. "Vicarious Moral Licensing: The Influence of Others' Past Moral Actions on Moral Behavior." *Journal of Personality and Social Psychology* 101, no. 4 (2011): 702–15. doi:10.1037/a0024552.

Laskow, Sarah. "Single-Stream Recycling Is Easier for Consumers, but Is It Better?" *Atlantic*, September 18, 2014. https://www.theatlantic.com/technology/archive/2014/09/single-stream-recycling-is-easier-for-consumers-but-is-it-better/380368/.

———. "Who Will Pay America's $1.5 Billion Recycling Bill?" *Next City*, February 9, 2015. https://nextcity.org/features/view/cost-of-recycling-america-extended-producer-responsibility-cities.

LeBlanc, Rick. "Electronics Recycling and E-Waste." *Balance*, July 1, 2017. https://www.thebalance.com/e-waste-and-the-importance-of-electronics-recycling-2877783.

———. "Impacts of Operation Green Fence on the Global Recycling Industry." *Balance*, November 3, 2016. https://www.thebalance.com/operation-green-fence-impacts-2878038.

———. "What Is a Waste Transfer Station?" *Balance*, January 31, 2017. https://www. thebalance.com/what-is-a-waste-transfer-station-2877735.

Leif, Dan. "WM Leader Says Contamination Is 'a Slow Ship to Turn.'" *Resource Recycling News*, June 20, 2017. https://resource-recycling.com/recycling/2017/06/20/wm-leader-says-contamination-slow-ship-turn/.

Leonard, Annie. *The Story of Stuff: With Annie Leonard*. Berkeley, CA: Free Range Studios, 2007.

Lloyd, John, and John Mitchinson. *The Book of General Ignorance*. London: Faber and Faber, 2006.

Local Tools. "Find Your Local Tool Lending Library." http://localtools.org/find/.

Lodge, George C., and Jeffrey F. Rayport. "Knee-Deep and Rising: America's Recycling Crisis." *Harvard Business Review*, August 1, 2014. https://hbr.org/1991/09/knee-deep-and-rising-americas-recycling-crisis.

Lombardi, Eric. "The Secret to San Francisco's Zero Waste Success." *Waste360*, April 13, 2016.   http://www.waste360.com/waste-reduction/secret-san-francisco-s-zero-waste-success.

London, Canada. "Sort It Right." February 17, 2015. https://www.london.ca/residents/ Garbage-Recycling/Recycling/Pages/Sort-it-Right.aspx.

Loughran, Jack. "European Recycling Rates Based on 'Flawed' Methodology." *Materials Recycling World*. June 2, 2015. https://www.mrw.co.uk/news/european-recycling-rates-based-on-flawed-methodology/8684107.article?blocktitle=Latest-news---recycling-and-waste-management&contentID=2182.

Madhusoodanan, Jyoti. "When Companies Praise Good Behavior, They May Encourage the Exact Opposite." *Kellogg Insight*, October 10, 2016. https://insight.kellogg.northwestern. edu/article/when-companies-praise-good-behavior-they-may-encourage-the-exact-opposite.

Margolis, Jason. "China's 'Green Fence' Is Cleaning Up America's Dirty Recycling." *Public Radio International*, February 18, 2014. https://www.pri.org/stories/2014-02-18/chinas-green-fence-cleaning-americas-dirty-recycling.

Marketplace. "FTC Punishes Companies for 'Greenwashing.'" March 9, 2017. http://www. cbc.ca/marketplace/blog/ftc-punishes-companies-for-greenwashing.

Marks, Jerry, and Chris Bayliss. "Aluminum: Meeting the Challenges of Climate Change." *Journal of the Minerals, Metals, and Materials Society* 62, no. 8 (August 2010): 33–36. doi:10.1007/s11837-010-0122-7.

Mars, Carole, and Christopher Nafe. "Electronics Recycling Landscape: Report Summary." May 2016. https://www.sustainabilityconsortium.org/wp-content/themes/enfold-child/ assets/pdf/TSC_Electronics_Recycling_Landscape_Report_Summary.pdf.

Martin, Florian. "What Happened to Houston's 'One Bin for All' Program?" *Houston Public Media*, January 18, 2016. https://www.houstonpublicmedia.org/articles/news/2016/01/18/ 134410/what-happened-to-houstons-one-bin-for-all-program/.

Master Recycler. "Home." http://www.masterrecycler.org/.

———. "What Is a Master Recycler?" http://www.masterrecycler.org/what-we-do/.

Mayer, Jane. "A Whistle-Blower Accuses the Kochs of 'Poisoning' an Arkansas Town." *New Yorker*, September 9, 2016. https://www.newyorker.com/news/news-desk/a-whistle-blower-accuses-the-kochs-of-poisoning-an-arkansas-town.

Mazar, Nina, and Chen-Bo Zhong. "Do Green Products Make Us Better People?" *Psychological Science* 21, no. 4 (2010). http://journals.sagepub.com/doi/abs/10.1177/ 0956797610363538.

McDonald, J., A. P. Sloan, and C. Stevens. *My Years with General Motors*. New York: Doubleday, 1972.

McGrane, Sally. "An Effort to Bury a Throwaway Culture One Repair at a Time." *New York Times*, May 8, 2012. http://www.nytimes.com/2012/05/09/world/europe/amsterdam-tries-to-change-culture-with-repair-cafes.html.

Mele, Christopher. "At Repair Cafes, 'Beloved but Broken' Possessions Find New Life." *New York Times*, January 18, 2017. www.nytimes.com/2017/01/18/us/repair-cafe.html.

Merriam-Webster. "System." December 2017. www.merriam-webster.com/dictionary/system.

Merritt, Anna C., Daniel A. Effron, and Benoit Monin. "Moral Self-Licensing: When Being Good Frees Us to Be Bad." *Social and Personality Psychology Compass* 4, no. 5 (2010): 344–57. doi:10.1111/j.1751-9004.2010.00263.x.

Merritt, Dawn. "90 Years of Conservation Success: 1950s and 1960s." *Izaak Walton League of America.* 2017. http://www.iwla.org/publications/outdoor-america/article/outdoor-america-2012-issue-3/90-years-of-conservation-success-1950s-and-1960s.

Michigan Department of Environmental Quality. "Why Does Recycling Cost Money?" April 2016. https://www.michigan.gov/documents/deq/deq-oea-owmrp-WhyRecyclingCosts_Web_523826_7.pdf.

MidAtlantic Solid Waste Consultants. "Litter in America: Results from the Nation's Largest Litter Study." *Keep America Beautiful.* January 2010. https://www.kab.org/sites/default/files/News%26Info_Research_LitterinAmerica_FactSheet_LitteringBehavior.pdf.

Miller, Chaz. "States Lead the Way: Pioneering Recycling Efforts in the US." *Waste Management World.* January 9, 2006. https://waste-management-world.com/a/states-lead-the-way-pioneering-recycling-efforts-in-the-us.

Miller, Gillian Zaharias, and Lauren Olson. "More Than You Bargained For: BPS and BPA in Receipts." January 17, 2018. https://www.ecocenter.org/sites/default/files/healthy-stuff/Ecology%20Center%20Receipt%20Study%202018%20Report%20final_0.pdf.

Minter, Adam. *Junkyard Planet: Travels in the Billion-Dollar Trash Trade.* New York: Bloomsbury, 2015.

Mitchell, Megan. "Tool-Sharing Service Comes to Kenton County." *WLWT,* July 18, 2017. http://www.wlwt.com/article/tool-sharing-service-comes-to-kenton-county/10245750.

Mohan, Anne Marie. "A Simple Recycling 'Fix' with Big Potential for Packaging." *Packaging World.* June 13, 2016. www.packworld.com/article/sustainability/recycling/simple-recycling-fix-big-potential-packaging.

Moran, Craig. "Solving Malaysia's Bauxite Mining Woes." *World Policy Institute.* March 3, 2016. http://www.worldpolicy.org/blog/2016/03/03/solving-malaysia%E2%80%99s-bauxite-mining-woes.

Morawski, Clarissa. "Understanding Economic and Environmental Impacts of Single-Stream Collection Systems." December 2009. http://www.container-recycling.org/assets/pdfs/reports/2009-SingleStream.pdf.

Mosbergen, Dominique. "The Oceans Are Drowning in Plastic—and No One's Paying Attention." *Huffington Post,* May 12, 2017. https://www.huffingtonpost.com/entry/plastic-waste-oceans_us_58fed37be4b0c46f0781d426.

Moulds, Josephine. "Child Labour in the Fashion Supply Chain." *Guardian.* https://labs.theguardian.com/unicef-child-labour/.

Mousseau, Timothy A., Gennadi Milinevsky, Jane Kenney-Hunt, and Anders Pape Miller. "Highly Reduced Mass Loss Rates and Increased Litter Layer in Radioactively Contaminated Areas." *Global Change Ecology* 175 (March 4, 2014): 429–37. https://link.springer.com/epdf/10.1007/s00442-014-2908-8?shared_access_token=3EGOiSXvyR0VTIVB2iw6H_e4RwlQNchNByi7wbcMAY7LZj_Pziie9KZM4nwUCjJEmIDcaZbC49c978dqVLXdW884oaN1aT1e-4PR_2ct8PC5dEQWuwfPWwHH6JZeskceuWvYNzkcVFoAbiC1jZkSNjSZkSrhRag_ALONBC9pYXo.

Naimi, Matthew. "Recycling in Detroit: You Made It Happen." *Model D,* April 23, 2013. http://www.modeldmedia.com/features/beegreen413.aspx.

National Recycling Coalition. "Fact Sheets." https://nrcrecycles.org/glossary-3/.

Nestor, Michele. "Can We Rescue Glass Recycling?" *Waste360,* February 4, 2016. http://www.waste360.com/glass/can-we-rescue-glass-recycling.

New York City Parks. "Freshkills Park." https://www.nycgovparks.org/park-features/freshkills-park.

Nine Dragons Paper. "Environmental, Social and Governance." http://www.ndpaper.com/eng/ir/esg.htm.

North Carolina Division of Pollution Prevention and Environmental Assistance. "Mixed Waste Processing." January 1997. http://infohouse.p2ric.org/ref/01/00028.htm.

Northeast Recycling Council. "Best Operational Practices for Recycling Drop-off Operations." Fall 2014. https://nerc.org/documents/recycling/BOP_Illinios%20Drop%20Off%20Man_FIN%2011.28.16.pdf.

Northeast Recycling Council. "Disposal Bans and Mandatory Recycling in the United States." May 1, 2017. https://nerc.org/documents/disposal_bans_mandatory_recycling_united_states.pdf.

Ocean Conservancy. "Plastics in the Ocean." 2017. https://oceanconservancy.org/trash-free-seas/plastics-in-the-ocean/.

O'Dell, Bruce. Interview with author. November 13, 2017.

O'Neill, William L. *A Democracy at War: America's Fight at Home and Abroad in World War II*. Cambridge, MA: Harvard University Press, 1997.

Oregon.gov. "Materials Management Home." http://www.oregon.gov/deq/mm/pages/default.aspx.

Organisation for Economic Co-operation and Development. "Extended Producer Responsibility: Guidance for Efficient Waste Management." September 2016. https://www.oecd.org/environment/waste/Extended-producer-responsibility-Policy-Highlights-2016-web.pdf.

Pacific Northwest Pollution Prevention Resource Center. "Should We Recycle Thermal Receipts That Contain BPA?" http://pprc.org/index.php/2015/pprc/should-we-recycle-thermal-receipts-that-contain-bpa/.

Papineschi, Joe, Peter Jones, and Rob Gillies. "Recycling—Who Really Leads the World?" *Eunomia*. March 2017. http://www.eunomia.co.uk/reports-tools/recycling-who-really-leads-the-world/.

Park, Tammy. "How Are Aluminum Cans Recycled?" *Environmental and Recycling Industry Center*. January 28, 2017. http://sprecycling.com/how-are-aluminum-cans-recycled/.

Parker, Diana. "Indigenous Communities Demand Forest Rights, Blame Land Grabs for Failure to Curb Deforestation." *Conservation News*. March 24, 2014. https://news.mongabay.com/2014/03/indigenous-communities-demand-forest-rights-blame-land-grabs-for-failure-to-curb-deforestation/.

Patterson, Sam H. *Bauxite Reserves and Potential Aluminum Resources of the World*. Geological Survey Bulletin 1228. Washington, DC: United States Government Printing Office, 1967. https://pubs.er.usgs.gov/publication/b1228.

Peacock, Danielle. "ReLoop: What Is Mixed Waste Processing or 'All in One/Dirty MRF' Recycling?" *GreenBlue*, http://greenblue.org/reloop-what-is-mixed-waste-processing-or-all-in-onedirty-mrf-recycling/.

Pellow, David N., Adam Weinberg, and Allan Schnaiberg. "The Environmental Justice Movement: Equitable Allocation of the Costs and Benefits of Environmental Management Outcomes." June 17, 2004. https://www.ipr.northwestern.edu/publications/papers/urban-policy-and-community-development/docs/schnaiberg/environmental-justice.pdf.

Pew Research Center. "Global Views on Morality." April 15, 2014. http://www.pewglobal.org/2014/04/15/global-morality/.

Pierre-Louis, Kendra. "These Billion-Dollar Natural Disasters Set a U.S. Record in 2017." *New York Times*, January 8, 2018. https://www.nytimes.com/2018/01/08/climate/2017-weather-disasters.html?smid=tw-nytimes&smtyp=cur.

Planning and Technical Support Division, California Air Resources Board, and California Environmental Protection Agency. "Method for Estimating Greenhouse Gas Emission Reductions from Recycling." November 14, 2011. https://www.arb.ca.gov/cc/protocols/localgov/pubs/recycling_method.pdf.

Plastic Oceans Foundation. "Facts about Plastic." 2017. https://www.plasticoceans.org/the-facts/.

Plastics for Change. "Why Are Plastic Recycling Rates So Low?" July 3, 2017. http://www.plasticsforchange.org/blog/category/why-are-plastic-recycling-rate-so-low.

Plastic Packaging Facts. "Resins and Types of Packaging." https://www.plasticpackagingfacts.org/plastic-packaging/resins-types-of-packaging/.

Product Stewardship Institute. "U.S. State EPR Laws." December 2017. http://www. productstewardship.us/?State_EPR_Laws_Map.

Profita, Cassandra, and Jes Burns. "Recycling Chaos in U.S. as China Bans 'Foreign Waste.'" *NPR.* December 9, 2017. https://www.npr.org/2017/12/09/568797388/recycling-chaos-in-u-s-as-china-bans-foreign-waste.

Pyper, Julia. "Does Burning Garbage to Produce Electricity Make Sense?" *Scientific American,* August 26, 2011. https://www.scientificamerican.com/article/does-burning-garbage-to-produce-energy-make-sense/.

Raghab, Safaa M., Ahmed M. Abd El Meguid, and Hala A. Hegazi. "Treatment of Leachate from Municipal Solid Waste Landfill." *HBRC Journal* 9, no. 2 (2013): 187–92. doi:10.1016/j.hbrcj.2013.05.007.

Raz, Nicole. "Republic Services: Nobody Else Can Handle Las Vegas' Trash." *Las Vegas Review-Journal,* March 2, 2017. https://www.reviewjournal.com/business/republic-services-nobody-else-can-handle-las-vegas-trash/.

Re3.org. *How Does a Material Recovery Facility (MRF) Work?* May 11, 2011. https://www. youtube.com/watch?v=7CFE5tD1CCI.

Recology. "Our Mission and Vision." https://www.recology.com/about-us/mission-vision/.

Recyclebank. "Because You Asked: Can Plastic Patio Furniture Be Recycled?" December 19, 2017. https://livegreen.recyclebank.com/because-you-asked-can-plastic-patio-furniture-be-recycled.

———. "Because You Asked: If I Can't Put Aseptic Cartons in My Recycling Bin, Do I Have to Trash Them?" January 5, 2016. https://livegreen.recyclebank.com/because-you-asked-if-i-can-t-put-aseptic-cartons-in-my-recycling-bin-do-i-have-to-trash-them.

RecycleMania. "History of RecycleMania." 2017. https://recyclemania.org/about-recyclemania/history/.

Richmond, Barry. "Systems Thinking/System Dynamics: Let's Just Get on with It." *System Dynamics Review* 10, nos. 2–3 (1994): 135–57. doi:10.1002/sdr.4260100204.

RISI. "Cheung Yan, Chairlady of Nine Dragons Paper Selected as This Year's Asia CEO of the Year." March 15, 2017. https://www.risiinfo.com/press-release/cheung-yan-chairlady-nine-dragons-paper-selected-years-asia-ceo-year/.

Robinson, Susan. "State of MRFs in 2016: Current Trends and Conditions." Lecture, Waste Management, October 16, 2017. http://www.recyclingstar.org/wp-content/uploads/2016/11/Robinson-MRF-panel-2016-Final.pdf.

Rochman, Chelsea M., Akbar Tahir, Susan L. Williams, Dolores V. Baxa, Rosalyn Lam, Jeffrey T. Miller, Foo-Ching Teh, Shinta Werorilangi, and Swee J. Teh. "Anthropogenic Debris in Seafood: Plastic Debris and Fibers from Textiles in Fish and Bivalves Sold for Human Consumption." *Scientific Reports* 5, no. 1 (2015). doi:10.1038/srep14340.

Rockoff, Hugh. *Keep on Scrapping: The Salvage Drives of World War II.* Cambridge, MA: National Bureau of Economic Research, 2007. http://www.nber.org/papers/w13418.pdf.

Rosenbloom, Cara. "Savvier Shoppers See through Misleading Food Labels. Here's How." *Washington Post,* January 2, 2018. https://www.washingtonpost.com/lifestyle/wellness/shoppers-are-getting-savvier-to-these-misleading-food-labels/2017/12/12/de40c7dc-d555-11e7-a986-d0a9770d9a3e_story.html?utm_term=.21d289d68229.

Rosengren, Cole. "Disruptor of the Year: China's Import Policies." *Waste Dive,* December 4, 2017. https://www.wastedive.com/news/disruptor-of-the-year-chinas-import-policies/510675/.

———. "Hauler Heroes: Hurricane Responders." *Waste Dive,* December 4, 2017. https://www.wastedive.com/news/hauler-heroes-hurricane-responders/510671/.

———. "How Taiwan Became a World Leader in Recycling." *Waste Dive,* May 19, 2016. https://www.wastedive.com/news/how-taiwan-became-a-world-leader-in-recycling/419463/.

———. "Pennsylvania County Bucks the Single-Stream Trend." *Waste Dive,* December 12, 2016. https://www.wastedive.com/news/pennsylvania-county-bucks-the-single-stream-trend/432109/.

————. "Survey: 5.1M Residents Have Access to Curbside Organics Collection." *Waste Dive*, December 15, 2017. https://www.wastedive.com/news/survey-51m-residents-have-access-to-curbside-organics-collection/513109/.

Rosenthal, Elisabeth. "By 'Bagging It,' Ireland Rids Itself of a Plastic Nuisance." *New York Times*, January 31, 2008. http://www.nytimes.com/2008/01/31/world/europe/31iht-bags.4.9650382.html.

RRS. "MRF Material Flow Study: Final Report." July 2015. https://www.plasticsrecycling.org/images/pdf/resources/MRF-material-flow-study-FINAL.pdf.

Ryan's Recycling. "About Ryan's Recycling." September 21, 2017. http://ryansrecycling.com/about/.

Rysavy, Tracy Fernandez. "Americans Are Really Bad at Recycling. But Only Because We're Not Trying Very Hard." *Green America*. https://www.greenamerica.org/rethinking-recycling/americans-are-really-bad-recycling-only-because-were-not-trying-very-hard.

————. "Reduce and Reuse: How One Couple Shrank Their Trash Output to One Can a Year." *Green American Magazine* (June 2016): 17.

Schiller, Ben. "Once Robots Are Sorting the Recycling, the Economics All Change." *Fast Company*, November 9, 2015. https://www.fastcompany.com/3052355/once-robots-are-sorting-the-recycling-the-economics-all-change.

Schrieberg, David. "Landmark French Lawsuit Attacks Epson, HP, Canon and Brother for 'Planned Obsolescence.'" *Forbes*, September 26, 2017. https://www.forbes.com/sites/davidschrieberg1/2017/09/26/landmark-french-lawsuit-attacks-epson-hp-canon-and-brother-for-planned-obsolescence/#52490c01b36a.

Schumaker, Erin. "The Psychology behind Why People Don't Recycle." *Huffington Post*, August 3, 2016. https://www.huffingtonpost.com/entry/psychology-of-why-people-dont-recycle_us_57697a7be4b087b70be605b3.

Scruggs, Melanie. "Recycling Will Stay—Zero Waste Should Be Next." *Texas Campaign for the Environment*. March 23, 2016. https://www.texasenvironment.org/recycling-will-stay-zero-waste-should-be-next/.

Seattle Public Utilities. "2016 Recycling Rate Report." July 1, 2016. http://www.seattle.gov/util/cs/groups/public/@spu/@garbage/documents/webcontent/1_064754.pdf.

Seldman, Neil. "Does the Citizens Recycling Movement Face a Hostile Takeover?" *Institute for Local Self-Reliance*, July 2013. http://ilsr.org/wp-content/uploads/downloads/2013/07/US-Citizens-Recycling-Movement-07.12.2013.pdf.

————. "Is the $236 Billion Recycling Sector Threatened by a Hostile Takeover?" *Institute for Local Self-Reliance*. July 8, 2013. https://ilsr.org/epr-recycling-sector-takeover/.

Simard, Suzanne. "How Trees Talk to Each Other." TED Talk, June 1, 2016. https://www.ted.com/talks/suzanne_simard_how_trees_talk_to_each_other/transcript?language=en.

Simbrunner, Philipp, and Bodo B. Schlegelmilch. "Influencing Factors on Moral Licensing Effect: A Meta-Analytic Approach: An Abstract." In *Back to the Future: Using Marketing Basics to Provide Customer*, edited by Nina Krey and Patricia Ross (p. 19). Value Developments in Marketing Science: Proceedings of the Academy of Marketing Science (Cham, Switzerland: Springer, 2017). doi:10.1007/978-3-319-66023-3_10.

Sinai, Mina. "How to Read How2Recycle Labels." *RecycleNation*, September 12, 2017. https://recyclenation.com/2017/09/how-to-read-how2recycle-labels/.

Smith, Kristin. "Similar but Different." *Recycling Today*, April 6, 2015. http://www.recyclingtoday.com/article/rt0415-mixed-waste-processing/.

Smith, Tovia. "How Green Are Reusable Bags?" *NPR*, August 7, 2009. http://www.npr.org/templates/story/story.php?storyId=111672574.

Society for Personality and Social Psychology. "How We Form Habits, Change Existing Ones." *Science Daily*, August 8, 2014. www.sciencedaily.com/releases/2014/08/140808111931.htm.

Somerville, Madeleine. "The Real Reason No One's Recycling Styrofoam—and How One Company Is Changing That." *Earth911*, July 27, 2017. https://earth911.com/uncategorized/recycling-styrofoam/.

Stanford University. "Frequently Asked Questions: Benefits of Recycling." https://lbrc. stanford.edu/pssistanford-recycling/frequently-asked-questions/frequently-asked-questions-benefits-recycling.

Stanislaus, Mathy. "The Economic Power of Recycling: Sustainable Materials Management." *EPA Blog.* November 15, 2016. https://blog.epa.gov/blog/2016/11/the-economic-power-of-recycling-sustainable-materials-management/.

Stockton Recycles. "What Do Those Recycling Symbols Mean, Anyway?" November 30, 2017. http://www.stocktonrecycles.com/recycling-symbols/.

Stoknes, Per Espen. "Wondering How to Get People to Go Green? Tell Them That's What Their Neighbors Are Doing." *Salon*, May 10, 2015. www.salon.com/2015/05/10/wondering_how_to_get_people_to_go_green_tell_them_thats_what_their_neighbors_are_doing/.

Stradling, Richard. "Recycle Those Plastic Bottles—It Means More Jobs for NC." *News and Observer*, April 7, 2017. http://www.newsobserver.com/news/business/article143301594. html.

Strange, Kit. "Overview of Waste Management Options: Their Efficacy and Acceptability." *Royal Society of Chemistry.* 2002.

Strutner, Suzy. "Here's What Goodwill Actually Does with Your Donated Clothes." *Huffington Post*, September 28, 2016. https://www.huffingtonpost.com/entry/what-does-goodwill-do-with-your-clothes_us_57e06b96e4b0071a6e092352.

Szaky, Tom. "The Many Challenges of Plastic Recycling." *Sustainable Brands.* April 22, 2015. http://www.sustainablebrands.com/news_and_views/waste_not/tom_szaky/many_challenges_plastic_recycling.

Tankersley, Shelby. "Meet the People Who Made Recycling Happen in Detroit." *Hour Detroit*, October 3, 2017. http://www.hourdetroit.com/Give-Detroit/Meet-the-People-Who-Made-Recycling-Happen-in-Detroit/.

Target. "How2Recycle Labels Coming to Target." November 21, 2013. https://corporate. target.com/article/2013/11/how2recycle-labels-coming-to-target.

Taylor, Steve. "Self-Sufficiency: An Essential Aspect of Well-Being." *Psychology Today*, March 25, 2013. https://www.psychologytoday.com/blog/out-the-darkness/201303/self-sufficiency-essential-aspect-well-being.

Tepperman, Jean. "Recycling's Dirty Little Secret." *East Bay Express*, April 25, 2012. https://www.eastbayexpress.com/oakland/recyclings-dirty-little-secret/Content?oid=3184736.

TerraCycle. "Candy and Snack Wrappers Zero Waste Box." https://www.terracycle.com/en-US/zero_waste_boxes/candy-and-snack-wrappers.

Tetra Pak. "Tetra Pak in Brief—A Company Overview." https://tetrapak.com/us/about/tetra-pak-in-brief.

Themelis, Nickolas J., and Jeffrey Morris. "Does Burning Garbage for Electricity Make Sense?" *Wall Street Journal*, November 15, 2015. https://www.wsj.com/articles/does-burning-garbage-make-sense-1447643515.

Theuws, Martje, and Pauline Overeem. *Flawed Fabrics: The Abuse of Girls and Women Workers in the South Indian Textile Industry.* Amsterdam: Centre for Research on Multi-national Corporations, India Committee of the Netherlands, 2014. www.indianet.nl/pdf/FlawedFabrics.pdf.

Thøgersen, John. "Psychology: Inducing Green Behaviour." *Nature Climate Change* 3 (2013): 100–101.

Thøgersen, John, and Tom Crompton. "Simple and Painless? The Limitations of Spillover in Environmental Campaigning." *Journal of Consumer Policy* 32, no. 2 (2009): 141–63.

Thompson, James. "Landfill Waste Costs Continued to Rise in 2016." *Solid Waste Environmental Excellence Protocol*, January 12, 2017. http://nrra.net/sweep/cost-to-landfill-waste-continues-to-rise-through-2016/.

Tiefenbeck, Verena, Thorsen Staake, Kurt Roth, and Olga Sachs. "For Better or for Worse? Empirical Evidence of Moral Licensing in a Behavioral Energy Conservation Campaign." *Energy Policy* 57 (June 2013): 160–71.

Trager, Rebecca. "US Bans Microbeads from Personal Care Products." *Chemistry World*, January 5, 2016. https://www.chemistryworld.com/news/us-bans-microbeads-from-personal-care-products/9309.article.

Trudel, Remi. "The Behavioral Economics of Recycling." *Harvard Business Review*, October 7, 2016. https://hbr.org/2016/10/the-behavioral-economics-of-recycling.

U.S. Energy Information Administration. "International Energy Outlook 2017." September 14, 2017. https://www.eia.gov/outlooks/ieo/pdf/0484(2017).pdf.

U.S. Environmental Protection Agency. "Advancing Sustainable Materials Management: Facts and Figures." August 10, 2017. https://www.epa.gov/smm/advancing-sustainable-materials-management-facts-and-figures.

———. "Basic Information." March 29, 2016. https://archive.epa.gov/epawaste/nonhaz/municipal/web/html/basic.html.

———. "Deepwater Horizon: BP Gulf of Mexico Oil Spill." April 19, 2017. https://www.epa.gov/enforcement/deepwater-horizon-bp-gulf-mexico-oil-spill.

———. "History of the Resource Conservation and Recovery Act (RCRA)." August 23, 2017. https://www.epa.gov/rcra/history-resource-conservation-and-recovery-act-rcra.

———. *Inventory of Greenhouse Gas Emissions and Sinks: 1990–2015*. 2015. https://www.epa.gov/sites/production/files/2017-02/documents/2017_complete_report.pdf.

———. "Municipal Solid Waste." March 29, 2016. https://archive.epa.gov/epawaste/nonhaz/municipal/web/html/.

———. "Municipal Solid Waste Generation, Recycling, and Disposal in the United States: Facts and Figures for 2012." February 2014. www.epa.gov/sites/production/files/2015-09/documents/2012_msw_fs.pdf.

———. "Overview of Greenhouse Gases." April 14, 2017. https://www.epa.gov/ghgemissions/overview-greenhouse-gases.

———. "Procurement and Use of Recycled Products: A Primer for Government Officials." 1993.

———. "Recycling and Waste Electrical and Electronic Equipment Management in Taiwan: A Case Study." December 2012. https://www.epa.gov/sites/production/files/2014-08/documents/taiwan_iemn_case_study_12.7_final.pdf.

———. "Sources of Greenhouse Gas Emissions." April 14, 2017. https://www.epa.gov/ghgemissions/sources-greenhouse-gas-emissions#industry.

———. "Summary of the Resource Conservation and Recovery Act." August 24, 2017. https://www.epa.gov/laws-regulations/summary-resource-conservation-and-recovery-act.

———. "Sustainable Materials Management: Non-Hazardous Materials and Waste Management Hierarchy." August 10, 2017. https://www.epa.gov/smm/sustainable-materials-management-non-hazardous-materials-and-waste-management-hierarchy.

———. "Zero Waste Case Study: San Francisco." June 12, 2017. https://www.epa.gov/transforming-waste-tool/zero-waste-case-study-san-francisco.

U.S. Environmental Protection Agency, Office of Air and Radiation, and Office of Air Quality Planning and Standards. "Municipal Solid Waste Landfills: Economic Impact Analysis for the Proposed New Subpart to the New Source Performance Standards." June 2014. https://www3.epa.gov/ttnecas1/regdata/EIAs/LandfillsNSPSProposalEIA.pdf.

U.S. Environmental Protection Agency, Office of Resource Conservation and Recovery. "Historic Tipping Fees and Commodity Values." February 2015. https://www.epa.gov/sites/production/files/2015-12/documents/historic_tipping_fees_and_commodity_values_02062015_508.pdf.

Vaidyanathan, Gayathri. "How Bad of a Greenhouse Gas Is Methane?" *Scientific American*, December 22, 2015. https://www.scientificamerican.com/article/how-bad-of-a-greenhouse-gas-is-methane/.

VandenBerg, Nancy, Susan Kinsella, and Carla S. Lallatin. "Source Reduction Opportunities." In *Resourceful Purchasing: A Hands-On Buyers' Manual with How-to-Do-It Guidance for Source Reduction and Recycled Products*. Oakland, CA: Alameda County Source Reduction and Recycling Board, 1996.

Van Ewijk, Stijn, Julia A. Stegemann, and Paul Ekins. "Global Life Cycle Paper Flows, Recycling Metrics, and Material Efficiency." *Journal of Industrial Ecology* (June 6, 2017).

Vedantam, Shankar. "Why Recycling Options Lead People to Waste More." *NPR*, June 2, 2017. https://www.npr.org/2017/06/02/531173499/why-recycling-options-lead-people-to-waste-more.

Vermont Department of Environmental Conservation. "Vermont's Universal Recycling Law: Status Report." December 2016. http://dec.vermont.gov/sites/dec/files/wmp/SolidWaste/Documents/Universal.Recycling.Status.Report.Dec_.2016.pdf.

Vossler, Bill. "When Plowshares Built Swords: Scrap Drives During World War II—Farm Life." *Farm Collector*, December 2015. https://www.farmcollector.com/farm-life/scrap-drives-zmbz15deczhur.

"Voyage of the Mobro 4000." *New York Times: Retro Report*, https://www.nytimes.com/video/booming/100000002206073/voyage-of-the-mobro-4000.html.

Wagner, Vivian. "Littering and Following the Crowd." *Atlantic*, August 1, 2014. https://www.theatlantic.com/health/archive/2014/08/littering-and-following-the-crowd/374913/.

Walsh, Edward J., D. Clayton. Smith, and Rex Warland. *Don't Burn It Here: Grassroots Challenges to Trash Incinerators*. University Park: Pennsylvania State University Press, 1997.

Weatherstone, Alan Watson. "Decomposition and Decay." *Trees for Life*. 2017. http://treesforlife.org.uk/forest/forest-ecology/decomposition-and-decay/.

Weimar, Jake. "The Cost of Recycling." *Economics 411: Monetary and Financial Theory*, Winter 2015. https://411w15.econ.lsa.umich.edu/?p=4459.

Weinberg, Adam S., David N. Pellow, and Allan Schnaiberg. *Urban Recycling and the Search for Sustainable Community Development*. Princeton, NJ: Princeton University Press, 2000.

Weinschenk, Susan. "Shopping, Dopamine, and Anticipation." *Psychology Today*, October 22, 2015. https://www.psychologytoday.com/blog/brain-wise/201510/shopping-dopamine-and-anticipation.

Whitman, Sylvia. *V Is for Victory: The American Home Front during World War II*. Minneapolis: Lerner, 1993.

Willers, W. B. *Learning to Listen to the Land*. Washington, DC: Island Press, 1991.

Willis, Rachael. "Malaysia's Bauxite Backlash." *Huffington Post*, January 15, 2016. https://www.huffingtonpost.com/rachael-willis-/malaysias-bauxite-backlas_b_8987234.html.

Winter, Debra. "The Violent Afterlife of a Recycled Plastic Bottle." *Atlantic*, December 4, 2015. https://www.theatlantic.com/technology/archive/2015/12/what-actually-happens-to-a-recycled-plastic-bottle/418326/.

Woodbridge Township, New Jersey. "'A Conversation with Greenable Woodbridge': Waste Management, Recycling, and Green Purchasing." http://www.twp.woodbridge.nj.us/DocumentCenter/View/3041.

World Coal Association. "How Is Steel Produced?" 2017. https://www.worldcoal.org/coal/uses-coal/how-steel-produced.

World Wide Fund for Nature. "Pulp and Paper." 2017. http://wwf.panda.org/about_our_earth/deforestation/forest_sector_transformation/pulp_and_paper/.

Worthy, Kenneth. "The Self-Deceptions of Recycling." *Psychology Today*, March 31, 2015. https://www.psychologytoday.com/blog/the-green-mind/201503/the-self-deceptions-recycling.

Wyatt, Edward. "F.T.C. Issues Guidelines for 'Eco-Friendly' Labels." *New York Times*, October 1, 2012. http://www.nytimes.com/2012/10/02/business/energy-environment/ftc-issues-guidelines-for-eco-friendly-labels.html.

Yardley, Jim. "Report on Deadly Factory Collapse in Bangladesh Finds Widespread Blame." *New York Times*, May 22, 2013. www.nytimes.com/2013/05/23/world/asia/report-on-bangladesh-building-collapse-finds-widespread-blame.html.

Yasar, Duygu, Haluk Damgacioglu, Mehrad Bastani, and Nurcin Celik. "Assessment of the Impact of Single Stream Recycling on Paper Contamination in Recovery Facilities and Paper Mills." Report no. 10916. February 28, 2017. http://www.coe.miami.edu/simlab/documents/Final-2016.pdf.

Yawn, Andrew J. "'Dirty' Goods May Have Sunk IREP." *Montgomery Advertiser*, November 14, 2015. http://www.montgomeryadvertiser.com/story/news/local/2015/11/13/dirty-goods-may-have-sunk-irep/74899002/.

Yawn, Andrew J. "Too Little Trash? Why Recycling Is Difficult in Montgomery." *Montgomery Advertiser*, March 10, 2017. http://www.montgomeryadvertiser.com/story/news/2017/03/10/too-little-trash-why-recycling-difficult-montgomery/98910236/.

Young, John E., and Aaron Sachs. "The Next Efficiency Revolution: Creating a Sustainable Materials Economy." *Resources Policy* 20, no. 4 (December 1994): 285–86. doi:10.1016/0301-4207(94)90011-6.

Zimring, Carl A. *Cash for Your Trash: Scrap Recycling in America*. New Brunswick, NJ: Rutgers University Press, 2009.

———. *Clean and White: A History of Environmental Racism in the United States*. New York: New York University Press, 2017.

Zukowsky, John. "Modern Design in the United States." *Encyclopædia Britannica*, May 25, 2017. https://www.britannica.com/topic/industrial-design/Modern-design-in-the-United-States#ref244796.

NOTES

1. THE ECOSYSTEM OF RECYCLING

1. U.S. Environmental Protection Agency, "Municipal Solid Waste," March 2016, https://archive.epa.gov/epawaste/nonhaz/municipal/web/html.

2. Barry Richmond, "Systems Thinking/System Dynamics: Let's Just Get on with It," *System Dynamics Review* 10, nos. 2–3 (1994): 135–57, doi:10.1002/sdr.4260100204.

3. Merriam-Webster, "System," December 2017, www.merriam-webster.com/dictionary/system.

4. Philip Angelides, Sophie Glass, and Frank Locantore, "Green in All Grades," Green America White Paper, July 23, 2012, https://www.greenamerica.org/sites/default/files/inline-files/GreeninAllGrade_72312_FINAL_z.pdf.

5. U.S. Environmental Protection Agency, "Deepwater Horizon: BP Gulf of Mexico Oil Spill," April 19, 2017, https://www.epa.gov/enforcement/deepwater-horizon-bp-gulf-mexico-oil-spill.

6. Associated Press, "BP's Reckless Conduct Caused Deepwater Horizon Oil Spill, Judge Rules," *Guardian*, September 4, 2014, https://www.theguardian.com/environment/2014/sep/04/bp-reckless-conduct-oil-spill-judge-rules.

7. Suzanne Goldenberg, "BP Oil Spill Blamed on Management and Communication Failures," *Guardian*, December 2, 2010, https://www.theguardian.com/business/2010/dec/02/bp-oil-spill-failures.

8. Paul R. Gregory and Robert C. Stuart, *The Global Economy and Its Economic Systems* (Mason, OH: South-Western Cengage Learning, 2014).

9. Suzanne Simard, "How Trees Talk to Each Other," TED Talk, June 1, 2016, https://www.ted.com/talks/suzanne_simard_how_trees_talk_to_each_other/transcript?language=en.

10. Complexity Labs, "System Boundary," October 17, 2016, http://complexitylabs.io/system-boundary/.

11. Alan Watson Weatherstone, "Decomposition and Decay," *Trees for Life*, 2017, http://treesforlife.org.uk/forest/forest-ecology/decomposition-and-decay/.

12. Timothy A. Mousseau, Gennadi Milinevsky, Jane Kenney-Hunt, and Anders Pape Miller, "Highly Reduced Mass Loss Rates and Increased Litter Layer in Radioactively Contaminated Areas," *Global Change Ecology* 175 (March 4, 2014): 429–37, https://link.springer.com/epdf/10.1007/s00442-014-2908-8?shared_access_token=3EGOiSXvyR0VTIVB2iw6H_e4RwlQNchNByi7wbcMAY7LZj_Pziie9KZM4nwUCjJEmIDcaZbC49c978dqVLXdW884oaN1aT1e-4PR_2ct8PC5dEQWuwfPWwHH6JZeskceuWvYNzkcVFoAbiC1jZkSNjSZkSrhRag_ALONBC9pYXo.

13. Annie Leonard, *The Story of Stuff: With Annie Leonard* (Berkeley, CA: Free Range Studios, 2007), transcript.

14. John E. Young and Aaron Sachs, "The Next Efficiency Revolution: Creating a Sustainable Materials Economy," *Resources Policy* 20, no. 4 (December 1994): 285–86, doi:10.1016/0301-4207(94)90011-6.

15. Ryan's Recycling, "About Ryan's Recycling," September 21, 2017, http://ryansrecycling.com/about/.

2. WHEN RECYCLING WAS PATRIOTIC

1. Hugh Rockoff, *Keep on Scrapping: The Salvage Drives of World War II* (Cambridge, MA: National Bureau of Economic Research, 2007), http://www.nber.org/papers/w13418.pdf.

2. Carl A. Zimring, *Cash for Your Trash: Scrap Recycling in America* (New Brunswick, NJ: Rutgers University Press, 2009), 134.

3. Carl A. Zimring, *Clean and White: A History of Environmental Racism in the United States* (New York: New York University Press, 2017).

4. Joe Duggan, "Remembering the 1942 Nebraska Scrap Metal Drive," *Lincoln Journal Star*, March 18, 2007, http://journalstar.com/news/local/remembering-the-nebraska-scrap-metal-drive/article_44b311bb-ca27-556b-b4d4-716a0fd9b801.html.

5. William L. O'Neill, *A Democracy at War: America's Fight at Home and Abroad in World War II* (Cambridge, MA: Harvard University Press, 1997).

6. Bill Vossler, "When Plowshares Built Swords: Scrap Drives during World War II—Farm Life," *Farm Collector*, December 2015, https://www. farmcollector.com/farm-life/scrap-drives-zmbz15deczhur.

7. Edwin C. Barringer, *The Story of Scrap* (Washington, DC: Institute of Scrap Iron and Steel, 1954).

8. Frank Ackerman, *Why Do We Recycle? Markets, Values, and Public Policy* (Washington, DC: Island Press, 2013).

9. O'Neill, *Democracy at War*.

10. Rockoff, *Keep on Scrapping*.

11. Keep America Beautiful, "Keep America Beautiful National Recycling Survey," November 2016, https://www.kab.org/sites/default/files/ARD_National_Recycling_Survey_Highlights_11.15.16.pdf.

12. O'Neill, *Democracy at War*.

13. Sylvia Whitman, *V Is for Victory: The American Home Front during World War II* (Minneapolis: Lerner, 1993).

14. O'Neill, *Democracy at War*.

15. Zimring, *Cash for Your Trash*.

16. Ben Cosgrove, "'Throwaway Living': When Tossing Out Everything Was All the Rage," *Time*, May 15, 2014, http://time.com/3879873/throwaway-living-when-tossing-it-all-was-all-the-rage/.

17. Zimring, *Cash for Your Trash*.

18. Annie Leonard, *The Story of Stuff: With Annie Leonard* (Berkeley, CA: Free Range Studios, 2007), transcript, 46.

19. J. McDonald, A. P. Sloan, and C. Stevens, *My Years with General Motors* (New York: Doubleday, 1972), 265.

20. David Schrieberg, "Landmark French Lawsuit Attacks Epson, HP, Canon and Brother For 'Planned Obsolescence,'" *Forbes*, September 26, 2017, https://www.forbes.com/sites/davidschrieberg1/2017/09/26/landmark-french-lawsuit-attacks-epson-hp-canon-and-brother-for-planned-obsolescence/#52490c01b36a.

21. John Zukowsky, "Modern Design in the United States." *Encyclopædia Britannica*, May 25, 2017, https://www.britannica.com/topic/industrial-design/Modern-design-in-the-United-States#ref244796.

22. Vivian Wagner, "Littering and Following the Crowd," *Atlantic*, August 1, 2014, https://www.theatlantic.com/health/archive/2014/08/littering-and-following-the-crowd/374913/.

23. Wagner, "Littering and Following."

24. Dawn Merritt, "90 Years of Conservation Success: 1950s and 1960s," *Izaak Walton League of America*, 2017, http://www.iwla.org/publications/outdoor-america/article/outdoor-america-2012-issue-3/90-years-of-conservation-success-1950s-and-1960s.

25.   Finis Dunaway, *Seeing Green: The Use and Abuse of American Environmental Images* (Chicago: University of Chicago Press, 2015), 92.

26.   Robert B. Cialdini, "Crafting Normative Messages to Protect the Environment," *American Psychological Society: Current Directions in Psychological Science*, 2003, http://www.pm-air.net/doc/cialcraf.pdf.

27.   Wagner, "Littering and Following."

28.   MidAtlantic Solid Waste Consultants for Keep America Beautiful, Inc., "Litter in America: Results from the Nation's Largest Litter Study," *Keep America Beautiful*, January 2010, https://www.kab.org/sites/default/files/News%26Info_Research_LitterinAmerica_FactSheet_LitteringBehavior.pdf.

29.   Matthew Gandy, *Recycling and the Politics of Urban Waste* (Abingdon: Routledge, 2017), 1.

30.   Nancy F. Koehn, "From Calm Leadership, Lasting Change," *New York Times*, October 27, 2012, http://www.nytimes.com/2012/10/28/business/rachel-carsons-lessons-50-years-after-silent-spring.html.

31.   Rachel Carson, *Silent Spring* (London: Penguin Books, in Association with Hamish Hamilton, 2015).

32.   Zimring, *Cash for Your Trash*, 122, 145.

33.   Dunaway, *Seeing Green*.

34.   Finn Arne Jørgensen, "A Pocket History of Bottle Recycling," *Atlantic*, February 27, 2013, https://www.theatlantic.com/technology/archive/2013/02/a-pocket-history-of-bottle-recycling/273575/.

3. RUNNING OUT OF ROOM

1.   Lee Davis, "DesignView—Garbage Design: Modesto Invented Curbside Recycling," *Modestoview*, May 3, 2017, https://www.modestoview.com/designview-curbside-recycling/.

2.   W. B. Willers, *Learning to Listen to the Land* (Washington, DC: Island Press, 1991), 252.

3.   Container Recycling Institute, "Bottle Bills Complement Curbside Recycling Programs," *Bottlebill.org*, 2016, http://www.bottlebill.org/about/benefits/curbside.htm.

4.   Carl A. Zimring, *Cash for Your Trash: Scrap Recycling in America* (New Brunswick, NJ: Rutgers University Press, 2009), 149.

5.   U.S. Environmental Protection Agency, "Summary of the Resource Conservation and Recovery Act," August 24, 2017, https://www.epa.gov/laws-regulations/summary-resource-conservation-and-recovery-act.

6.   John Lloyd and John Mitchinson, *The Book of General Ignorance* (London: Faber and Faber, 2006), 114–15.

7. Matthew Gandy, *Recycling and the Politics of Urban Waste* (Abingdon: Routledge, 2017).

8. U.S. Environmental Protection Agency, Office of Resource Conservation and Recovery, "Historic Tipping Fees and Commodity Values," February 2015, https://www.epa.gov/sites/production/files/2015-12/documents/historic_tipping_fees_and_commodity_values_02062015_508.pdf.

9. U.S. Environmental Protection Agency, "Basic Information," March 29, 2016, https://archive.epa.gov/epawaste/nonhaz/municipal/web/html/basic.html.

10. U.S. Environmental Protection Agency, "Basic Information."

11. Edward J. Walsh, D. Clayton Smith, and Rex Warland, *Don't Burn It Here: Grassroots Challenges to Trash Incinerators* (University Park: Pennsylvania State University Press, 1997), 11.

12. Walsh, Smith, and Warland, *Don't Burn It Here*, 13.

13. Robert Doyle Bullard, *Dumping in Dixie: Race, Class, and Environmental Quality*, 2nd ed. (Boulder, CO: Westview Press, 2000), 4–32.

14. Adam S. Weinberg, David N. Pellow, and Allan Schnaiberg, *Urban Recycling and the Search for Sustainable Community Development* (Princeton, NJ: Princeton University Press, 2000), 79.

15. David N. Pellow, Adam Weinberg, and Allan Schnaiberg, "The Environmental Justice Movement: Equitable Allocation of the Costs and Benefits of Environmental Management Outcomes," June 17, 2004, https://www.ipr.northwestern.edu/publications/papers/urban-policy-and-community-development/docs/schnaiberg/environmental-justice.pdf.

16. Woodbridge Township, New Jersey, "'A Conversation with Greenable Woodbridge': Waste Management, Recycling, and Green Purchasing," http://www.twp.woodbridge.nj.us/DocumentCenter/View/3041.

17. "Voyage of the Mobro 4000," *New York Times: Retro Report*, https://www.nytimes.com/video/booming/100000002206073/voyage-of-the-mobro-4000.html.

18. Seldman, Neil. "Recycling: History in the United States." *Encyclopedia of Energy Technology and the Environment*, Edited by Attilio Bisio and Sharon Boots, Wiley & Sons, Inc., 1995, 2352–68.

19. Zimring, *Cash for Your Trash*, 134.

20. U.S. Environmental Protection Agency, "Municipal Solid Waste," March 29, 2016, https://archive.epa.gov/epawaste/nonhaz/municipal/web/html.

21. Green Spectrum Consulting, LLC, and Resource Recycling, Inc., "Making Sense of the Mix: Analysis and Implications of the Changing Curbside Recycling Stream," February 2015, https://plastics.americanchemistry.com/Education-Resources/Publications/Making-Sense-of-the-Mix.pdf.

22.   Richard A. Denison and John F. Ruston, "Recycling Is Not Garbage," *MIT Technology Review*, December 30, 2013, https://www.technologyreview. com/s/400100/recycling-is-not-garbage/.

23.   George C. Lodge and Jeffrey F. Rayport, "Knee-Deep and Rising: America's Recycling Crisis," *Harvard Business Review* August 1, 2014, https:// hbr.org/1991/09/knee-deep-and-rising-americas-recycling-crisis.

24.   Weinberg, Pellow, and Schnaiberg, *Urban Recycling*, 3.

25.   Grandmont Rosedale Development Corporation, "Rosedale Recycles Turned 24 This April," 2017, http://grandmontrosedale.com/rosedale-recycles-turned-24-april/.

26.   Gandy, *Recycling and the Politics*.

27.   Conservatree, "Conservatree Staff," http://www.conservatree.org/about/Who.shtml.

28.   New York City Parks, "Freshkills Park," https://www.nycgovparks.org/park-features/freshkills-park.

29.   Fresh Kills Park Alliance, "The Park Plan," http://freshkillspark.org/the-park/the-park-plan.

4. WHY REDUCE AND REUSE COME FIRST

1.   U.S. Environmental Protection Agency, "Sustainable Materials Management: Non-Hazardous Materials and Waste Management Hierarchy," August 10, 2017, https://www.epa.gov/smm/sustainable-materials-management-non-hazardous-materials-and-waste-management-hierarchy.

2.   Environmental Protection Agency. "Sustainable Materials Management."

3.   Eleanor Greene, "What Does It Mean to Vote with Your Dollar?" *Green America*, June 20, 2017, https://www.greenamerica.org/blog/what-does-it-mean-vote-your-dollar.

4.   Nancy VandenBerg, Susan Kinsella, and Carla S. Lallatin, "Source Reduction Opportunities," in *Resourceful Purchasing: A Hands-On Buyers' Manual with How-to-Do-It Guidance for Source Reduction and Recycled Products* (Oakland, CA: Alameda County Source Reduction and Recycling Board, 1996).

5.   U.S. Environmental Protection Agency, "Municipal Solid Waste Generation, Recycling, and Disposal in the United States: Facts and Figures for 2012," February 2014, www.epa.gov/sites/production/files/2015-09/documents/2012_msw_fs.pdf.

6. Kristin Heist, "How Packaging Protects the Environment," *Harvard Business Review*, July 23, 2014, https://hbr.org/2012/06/how-packaging-protects-the-env.

7. Industry Council for Research on Packaging and the Environment, "Facts about Packaging," www.incpen.org/displayarticle.asp?a=2&c=2.

8. Tracy Fernandez Rysavy, "Reduce and Reuse: How One Couple Shrank Their Trash Output to One Can a Year," *Green American Magazine*, June 2016, 17.

9. Tovia Smith, "How Green Are Reusable Bags?" *NPR*, August 7, 2009, http://www.npr.org/templates/story/story.php?storyId=111672574.

10. Elbert Dijkgraaf and Raymond Gradus, "An EU Recycling Target: What Does the Dutch Evidence Tell Us?" *Environmental and Resource Economics* 68, no. 3 (2016): 501–26, doi:10.1007/s10640-016-0027-1.

11. Becky Hammad, "Trash Planet: The Netherlands," *Earth911*, July 6, 2009, https://earth911.com/earth-watch/trash-planet-the-netherlands/.

12. Christopher Mele, "At Repair Cafés, 'Beloved but Broken' Possessions Find New Life," *New York Times*, January 18, 2017, www.nytimes.com/2017/01/18/us/repair-cafe.html.

13. Steve Taylor, "Self-Sufficiency: An Essential Aspect of Well-Being," *Psychology Today*, March 25, 2013, https://www.psychologytoday.com/blog/out-the-darkness/201303/self-sufficiency-essential-aspect-well-being.

14. Jo Confino, "We Buy a Staggering Amount of Clothing, and Most of It Ends up in Landfills," *Huffington Post*, September 14, 2016, https://www.huffingtonpost.com/entry/transforming-the-fashion-industry_us_57ceee96e4b0a48094a58d39.

15. Elizabeth Cline, "Where Does Discarded Clothing Go?" *Atlantic*, July 18, 2014, https://www.theatlantic.com/business/archive/2014/07/where-does-discarded-clothing-go/374613/.

16. Suzy Strutner, "Here's What Goodwill Actually Does with Your Donated Clothes," *Huffington Post*, September 28, 2016, https://www.huffingtonpost.com/entry/what-does-goodwill-do-with-your-clothes_us_57e06b96e4b0071a6e092352.

17. Sara Boboltz, "We Buy an Obscene Amount of Clothes: Here's What It's Doing to Secondhand Stores," *Huffington Post*, November 20, 2014, www.huffingtonpost.com/2014/11/20/fast-fashion-thrift-stores_n_5798612.html.

18. Cline, "Discarded Clothing."

19. Council for Textile Recycling, "The Facts about Textile Waste," 2017, www.weardonaterecycle.org/about/issue.html.

20. Jim Yardley, "Report on Deadly Factory Collapse in Bangladesh Finds Widespread Blame," *New York Times*, May 22, 2013, www.nytimes.com/2013/

05/23/world/asia/report-on-bangladesh-building-collapse-finds-widespread-blame.html.

21.   Harpreet Kaur, "Low Wages, Unsafe Conditions and Harassment: Fashion Must Do More to Protect Female Workers," *Guardian*, March 8, 2016, www.theguardian.com/sustainable-business/2016/mar/08/fashion-industry-protect-women-unsafe-low-wages-harassment.

22.   "Child Labor, Forced Labor & Human Trafficking." United States Department of Labor. May 9, 2018. https://www.dol.gov/agencies/ilab/our-work/child-forced-labor-trafficking.

23.   Josephine Moulds, "Child Labour in the Fashion Supply Chain," *Guardian*, http://labs.theguardian.com/unicef-child-labour/.

24.   Green America, "What Is Fair Trade/Fair Labor?" 2017, www.greenamerica.org/end-child-labor-cocoa/dean-foods/what-fair-tradefair-labor.

25.   Green America, "Sweatshop-Free Clothing," 2017, www.greenamerica.org/green-living/sweatshop-free-clothing.

26.   Boboltz, "Obscene Amount of Clothes," https://www.huffingtonpost.com/2014/11/20/fast-fashion-thrift-stores_n_5798612.html.

5. WHAT'S THE POINT OF RECYCLING?

1.   U.S. Environmental Protection Agency, "Municipal Solid Waste," March 29, 2016, https://archive.epa.gov/epawaste/nonhaz/municipal/web/html.

2.   U.S. Environmental Protection Agency, "History of the Resource Conservation and Recovery Act (RCRA)," August 23, 2017, https://www.epa.gov/rcra/history-resource-conservation-and-recovery-act-rcra.

3.   U.S. Environmental Protection Agency, "Advancing Sustainable Materials Management: Facts and Figures," August 10, 2017, https://www.epa.gov/smm/advancing-sustainable-materials-management-facts-and-figures.

4.   Bruce O'Dell, interview by author, November 13, 2017.

5.   Safaa M. Raghab, Ahmed M. Abd El Meguid, and Hala A. Hegazi, "Treatment of Leachate from Municipal Solid Waste Landfill," *HBRC Journal* 9, no. 2 (2013): 187–92, doi:10.1016/j.hbrcj.2013.05.007.

6.   U.S. Environmental Protection Agency, "History of the RCRA."

7.   Amalendu Bagchi, *Design of Landfills and Integrated Solid Waste Management* (New York: Wiley, 2004), 450–51.

8.   Gayathri Vaidyanathan, "How Bad of a Greenhouse Gas Is Methane?" *Scientific American*, December 22, 2015, https://www.scientificamerican.com/article/how-bad-of-a-greenhouse-gas-is-methane/.

9. U.S. Environmental Protection Agency, "Overview of Greenhouse Gases," April 14, 2017, https://www.epa.gov/ghgemissions/overview-greenhouse-gases.

10. Olga Grigoryants, "Turning Garbage into Profit," *Pacific Standard*, September 2, 2015, https://psmag.com/environment/turning-garbage-into-profit.

11. Agency for Toxic Substances and Disease Registry, "Landfill Gas Primer: An Overview for Environmental Health Professionals," November 1, 2001, https://www.atsdr.cdc.gov/HAC/landfill/html/ch2.html.

12. Allan Gerlat, "Casella Waste Partners on Solar Project at Vermont Landfill," *Waste360*, May 6, 2014, http://www.waste360.com/landfill-gas-energy-lfgte/casella-waste-partners-solar-project-vermont-landfill.

13. U.S. Environmental Protection Agency, "Zero Waste Case Study: San Francisco," June 12, 2017, https://www.epa.gov/transforming-waste-tool/zero-waste-case-study-san-francisco.

14. Seattle Public Utilities, "2016 Recycling Rate Report," July 1, 2016, http://www.seattle.gov/util/cs/groups/public/@spu/@garbage/documents/webcontent/1_064754.pdf.

15. ClimateWatch, "CAIT Emissions Data (Except PIK or UNFCCC Data Sets)," 2017, https://www.climatewatchdata.org/ghg-emissions.

16. ClimateWatch, "CAIT Emissions Data."

17. U.S. Energy Information Administration, "International Energy Outlook 2017," September 14, 2017, https://www.eia.gov/outlooks/ieo/pdf/0484(2017).pdf.

18. U.S. Environmental Protection Agency, "Sources of Greenhouse Gas Emissions," April 14, 2017, https://www.epa.gov/ghgemissions/sources-greenhouse-gas-emissions#industry.

19. Jane Mayer, "A Whistle-Blower Accuses the Kochs of 'Poisoning' an Arkansas Town," *New Yorker*, September 9, 2016, https://www.newyorker.com/news/news-desk/a-whistle-blower-accuses-the-kochs-of-poisoning-an-arkansas-town.

20. Clean Water Action Council of Northeast Wisconsin, "Environmental Impacts of the Paper Industry," 2017, http://www.cleanwateractioncouncil.org/issues/resource-issues/paper-industry/.

21. Diana Parker, "Indigenous Communities Demand Forest Rights, Blame Land Grabs for Failure to Curb Deforestation," *Conservation News*, March 24, 2014, https://news.mongabay.com/2014/03/indigenous-communities-demand-forest-rights-blame-land-grabs-for-failure-to-curb-deforestation/.

22. Alain Frechette, Katie Reytar, Sonia Saini, and Wayne Walker, "Toward a Global Baseline of Carbon Storage in Collective Lands," November

2016, http://rightsandresources.org/wp-content/uploads/2016/10/Toward-a-Global-Baseline-of-Carbon-Storage-in-Collective-Lands-November-2016-RRI-WHRC-WRI-report.pdf.

23.   Linda Etchart, "The Role of Indigenous Peoples in Combating Climate Change," *Palgrave Communications* 3, no. 17085 (2017), doi:10.1057/palcomms.2017.85.

24.   Valentin Bellassen and Sebastiaan Luyssaert, "Carbon Sequestration: Managing Forests in Uncertain Times," *Nature News*, February 12, 2014, www.nature.com/news/carbon-sequestration-managing-forests-in-uncertain-times-1.14687.

25.   World Wide Fund for Nature, "Pulp and Paper," 2017, http://wwf.panda.org/about_our_earth/deforestation/forest_sector_transformation/pulp_and_paper/.

26.   Philip Angelides, Sophie Glass, and Frank Locantore, "Green in All Grades," Green America White Paper, July 23, 2012, https://www.greenamerica.org/sites/default/files/inline-files/GreeninAllGrade_72312_FINAL_z.pdf.

27.   Environmental Paper Network, "Paper Calculator," 2017, http://c.environmentalpaper.org/home.

28.   Food and Agriculture Organization of the United Nations, *Global Forest Products Facts and Figures: 2016.* http://www.fao.org/3/17034EN/i7034en.pdf.

29.   Stijn Van Ewijk, Julia A. Stegemann, and Paul Ekins, "Global Life Cycle Paper Flows, Recycling Metrics, and Material Efficiency," *Journal of Industrial Ecology* (June 6, 2017).

30.   Aluminum Association, "Recycling," September 24, 2014, http://www.aluminum.org/industries/production/recycling.

31.   Sam H. Patterson, *Bauxite Reserves and Potential Aluminum Resources of the World*, Geological Survey Bulletin 1228 (Washington, DC: United States Government Printing Office, 1967), https://pubs.er.usgs.gov/publication/b1228.

32.   Jonathan Head, "Bauxite in Malaysia: The Environmental Cost of Mining," *BBC News*, January 19, 2016, http://www.bbc.com/news/world-asia-35340528.

33.   Rachael Willis, "Malaysia's Bauxite Backlash," *Huffington Post*, January 15, 2016, https://www.huffingtonpost.com/rachael-willis-/malaysias-bauxite-backlas_b_8987234.html.

34.   Emily Chow, "Malaysia's Bauxite Exports Rise Despite Mining Ban," *Reuters*, July 5, 2017, https://www.reuters.com/article/us-malaysia-bauxite/malaysias-bauxite-exports-rise-despite-mining-ban-idUSKBN19Q32I.

35. Craig Moran, "Solving Malaysia's Bauxite Mining Woes," *World Policy Institute*, March 3, 2016, http://www.worldpolicy.org/blog/2016/03/03/solving-malaysia%E2%80%99s-bauxite-mining-woes.

36. Jerry Marks and Chris Bayliss, "Aluminum: Meeting the Challenges of Climate Change," *Journal of the Minerals, Metals, and Materials Society* 62, no. 8 (August 2010): 33–36, doi:10.1007/s11837-010-0122-7.

6. WHERE YOUR RECYCLABLES GO

1. Sarah Laskow, "Single-Stream Recycling Is Easier for Consumers, but Is It Better?" *Atlantic*, September 18, 2014, https://www.theatlantic.com/technology/archive/2014/09/single-stream-recycling-is-easier-for-consumers-but-is-it-better/380368/.

2. Adam Gendell, "2015–16 Centralized Study on Availability of Recycling," *Sustainable Packaging Coalition*, 2016, http://sustainablepackaging.org/resources/spcs-centralized-availability-recycling-study/.

3. Northeast Recycling Council, "Best Operational Practices for Recycling Drop-off Operations," Fall 2014, https://nerc.org/documents/recycling/BOP_Illinios%20Drop%20Off%20Man_FIN%2011.28.16.pdf.

4. Northeast Recycling Council, "Best Operational Practices."

5. Gendell, "2015–16 Centralized Study."

6. Gershman, Brickner, and Bratton, "The Evolution of Mixed Waste Processing Facilities: 1970–Today," June 2015, https://plastics.americanchemistry.com/Education-Resources/Publications/The-Evolution-of-Mixed-Waste-Processing-Facilities.pdf.

7. Susan Robinson, "State of MRFs in 2016: Current Trends and Conditions," lecture, Waste Management, October 16, 2017, http://www.recyclingstar.org/wp-content/uploads/2016/11/Robinson-MRF-panel-2016-Final.pdf.

8. Dan Leif, "WM Leader Says Contamination Is 'a Slow Ship to Turn.'" *Resource Recycling News*, June 20, 2017, https://resource-recycling.com/recycling/2017/06/20/wm-leader-says-contamination-slow-ship-turn/.

9. *Environmental Research and Education Foundation Newsletter* 19, no. 2 (2015), https://erefdn.org/wp-content/uploads/2016/04/Winter-2015-EREF-Newsletter.pdf.

10. Northeast Recycling Council, "Best Operational Practices."

11. Robert Carr, "Contamination Continues to Hurt Recycling Efforts," *Waste360*, January 26, 2016, http://www.waste360.com/source-separation/contamination-continues-hurt-recycling-efforts.

12.   Debra Winter, "The Violent Afterlife of a Recycled Plastic Bottle," *Atlantic*, December 4, 2015, https://www.theatlantic.com/technology/archive/2015/12/what-actually-happens-to-a-recycled-plastic-bottle/418326/.

13.   Rick LeBlanc, "What Is a Waste Transfer Station?" *Balance*, January 31, 2017, https://www.thebalance.com/what-is-a-waste-transfer-station-2877735.

14.   Alexander J. Dubanowitz, "Design of a Materials Recovery Facility (MRF) for Processing the Recyclable Materials of New York City's Municipal Solid Waste," PhD diss., Columbia University, 2000, http://www.seas.columbia.edu/earth/dubanmrf.pdf.

15.   Re3.org, *How Does a Material Recovery Facility (MRF) Work?* May 11, 2011, https://www.youtube.com/watch?v=7CFE5tD1CCI.

16.   Planning and Technical Support Division, California Air Resources Board, and California Environmental Protection Agency, "Method for Estimating Greenhouse Gas Emission Reductions from Recycling," November 14, 2011, https://www.arb.ca.gov/cc/protocols/localgov/pubs/recycling_method.pdf.

17.   Government Advisory Associates, *Materials Recovery and Processing Yearbook and Directory*, November 2016, https://governmentaladvisory.com/ordering/.

18.   Cole Rosengren, "Pennsylvania County Bucks the Single-Stream Trend," *Waste Dive*, December 12, 2016, https://www.wastedive.com/news/pennsylvania-county-bucks-the-single-stream-trend/432109/.

19.   London, Canada, "Sort It Right," February 17, 2015, https://www.london.ca/residents/Garbage-Recycling/Recycling/Pages/Sort-it-Right.aspx.

20.   Robinson, "State of MRFs."

21.   J. Poyry and Skumatz Economic Research Associates, "Paper Recycling: Quality Is Key to Long-Term Success," March 2004, 32.

22.   Clarissa Morawski, "Understanding Economic and Environmental Impacts of Single-Stream Collection Systems," December 2009, http://www.container-recycling.org/assets/pdfs/reports/2009-SingleStream.pdf.

23.   Robert Bullard, "Houston Recycling Plan Will Hit Minorities Hardest," *TribTalk*, September 8, 2014, https://www.tribtalk.org/2014/09/08/houston-recycling-plan-will-hit-minorities-hardest/.

24.   Danielle Peacock, "ReLoop: What Is Mixed Waste Processing or 'All in One/Dirty MRF' Recycling?" *GreenBlue*, http://greenblue.org/reloop-what-is-mixed-waste-processing-or-all-in-onedirty-mrf-recycling/.

25.   City of Houston, "One Bin for All: Recycling Reimagined in Houston," https://www.houstontx.gov/onebinforall/.

26.   Andrew J. Yawn, "'Dirty' Goods May Have Sunk IREP," *Montgomery Advertiser*, November 14, 2015, http://www.montgomeryadvertiser.com/story/news/local/2015/11/13/dirty-goods-may-have-sunk-irep/74899002/.

27.   Andrew J. Yawn, "Too Little Trash? Why Recycling Is Difficult in Montgomery," *Montgomery Advertiser*, March 10, 2017, http://www.montgomeryadvertiser.com/story/news/2017/03/10/too-little-trash-why-recycling-difficult-montgomery/98910236/.

28.   Melanie Scruggs, "Recycling Will Stay—Zero Waste Should Be Next," *Texas Campaign for the Environment*, March 23, 2016, https://www.texasenvironment.org/recycling-will-stay-zero-waste-should-be-next/.

29.   Florian Martin, "What Happened to Houston's 'One Bin for All' Program?" *Houston Public Media*, January 18, 2016, https://www.houstonpublicmedia.org/articles/news/2016/01/18/134410/what-happened-to-houstons-one-bin-for-all-program/.

30.   Meagan Flynn, "The Long Rise and Fast Fall of the Ambitious One-Bin Recycling Program," *Houston Press*, July 13, 2017, http://www.houstonpress.com/news/what-happened-to-ecohub-and-houstons-one-bin-for-all-recycling-plan-9601564.

31.   Mike Breslin, "Advanced Waste MRFs Tackle Diverse Challenges," *American Recycler News*, January 2016, http://americanrecycler.com/8568759/index.php/news/waste-news/1460-advanced-mixed-waste-mrfs-tackle-diverse-challenges.

32.   North Carolina Division of Pollution Prevention and Environmental Assistance, "Mixed Waste Processing," January 1997, http://infohouse.p2ric.org/ref/01/00028.htm.

33.   Gershman, Brickner, and Bratton, "Evolution of Mixed Waste."

34.   Cole Rosengren, "Survey: 5.1M Residents Have Access to Curbside Organics Collection," *Waste Dive*, December 15, 2017, https://www.wastedive.com/news/survey-51m-residents-have-access-to-curbside-organics-collection/513109/.

35.   Kristin Smith, "Similar but Different," *Recycling Today*, April 6, 2015, http://www.recyclingtoday.com/article/rt0415-mixed-waste-processing/.

36.   Earth911, "Mixed Feelings on Mixed Waste, Still," November 8, 2016, https://earth911.com/business-policy/mixed-waste-mixed-feelings/.

37.   Kit Strange, "Overview of Waste Management Options: Their Efficacy and Acceptability," *Royal Society of Chemistry*, 2002, 15.

38.   Jack Loughran, "European Recycling Rates Based on 'Flawed' Methodology," *Materials Recycling World*, June 2, 2015, https://www.mrw.co.uk/news/european-recycling-rates-based-on-flawed-methodology/8684107.article?blocktitle=Latest-news—-recycling-and-waste-management&contentID=2182.

39.   Duygu Yasar, Haluk Damgacioglu, Mehrad Bastani, and Nurcin Celik, "Assessment of the Impact of Single Stream Recycling on Paper Contamination in Recovery Facilities and Paper Mills," Report no. 10916, February 28, 2017, http://www.coe.miami.edu/simlab/documents/Final-2016.pdf.

40.   Roland Geyer, Jenna R. Jambeck, and Kara Lavender Law, "Production, Use, and Fate of All Plastics Ever Made," *Science Advances* 3, no. 7 (July 19, 2017), doi:10.1126/sciadv.1700782.

41.   Jenna R. Jambeck, Roland Geyer, Chris Wilcox, Theodore R. Siegler, Miriam Perryman, Anthony Andrady, Ramani Narayan, and Kara Lavender Law, "Plastic Waste Inputs from Land into the Ocean," *Science*, February 13, 2015, http://science.sciencemag.org/content/347/6223/768.full?ijkey=BXtBaPzbQgagE&keytype=ref&siteid=sci.

42.   Ocean Conservancy, "Plastics in the Ocean," 2017, https://oceanconservancy.org/trash-free-seas/plastics-in-the-ocean/.

43.   Chelsea M. Rochman, Akbar Tahir, Susan L. Williams, Dolores V. Baxa, Rosalyn Lam, Jeffrey T. Miller, Foo-Ching Teh, Shinta Werorilangi, and Swee J. Teh, "Anthropogenic Debris in Seafood: Plastic Debris and Fibers from Textiles in Fish and Bivalves Sold for Human Consumption," *Scientific Reports* 5, no. 1 (2015), doi:10.1038/srep14340.

44.   Eco-Cycle, "Be Straw Free Campaign: Frequently Asked Questions," 2016, http://ecocycle.org/bestrawfree/faqs.

45.   Dominique Mosbergen, "The Oceans Are Drowning in Plastic—and No One's Paying Attention," *Huffington Post*, May 12, 2017, https://www.huffingtonpost.com/entry/plastic-waste-oceans_us_58fed37be4b0c46f0781d426.

46.   Plastic Oceans, "Facts about Plastic," 2017, https://www.plasticoceans.org/the-facts/.

47.   Plastics for Change, "Why Are Plastic Recycling Rates So Low?" July 3, 2017, http://www.plasticsforchange.org/blog/category/why-are-plastic-recycling-rate-so-low.

48.   Plastic Packaging Facts, "Resins and Types of Packaging," https://www.plasticpackagingfacts.org/plastic-packaging/resins-types-of-packaging/.

49.   George C. Lodge and Jeffrey F. Rayport, "Knee-Deep and Rising: America's Recycling Crisis," *Harvard Business Review*, August 1, 2014, https://hbr.org/1991/09/knee-deep-and-rising-americas-recycling-crisis.

50.   Tom Szaky, "The Many Challenges of Plastic Recycling," *Sustainable Brands*, April 22, 2015, http://www.sustainablebrands.com/news_and_views/waste_not/tom_szaky/many_challenges_plastic_recycling.

51.   Greentumble Editorial Team, "How Is Plastic Recycled: Step by Step," *Greentumble*, October 22, 2015, https://greentumble.com/how-is-plastic-recycled-step-by-step/.

52. Global Aluminium Recycling Committee, "Global Aluminium Recycling: A Cornerstone of Sustainable Development," 2009, http://www.world-aluminium.org/media/filer_public/2013/01/15/fl0000181.pdf.

53. Aluminum Association, "Study Finds Aluminum Cans the Sustainable Package of Choice," May 20, 2015, http://www.aluminum.org/news/study-finds-aluminum-cans-sustainable-package-choice.

54. Aluminum Association, "Recycling," 2017, http://www.aluminum.org/industries/production/recycling.

55. Tammy Park, "How Are Aluminum Cans Recycled?" *Environmental and Recycling Industry Center*, January 28, 2017, http://sprecycling.com/how-are-aluminum-cans-recycled/.

56. Lobet, Ingrid. "Danger in Air near Metal Recyclers." *Houston Chronicle*. December 29, 2012. https://www.houstonchronicle.com/news/houston-texas/houston/article/Danger-in-air-near-metal-recyclers-4154951.php.

57. Lobet, Ingrid. "City Plans Further Testing outside Metal Recyclers." *Houston Chronicle*. January 08, 2013. https://www.houstonchronicle.com/news/houston-texas/houston/article/City-plans-further-testing-outside-metal-recyclers-4173303.php.

58. American Iron and Steel Institute, "Steel Is the World's Most Recycled Material," *SteelWorks*, 2017, http://www.steel.org/sustainability/steel-recycling.aspx.

59. Editorial Staff, "US Steel Recycling Rate Hits 92%," *Recycling International*, November 29, 2012, https://www.recyclinginternational.com/recycling-news/6718/ferrous-metals/united-states/us-steel-recycling-rate-hits-92.

60. World Coal Association, "How Is Steel Produced?" 2017, https://www.worldcoal.org/coal/uses-coal/how-steel-produced.

61. David L. Chandler, "One Order of Steel; Hold the Greenhouse Gases," *MIT News*, May 8, 2013, http://news.mit.edu/2013/steel-without-greenhouse-gas-emissions-0508.

62. U.S. Environmental Protection Agency, *Inventory of Greenhouse Gas Emissions and Sinks: 1990–2015*, 2015, https://www.epa.gov/sites/production/files/2017-02/documents/2017_complete_report.pdf.

63. Bureau of International Recycling, "Ferrous Metals," http://www.bir.org/industry/ferrous-metals/.

64. European Container Glass Federation, "Glass Recycling Hits 73% in the EU," press release, September 2015, http://feve.org/wp-content/uploads/2016/04/Press-Release-EU.pdf.

65. Glass Packaging Institute, "Recycling," 2017, http://www.gpi.org/recycling/glass-recycling-facts.

66. Trey Granger, "Truth about Glass Recycling," *Earth911*, June 22, 2009, https://earth911.com/earth-watch/truth-about-glass-recycling/.

67. Glass Packaging Institute, "Recycling."

68. Carr, "Contamination Continues."

69. Glass Packaging Institute, "Recycling."

70. Jessica Harlan, "The List: 7 Truths about Glass Recycling," *Recyclebank*, March 17, 2017, https://livegreen.recyclebank.com/the-list-7-truths-about-glass-recycling.

71. Michele Nestor, "Can We Rescue Glass Recycling?" *Waste360*, February 4, 2016, http://www.waste360.com/glass/can-we-rescue-glass-recycling.

72. Glass Packaging Institute, "Recycling."

73. International Council of Forest and Paper Associations, "2017 ICFPA: Sustainability Progress Report," 2017, http://www.icfpa.org/uploads/Modules/Publications/2017-icfpa-sustainability-report.pdf.

74. American Forest and Paper Association, "U.S. Paper Recovery Rate Reaches Record 67.2 Percent in 2016," May 9, 2017, http://afandpa.org/media/news/2017/05/09/u.s.-paper-recovery-rate-reaches-record-67.2-percent-in-2016.

75. Complete Recycling, "Paper Recycling and Refining Process," https://www.completerecycling.com/resources/paper-recycling/process.

7. HOW PSYCHOLOGY AFFECTS RECYCLING AND WASTE

1. Shankar Vedantam, "Why Recycling Options Lead People to Waste More," *NPR*, June 2, 2017, https://www.npr.org/2017/06/02/531173499/why-recycling-options-lead-people-to-waste-more.

2. Remi Trudel, "The Behavioral Economics of Recycling," *Harvard Business Review*, October 7, 2016, https://hbr.org/2016/10/the-behavioral-economics-of-recycling.

3. Adam Minter, *Junkyard Planet: Travels in the Billion-Dollar Trash Trade* (New York: Bloomsbury Press, 2015), 5.

4. Anna C. Merritt, Daniel A. Effron, and Benoît Monin, "Moral Self-Licensing: When Being Good Frees Us to Be Bad," *Social and Personality Psychology Compass* 4, no. 5 (2010): 344–57, doi:10.1111/j.1751-9004.2010.00263.x.

5. Maryam Kouchaki, "Vicarious Moral Licensing: The Influence of Others' Past Moral Actions on Moral Behavior," *Journal of Personality and Social Psychology* 101, no. 4 (2011): 702–15, doi:10.1037/a0024552.

6. Jyoti Madhusoodanan, "When Companies Praise Good Behavior, They May Encourage the Exact Opposite," *Kellogg Insight*, October 10, 2016, https://insight.kellogg.northwestern.edu/article/when-companies-praise-good-behavior-they-may-encourage-the-exact-opposite.

7. Madhusoodanan, "When Companies Praise."

8. Nina Mazar and Chen-Bo Zhong, "Do Green Products Make Us Better People?" *Psychological Science* 21, no. 4 (2010), http://journals.sagepub.com/doi/abs/10.1177/0956797610363538.

9. Verena Tiefenbeck, Thorsten Staake, Kurt Roth, and Olga Sachs, "For Better or for Worse? Empirical Evidence of Moral Licensing in a Behavioral Energy Conservation Campaign," *Energy Policy* 57 (June 2013): 160–71.

10. Kenneth Worthy, "The Self-Deceptions of Recycling," *Psychology Today*, March 31, 2015, https://www.psychologytoday.com/blog/the-green-mind/201503/the-self-deceptions-recycling.

11. Pew Research Center, "Global Views on Morality," April 15, 2014, http://www.pewglobal.org/2014/04/15/global-morality/.

12. Philipp Simbrunner and Bodo B. Schlegelmilch, "Influencing Factors on Moral Licensing Effect: A Meta-Analytic Approach: An Abstract," in *Back to the Future: Using Marketing Basics to Provide Customer Value*, edited by Nina Krey and Patricia Rossi (p. 19), Developments in Marketing Science: Proceedings of the Academy of Marketing Science (Cham, Switzerland: Springer, 2017), doi:10.1007/978-3-319-66023-3_10.

13. Neel Burton, "The Psychology of Embarrassment, Shame, and Guilt," *Psychology Today*, August 26, 2014, https://www.psychologytoday.com/blog/hide-and-seek/201408/the-psychology-embarrassment-shame-and-guilt.

14. Joseph Burgo, "The Difference between Guilt and Shame," *Psychology Today*, May 30, 2013, https://www.psychologytoday.com/blog/shame/201305/the-difference-between-guilt-and-shame.

15. Diana Ivanova, Konstantin Stadler, Kjartan Steen-Olsen, Richard Wood, Gibran Vita, Arnold Tukker, and Edgar G. Hertwich, "Environmental Impact Assessment of Household Consumption," *Journal of Industrial Ecology* 20, no. 3 (December 18, 2015), https://onlinelibrary.wiley.com/doi/abs/10.1111/jiec.12371.

16. Shawn Healy, "When Good Deeds Lead to Bad—Moral Self-Licensing," *Lawyers Concerned for Lawyers*, June 28, 2017, http://www.lclma.org/2016/06/28/when-good-deeds-lead-to-bad-deeds-moral-self-licensing/.

17. Mark Hertsgaard, "John Francis, a 'Planetwalker' Who Lived Car-Free and Silent for 17 Years, Chats with Grist," *Grist*, May 10, 2005, https://grist.org/article/hertsgaard-francis/.

18. John Francis, "Experience: I Didn't Speak for 17 Years," *Guardian*, November 25, 2016, https://www.theguardian.com/lifeandstyle/2016/nov/25/i-didnt-speak-for-17-years-experience-planetwalker.

19. Samuel Bowles, "When Economic Incentives Backfire," *Harvard Business Review*, July 31, 2014, https://hbr.org/2009/03/when-economic-incentives-backfire.

20.   Elisabeth Rosenthal, "By 'Bagging It,' Ireland Rids Itself of a Plastic Nuisance," *New York Times*, January 31, 2008, http://www.nytimes.com/2008/01/31/world/europe/31iht-bags.4.9650382.html.

21.   Jan Willem Bolderdijk and Linda Steg, "Promoting Sustainable Consumption: The Risks of Using Financial Incentives," http://www.verdus.nl/upload/documents/Bolderdijk%20%26%20Steg%20-%20REVISED.pdf.

22.   John Thøgersen, "Psychology: Inducing Green Behaviour," *Nature Climate Change* 3 (2013): 100–101.

23.   John Thøgersen and Tom Crompton, "Simple and Painless? The Limitations of Spillover in Environmental Campaigning," *Journal of Consumer Policy* 32, no. 2 (June 2009): 141–63.

24.   Susan Weinschenk, "Shopping, Dopamine, and Anticipation," *Psychology Today*, October 22, 2015, https://www.psychologytoday.com/blog/brainwise/201510/shopping-dopamine-and-anticipation.

25.   Denis Diderot, "Regrets for My Old Dressing Gown; or, A Warning to Those Who Have More Taste than Fortune" (1769), in *Oeuvres Complètes*, vol. 4 (Paris: Garnier Fréres, 1875), https://www.marxists.org/reference/archive/diderot/1769/regrets.htm.

26.   James Clear, "The Diderot Effect: Why We Want Things We Don't Need—and What to Do about It," *Huffington Post*, November 1, 2016, https://www.huffingtonpost.com/james-clear/the-diderot-effect-why-we_b_12756576.html.

27.   Patrick Allan, "How to Program Your Mind to Stop Buying Crap You Don't Need," *Lifehacker*, March 9, 2015, https://lifehacker.com/how-to-program-your-mind-to-stop-buying-crap-you-don-t-1690268064.

28.   American Psychological Association, "Making Lifestyle Changes That Last," http://www.apa.org/helpcenter/lifestyle-changes.aspx.

29.   Society for Personality and Social Psychology, "How We Form Habits, Change Existing Ones," *Science Daily*, August 8, 2014, www.sciencedaily.com/releases/2014/08/140808111931.htm.

30.   Erin Schumaker, "The Psychology behind Why People Don't Recycle," *Huffington Post*, August 3, 2016, https://www.huffingtonpost.com/entry/psychology-of-why-people-dont-recycle_us_57697a7be4b087b70be605b3.

31.   Column Five, "Infographic: Why Don't Americans Recycle?" *GOOD Magazine*, April 6, 2012, https://www.good.is/infographics/infographic-why-don-t-americans-recycle.

32.   Drew DeSilver, "Perceptions and Realities of Recycling Vary Widely from Place to Place," *Pew Research Center*, October 7, 2016, http://www.pewresearch.org/fact-tank/2016/10/07/perceptions-and-realities-of-recycling-vary-widely-from-place-to-place/.

33.   Trudel, "Behavioral Economics."

34. Jeffrey M. Jones, "Americans' Identification as 'Environmentalists' Down to 42%," *Gallup*, April 22, 2016, http://news.gallup.com/poll/190916/americans-identification-environmentalists-down.aspx.

35. Clare Goldsberry, "New Poll Reveals That Many Americans Are Confused about Recycling," *PlasticsToday*, January 5, 2017, https://www.plasticstoday.com/recycling/new-poll-reveals-many-americans-are-confused-about-recycling/44320612647240.

8. ECONOMICS OF RECYCLING

1. Rebecca Heisman, "When a Tree Falls in a Forest," *Northern Woodlands*, January 20, 2016, https://northernwoodlands.org/knots_and_bolts/tree-falls-in-a-forest.

2. Michigan Department of Environmental Quality, "Why Does Recycling Cost Money?" April 2016, https://www.michigan.gov/documents/deq/deq-oea-owmrp-WhyRecyclingCosts_Web_523826_7.pdf.

3. E Magazine, *Earthtalk: Expert Answers to Everyday Questions about the Environment: Selections from* E—The Environmental Magazine's *Nationally Syndicated Column* (New York: Plume, 2009), 97.

4. E Magazine, *Earthtalk*, 97.

5. James Thompson, "Landfill Waste Costs Continued to Rise in 2016," *Solid Waste Environmental Excellence Protocol*, January 12, 2017, http://nrra.net/sweep/cost-to-landfill-waste-continues-to-rise-through-2016/.

6. U.S. Environmental Protection Agency, Office of Air and Radiation, and Office of Air Quality Planning and Standards, "Municipal Solid Waste Landfills: Economic Impact Analysis for the Proposed New Subpart to the New Source Performance Standards," June 2014, https://www3.epa.gov/ttnecas1/regdata/EIAs/LandfillsNSPSProposalEIA.pdf.

7. Nicole Raz, "Republic Services: Nobody Else Can Handle Las Vegas' Trash," *Las Vegas Review-Journal*, March 2, 2017, https://www.reviewjournal.com/business/republic-services-nobody-else-can-handle-las-vegas-trash/.

8. Tracy Fernandez Rysavy, "Americans Are Really Bad at Recycling. But Only Because We're Not Trying Very Hard," *Green America*, https://www.greenamerica.org/rethinking-recycling/americans-are-really-bad-recycling-only-because-were-not-trying-very-hard.

9. U.S. Environmental Protection Agency, "Municipal Solid Waste," https://archive.epa.gov/epawaste/nonhaz/municipal/web/html/.

10. Nickolas J. Themelis and Jeffrey Morris, "Does Burning Garbage for Electricity Make Sense?" *Wall Street Journal*, November 15, 2015, https://

www.wsj.com/articles/does-burning-garbage-for-electricity-make-sense-1447643515.

11.   Alexander C. Kaufman, "The Trash Incinerator Industry Is Trying to Tank a Massive Renewable-Energy Effort," *Huffington Post*, June 27, 2017, https://www.huffingtonpost.com/entry/trash-incinerator-renewable-energy_us_594d7fede4b05c37bb767c15.

12.   Julia Pyper, "Does Burning Garbage to Produce Electricity Make Sense?" *Scientific American*, August 26, 2011, https://www.scientificamerican.com/article/does-burning-garbage-to-produce-energy-make-sense/.

13.   Themelis and Morris, "Burning Garbage for Electricity."

14.   Thomas Helbling, "Externalities," *International Monetary Fund*, December 2010, http://www.imf.org/external/pubs/ft/fandd/basics/index.htm.

15.   Douglas Koplow, Kevin Dietly, and Terry Dinan, "Federal Disincentives: A Study of Federal Tax Subsidies and Other Programs Affecting Virgin Industries and Recycling," August 1994. https://nepis.epa.gov/.

16.   Douglas Koplow, "Federal Energy Subsidies and Recycling: A Case Study," *Resource Recycling*, November 1994, 31–32, https://earthtrack.net/sites/default/files/Alum%20Subs%2C%20Res%20Recyc%20Article.pdf.

17.   Frank Ackerman, *Why Do We Recycle? Markets, Values, and Public Policy* (Washington, DC: Island Press, 2013), 34.

18.   Jake Weimar, "The Cost of Recycling," *Economics 411: Monetary and Financial Theory*, Winter 2015, https://411w15.econ.lsa.umich.edu/?p=4459.

19.   Kendra Pierre-Louis, "These Billion-Dollar Natural Disasters Set a U.S. Record in 2017," *New York Times*, January 8, 2018, https://www.nytimes.com/2018/01/08/climate/2017-weather-disasters.html?smid=tw-nytimes&smtyp=cur.

20.   Helbling, "Externalities."

21.   EarthTalk, "Is Recycling Worth It?" *Scientific American*, November 5, 2015, https://www.scientificamerican.com/article/is-recycling-worth-it/.

22.   Jon Frandsen, "The Money in Recycling Has Vanished: What Do States, Cities Do Now?" *Pew Charitable Trusts*, March 29, 2016, http://www.pewtrusts.org/en/research-and-analysis/blogs/stateline/2016/03/29/the-money-in-recycling-has-vanished-what-do-states-cities-do-now.

23.   CostOwl.com, "How Much Does a Recycling Pickup Service Cost?" http://www.costowl.com/home-improvement/home-services-recycling-pickup-cost.html.

24.   Organisation for Economic Co-operation and Development, "Extended Producer Responsibility: Guidance for Efficient Waste Management," September 2016, https://www.oecd.org/environment/waste/Extended-producer-responsibility-Policy-Highlights-2016-web.pdf.

25. Sarah Laskow, "Who Will Pay America's $1.5 Billion Recycling Bill?" *Next City*, February 9, 2015, https://nextcity.org/features/view/cost-of-recycling-america-extended-producer-responsibility-cities.

26. Laskow, "Who Will Pay."

27. Extended Producer Responsibility Alliance, "Extended Producer Responsibility at a Glance," http://www.expra.eu/uploads/downloads/EXPRA%20EPR%20Paper_March_2016.pdf.

28. Extended Producer Responsibility Alliance, "Belgium," http://www.expra.eu/countries/belgium/2.

29. Product Stewardship Institute, "U.S. State EPR Laws," December 2017, http://www.productstewardship.us/?State_EPR_Laws_Map.

30. Seldman, Neil. "EPR: The Good, the Bad and the Ugly." *Waste Dive*. March 22, 2018. https://www.wastedive.com/news/epr-good-bad-ugly/519582/.

31. Connecticut General Assembly Task Force. *Task Force to Study Methods for Reducing Consumer Packaging That Generates Solid Waste: Recommendations*. Feb. 2018, https://www.cga.ct.gov/env/taskforce.asp?TF= 20170216_
Task%20Force%20to%20Study%20Methods%20for%20Reducing%20Consumer%20Packaging%20that%20Generates%20Solid%20Waste.

32. Lianna Brinded, "The 9 Richest Self-Made Female Billionaires in the World," *Business Insider*, March 10, 2017, http://www.businessinsider.com/hurun-global-self-made-women-billionaires-list-2017-3/#9-peggy-cherng-and-husband-andrew-cherng-net-worth-44-billion-cherng-and-her-husband-found-their-fortune-through-panda-express-in-the-us-which-is-now-one-of-the-worlds-largest-family-owned-restaurant-chains-1.

33. David Barboza, "China's 'Queen of Trash' Finds Riches in Waste Paper—Business—International Herald Tribune," *New York Times*, January 15, 2007, http://www.nytimes.com/2007/01/15/business/worldbusiness/15iht-trash.4211783.html.

34. Nine Dragons Paper, "Environmental, Social and Governance," http://www.ndpaper.com/eng/ir/esg.htm.

35. RISI, "Cheung Yan, Chairlady of Nine Dragons Paper Selected as This Year's Asia CEO of the Year," March 15, 2017, https://www.risiinfo.com/press-release/cheung-yan-chairlady-nine-dragons-paper-selected-years-asia-ceo-year/.

36. Rick LeBlanc, "Impacts of Operation Green Fence on the Global Recycling Industry," *Balance*, November 3, 2016, https://www.thebalance.com/operation-green-fence-impacts-2878038.

37. Betsy Dorn and Susan Bush, "In Our Opinion: How to Develop Resilient Markets at Home," *Resource Recycling News*, November 17, 2017, https://

resource-recycling.com/recycling/2017/11/14/opinion-develop-resilient-markets-home/.

38. Jason Margolis, "China's 'Green Fence' Is Cleaning Up America's Dirty Recycling," *Public Radio International*, February 18, 2014, https://www.pri.org/stories/2014-02-18/chinas-green-fence-cleaning-americas-dirty-recycling.

39. LeBlanc, "Impacts of Operation Green Fence."

40. Katharine Earley, "Could China's 'Green Fence' Prompt a Global Recycling Innovation?" *Guardian*, August 27, 2013, https://www.theguardian.com/sustainable-business/china-green-fence-global-recycling-innovation.

41. Cole Rosengren, "Disruptor of the Year: China's Import Policies," *Waste Dive*, December 4, 2017, https://www.wastedive.com/news/disruptor-of-the-year-chinas-import-policies/510675/.

42. Cassandra Profita and Jes Burns, "Recycling Chaos in U.S. as China Bans 'Foreign Waste.'" *NPR*, December 9, 2017, https://www.npr.org/2017/12/09/568797388/recycling-chaos-in-u-s-as-china-bans-foreign-waste.

43. Boteler, Cody, and Cole Rosengren. "What Chinese Import Policies Mean for All 50 States." *Waste Dive*, 20 Apr. 2018, https://www.wastedive.com/news/what-chinese-import-policies-mean-for-all-50-states/510751/.

44. Association of Plastic Recyclers, "APR Announces Recycling Demand Champion Campaign," October 18, 2017, https://plasticsrecycling.org/news-and-media/735-october-18-2017-apr-recycling-demand-champion-release.

45. Dorn and Bush, "In Our Opinion."

46. Recology, "Our Mission and Vision," https://www.recology.com/about-us/mission-vision/.

47. Eric Lombardi, "The Secret to San Francisco's Zero Waste Success," *Waste360*, April 13, 2016, http://www.waste360.com/waste-reduction/secret-san-francisco-s-zero-waste-success.

48. Chaz Miller, "States Lead the Way: Pioneering Recycling Efforts in the US," *Waste Management World*, January 9, 2006, https://waste-management-world.com/a/states-lead-the-way-pioneering-recycling-efforts-in-the-us.

49. National Recycling Coalition, "Fact Sheets," https://nrcrecycles.org/glossary-3/.

50. Ron Gonen, "Yes, Recycling Is Still Good Business—If This Happens," *GreenBiz*, July 30, 2015, https://www.greenbiz.com/article/yes-recycling-still-good-business-if-happens.

51. Glass Packaging Institute, "Recycling," 2017, http://www.gpi.org/recycling/glass-recycling-facts.

52. Stanford University, "Frequently Asked Questions: Benefits of Recycling," https://lbre.stanford.edu/pssistanford-recycling/frequently-asked-questions/frequently-asked-questions-benefits-recycling.

53.   Ed Grabianowski, "How Recycling Works," *How StuffWorks Science*, https://science.howstuffworks.com/environmental/green-science/recycling2. htm.

54.   Cole Rosengren, "Hauler Heroes: Hurricane Responders," *Waste Dive*, December 4, 2017, https://www.wastedive.com/news/hauler-heroes-hurricane-responders/510671/.

55.   Profita and Burns, "Recycling Chaos."

56.   Ben Schiller, "Once Robots Are Sorting the Recycling, the Economics All Change," *Fast Company*, November 9, 2015, https://www.fastcompany. com/3052355/once-robots-are-sorting-the-recycling-the-economics-all-change.

57.   David Johnson, "The Top 10 Most Dangerous Jobs in America," *Time*, December 22, 2017, http://time.com/5074471/most-dangerous-jobs/.

58.   Jean Tepperman, "Recycling's Dirty Little Secret," *East Bay Express*, April 25, 2012, https://www.eastbayexpress.com/oakland/recyclings-dirty-little-secret/Content?oid=3184736.

59.   Leon Kaye, "Recycling Jobs Now Even More Dirty and Dangerous," *Triple Pundit: People, Planet, Profit*, September 6, 2012, https://www. triplepundit.com/2012/09/recycling-jobs-dirty-dangerous/.

60.   Carl A. Zimring, *Cash for Your Trash: Scrap Recycling in America* (New Brunswick, NJ: Rutgers University Press, 2009), 138.

61.   Debra Winter, "The Violent Afterlife of a Recycled Plastic Bottle," *Atlantic*, December 4, 2015, https://www.theatlantic.com/technology/archive/ 2015/12/what-actually-happens-to-a-recycled-plastic-bottle/418326/.

62.   Mathy Stanislaus, "The Economic Power of Recycling: Sustainable Materials Management," *EPA Blog*, November 15, 2016, https://blog.epa.gov/ blog/2016/11/the-economic-power-of-recycling-sustainable-materials-management/.

9. TAKING ACTION FROM YOUR CURBSIDE TO CAPITOL HILL

1.   Adam Minter, *Junkyard Planet: Travels in the Billion-Dollar Trash Trade* (New York: Bloomsbury, 2015), 5.

2.   RRS, "MRF Material Flow Study: Final Report," July 2015, https:// www.plasticsrecycling.org/images/pdf/resources/MRF-material-flow-study-FINAL.pdf.

3.   Trey Granger, "The Verdict Is In: Keep the Bottle Caps On," *Earth911*, July 1, 2010, https://earth911.com/food/the-verdict-is-in-keep-the-bottle-caps-on/.

4.   TerraCycle, "Candy and Snack Wrappers Zero Waste Box," https:// www.terracycle.com/en-US/zero_waste_boxes/candy-and-snack-wrappers. You

can also options purchase a box from Terracycle to collect lots of items like candy wrappers to mail in. For example, around Halloween you could acquire a Terracycle box and tell your neighbors to drop their empty wrappers off at your house.

5. Gillian Zaharias Miller and Lauren Olson, "More than You Bargained For: BPS and BPA in Receipts," January 17, 2018, https://www.ecocenter.org/sites/default/files/healthy-stuff/Ecology%20Center%20Receipt%20Study%202018%20Report%20final_0.pdf.

6. Pacific Northwest Pollution Prevention Resource Center, "Should We Recycle Thermal Receipts That Contain BPA?" http://pprc.org/index.php/2015/pprc/should-we-recycle-thermal-receipts-that-contain-bpa/.

7. American Disposal Services, "The Rundown on Plastic #6 (Styrofoam)," https://www.americandisposal.com/blog/the-rundown-on-plastic-6-styrofoam.

8. Madeleine Somerville, "The Real Reason No One's Recycling Styrofoam—and How One Company Is Changing That," *Earth911*, July 27, 2017, https://earth911.com/uncategorized/recycling-styrofoam/.

9. Earth911, "How to Recycle Glass," https://earth911.com/recycling-guide/how-to-recycle-glass/

10. Tetra Pak, "Tetra Pak in Brief: A Company Overview," https://tetrapak.com/us/about/tetra-pak-in-brief.

11. Advanced Disposal, "Recycle Right," http://www.advanceddisposal.com/for-mother-earth/recycling-tips-trivia/recycle-right.aspx.

12. Recyclebank, "Because You Asked: If I Can't Put Aseptic Cartons in My Recycling Bin, Do I Have to Trash Them?" January 5, 2016, https://livegreen.recyclebank.com/because-you-asked-if-i-can-t-put-aseptic-cartons-in-my-recycling-bin-do-i-have-to-trash-them.

13. Carton Council, "Communities: Steps to Take," http://www.cartonopportunities.org/add-carton/communities-steps-take.

14. Carton Council, "About Carton Recycling," http://www.cartonopportunities.org/carton-recycling.

15. Recyclebank, "Because You Asked: Can Plastic Patio Furniture Be Recycled?" December 19, 2017, https://livegreen.recyclebank.com/because-you-asked-can-plastic-patio-furniture-be-recycled.

16. Battery Solutions, "Battery Recycling Benefits," https://www.batterysolutions.com/recycling-information/recycling-benefits/.

17. Constance Gibbs, "UN Sees Global Rise in E-Waste, but Very Little Is Recycled," *New York Daily News*, December 13, 2017, http://www.nydailynews.com/life-style/u-n-sees-global-rise-e-waste-properly-rec-article-1.3696437.

18. C. P. Baldé, V. Forti, V. Gray, R. Kuehr, and P. Stegmann. *The Global E-Waste Monitor 2017: Quantities, Flows, and Resources* (Bonn, Germany:

United Nations University, International Telecommunication Union, and International Solid Waste Association, 2017).

19. Rick LeBlanc, "Electronics Recycling and E-Waste," *Balance*, July 1, 2017, https://www.thebalance.com/e-waste-and-the-importance-of-electronics-recycling-2877783.

20. Baldé et al., *Global E-Waste Monitor*.

21. iFixIt.Org, "It's Time for a Repair Jobs Revolution," https://ifixit.org/revolution.

22. Carole Mars and Christopher Nafe, "Electronics Recycling Landscape: Report Summary," May 2016, https://www.sustainabilityconsortium.org/wp-content/themes/enfold-child/assets/pdf/TSC_Electronics_Recycling_Landscape_Report_Summary.pdf.

23. Consumer Reports, "How to Recycle Old Electronics," April 22, 2017, https://www.consumerreports.org/recycling/how-to-recycle-electronics/.

24. Mars and Nafe, "Electronics Recycling Landscape."

25. Steve Douglas, "History and Design of the Recycle Logo," *Logo Factory*, September 11, 2015, http://www.thelogofactory.com/history-design-recycle-logo/.

26. Penny Jones and Jerry Powell, "Gary Anderson Has Been Found!" *Resource Recycling*, May 1999, https://logoblink.com/wp-content/uploads/2008/03/recycling_symbol_garyanderson.pdf+.

27. Harvey Mudd College, "The Möbius Strip," https://www.math.hmc.edu/~gu/curves_and_surfaces/surfaces/moebius.html.

28. Marketplace, "FTC Punishes Companies for 'Greenwashing,'" March 9, 2017, http://www.cbc.ca/marketplace/blog/ftc-punishes-companies-for-greenwashing.

29. Cara Rosenbloom, "Savvier Shoppers See through Misleading Food Labels. Here's How," *Washington Post*, January 2, 2018, https://www.washingtonpost.com/lifestyle/wellness/shoppers-are-getting-savvier-to-these-misleading-food-labels/2017/12/12/de40c7dc-d555-11e7-a986-d0a9770d9a3e_story.html?utm_term=.21d289d68229.

30. Edward Wyatt, "F.T.C. Issues Guidelines for 'Eco-Friendly' Labels," *New York Times*, October 1, 2012, http://www.nytimes.com/2012/10/02/business/energy-environment/ftc-issues-guidelines-for-eco-friendly-labels.html.

31. Federal Trade Commission, "Green Guides for the Use of Environmental Marketing Claims," October 12, 2012, https://www.ftc.gov/sites/default/files/attachments/press-releases/ftc-issues-revised-green-guides/greenguides.pdf.

32. U.S. Environmental Protection Agency, "Procurement and Use of Recycled Products: A Primer for Government Officials," 1993.

33. Drew DeSilver, "Perceptions and Realities of Recycling Vary Widely from Place to Place," *Pew Research Center*, October 7, 2016, http://www.pewresearch.org/fact-tank/2016/10/07/perceptions-and-realities-of-recycling-vary-widely-from-place-to-place/.

34. Chrystal Johnson, "Recycling Label Seeks to Clear Consumer Confusion," *Earth911*, April 20, 2016, https://earth911.com/business-policy/recycling-label-how2recycle/.

35. Mina Sinai, "How to Read How2Recycle Labels," *RecycleNation*, September 12, 2017, https://recyclenation.com/2017/09/how-to-read-how2recycle-labels/.

36. Target, "How2Recycle Labels Coming to Target," November 21, 2013, https://corporate.target.com/article/2013/11/how2recycle-labels-coming-to-target.

37. Per Espen Stoknes, "Wondering How to Get People to Go Green? Tell Them That's What Their Neighbors Are Doing," *Salon*, May 10, 2015, www.salon.com/2015/05/10/wondering_how_to_get_people_to_go_green_tell_them_thats_what_their_neighbors_are_doing/.

38. Master Recycler, "Home," http://www.masterrecycler.org/.

39. Oregon.gov, "Materials Management Home," http://www.oregon.gov/deq/mm/pages/default.aspx.

40. Master Recycler, "What Is a Master Recycler?" http://www.masterrecycler.org/what-we-do/.

41. Local Tools, "Find Your Local Tool Lending Library," http://localtools.org/find/.

42. Megan Mitchell, "Tool-Sharing Service Comes to Kenton County," *WLWT*, July 18, 2017, http://www.wlwt.com/article/tool-sharing-service-comes-to-kenton-county/10245750.

43. RecycleMania, "History of RecycleMania," 2017, https://recyclemania.org/about-recyclemania/history/.

44. City of Laurel, Maryland, "Recycling Competition," January 18, 2018, https://www.cityoflaurel.org/dpw/collections/recycling-program/recycling-competition.

45. Goldman Environmental Prize, "Destiny Watford: 2016 Goldman Prize Recipient North America," http://www.goldmanprize.org/recipient/destiny-watford/.

46. Curtin, Joe. "Ireland Can Lead Charge in War against Plastic." *Irish Times*. January 31, 2018. https://www.irishtimes.com/opinion/ireland-can-lead-charge-in-war-against-plastic-1.3374066.

47. U.S. Environmental Protection Agency, "Recycling and Waste Electrical and Electronic Equipment Management in Taiwan: A Case Study," De-

cember 2012, https://www.epa.gov/sites/production/files/2014-08/documents/taiwan_iemn_case_study_12.7_final.pdf.

48. Cole Rosengren, "How Taiwan Became a World Leader in Recycling," *Waste Dive*, May 19, 2016, https://www.wastedive.com/news/how-taiwan-became-a-world-leader-in-recycling/419463/.

49. Jessica Bush, "Taiwan Has Found a Brilliant Way to Get People to Recycle More," *Buzzworthy*, August 30, 2017, https://www.buzzworthy.com/taiwan-garbage-disposal/.

50. Joe Papineschi, Peter Jones, and Rob Gillies, "Recycling—Who Really Leads the World?" *Eunomia*, March 2017, http://www.eunomia.co.uk/reports-tools/recycling-who-really-leads-the-world/.

51. Bush, "Taiwan Has Found."

52. Rosengren, "How Taiwan Became."

53. HowMuchIsIt.org, "How Much Does Garbage Pickup Cost?" http://www.howmuchisit.org/garbage-service-cost/.

54. Northeast Recycling Council, "Disposal Bans and Mandatory Recycling in the United States," May 1, 2017, https://nerc.org/documents/disposal_bans_mandatory_recycling_united_states.pdf.

55. Richard Stradling, "Recycle Those Plastic Bottles—It Means More Jobs for NC," *News and Observer*, April 7, 2017, http://www.newsobserver.com/news/business/article143301594.html.

56. Bottle Bill Resource Guide, "What Is a Bottle Bill?" http://www.bottlebill.org/about/whatis.htm#how.

57. Neil Seldman, "Does the Citizens Recycling Movement Face a Hostile Takeover?" *Institute for Local Self-Reliance*, July 2013, http://ilsr.org/wp-content/uploads/downloads/2013/07/US-Citizens-Recycling-Movement-07.12.2013.pdf.

58. Paris Achen, "Mandatory Recycling? There's Little Enforcement," *Burlington Free Press*, July 18, 2015, http://www.burlingtonfreepress.com/story/news/local/2015/07/17/mandatory-recycling-little-enforcement/30327889/.

59. Vermont Department of Environmental Conservation, "Vermont's Universal Recycling Law: Status Report," December 2016, http://dec.vermont.gov/sites/dec/files/wmp/SolidWaste/Documents/Universal.Recycling.Status.Report.Dec_.2016.pdf.

60. Vermont Department of Environmental Conservation, "Vermont's Universal Recycling Law."

INDEX

ABOUT THE AUTHOR

Beth Porter has helped thousands of individuals and businesses live and operate more sustainably. As a nonprofit program director, she has spearheaded many campaigns that identify the waste of resources and energy in varying sectors and has authored comprehensive reports of proposed solutions. She loves to help people find answers to their recycling questions and try new ways to reduce waste. Beth is originally from North Carolina and lives in Washington, D.C. *Reduce, Reuse, Reimagine* is her first book.